The Complete Book of Bible Answers

Ron Rhodes

HARVEST HOUSE PUBLISHERS
Eugene, Oregon 97402

Cover by Paz Design, Salem, Oregon

Cover images © 1997 PhotoDisc, Inc.

THE COMPLETE BOOK OF BIBLE ANSWERS

Copyright © 1997 by Ron Rhodes
Published by Harvest House Publishers
Eugene, Oregon 97402

Library of Congress Cataloging-in-Publication Data
Rhodes, Ron
    The complete book of Bible answers / Ron Rhodes
      p. cm.
    Includes bibliographical references (p. 384) and index.
    ISBN 1-56507-721-0
    1. Bible—Criticism, interpretation, etc. 2. Bible—Miscellanea. I. Title.
BS511.2.R48 1997
220—dc21   97-8440
                                                  CIP

Printed in the United States of America.

97   98   99   00   01   02   / BC /   10   9   8   7   6   5   4   3   2

To my beloved son, David

Acknowledgments

I want to thank my wife, Kerri, and my children, David and Kylie, for their continual support and encouragement during the writing of this book. Without them my work of ministry would truly be an impossible task.

~

CONTENTS

Part 10: Ethics

~

Come Let Us Reason

When I was first asked to become a "regular" on the Christian Research Institute's *Bible Answer Man* call-in radio broadcast in 1990, I was initially very resistant. Who in his right mind wants to go on national radio, with millions of people listening, and get asked very hard questions for an hour each day?

After a while, though, I became quite comfortable and even grew to enjoy the challenge of responding to these tough questions on live radio. A side benefit of doing that show was that it forced me to give thoughtful (and *biblical*) attention to issues I'd really not thought that much about. And the more I wrestled with these issues, digging through the Scriptures each day for answers, the more I came to see that the Bible really does provide wisdom and insight on a plethora of relevant issues.

Over the five years or so that I was on the *Bible Answer Man*, I noticed that many questions seemed to come up quite regularly. In fact, over time, I developed and periodically updated a detailed listing of the most frequently asked questions. The book you're holding in your hands is largely the fruit of that list.

I need to mention at the outset that this book does not attempt to provide a full treatment of every Christian doctrine. This is not a theology textbook. My goal in this book is simply to answer common questions people are asking about some of these doctrines. If you want a fuller treatment of individual doctrines, you might be interested in reading some of my other books, like *The Heart of Christianity*, *Heaven: The Undiscovered Country*, *Angels Among Us*, and *Christ Before the Manger*.

As you read this book, you'll notice that I answer some questions very briefly, while others are allocated a number of pages to answer. This is much like it was on the *Bible Answer Man* show. The fact is, some questions are easily answered, while others require a lot more detail.

My prayer as you read this book is that you will become truly comfortable in answering questions people ask you about the Bible. You will find that God will open many opportunities for you to engage in dialogue with others *if you make yourself available to Him.*

Dig in! And by all means, as you go through this book, look up some of the Scripture references I cite. Like the ancient Bereans, we should make a regular habit of testing all things against Scripture (Acts 17:11). If you do this consistently, you'll soon become a formidable warrior of the Word, or, as I jokingly used to say among my apologetics colleagues, an Apolo-Jedi Master.

—Ron Rhodes
Rancho Santa Margarita, California
1997

PART 1

~

GOD'S BOOK—THE BIBLE

The Inspiration of Scripture
The Reliability of Scripture
The Canon of Scripture
Interpreting Scripture

1

~

The Inspiration of Scripture

What does it mean to say that the Bible is "inspired"?

Inspiration doesn't mean the biblical writer just felt enthusiastic, like the composer of "The Star-Spangled Banner." Nor does it mean the writings are necessarily inspiring to read, like an uplifting poem. The biblical Greek word for *inspiration* literally means "God-breathed." Because Scripture is breathed out by God—because it *originates* from Him—it is true and inerrant.

Biblical inspiration may be defined as God's superintending of the human authors so that, using their own individual personalities—and even their writing styles—they composed and recorded *without error* His revelation to humankind in the words of the original autographs. In other words, the original documents of the Bible were written by men, who, though permitted to exercise their own personalities and literary talents, wrote under the control and guidance of the Holy Spirit, the result being a perfect and errorless recording of the exact message God desired to give to man.

Hence, the writers of Scripture were not mere writing machines. God did not use them like keys on a typewriter to mechanically reproduce His message. Nor did He dictate the words, page by page. The biblical evidence makes it clear that each writer had a style of his own. (Isaiah had a powerful literary style; Jeremiah had a mournful tone;

Luke's style had medical overtones; and John was very simple in his approach.) The Holy Spirit infallibly worked through each of these writers, through their individual styles, to inerrantly communicate His message to human-kind.

To what extent were the biblical writers controlled by the Holy Spirit as they wrote?

In his second letter, Peter provides a key insight regarding the human-divine interchange in the process of inspiration. This verse informs us that "prophecy [or Scripture] never had its origin in the will of man, but men spoke from God as they were carried along by the Holy Spirit" (2 Peter 1:21). The phrase *carried along* in this verse literally means "forcefully borne along."

Even though human beings were used in the process of writing down God's Word, they were all literally "borne along" by the Holy Spirit. The human wills of the authors were not the originators of God's message. God did not permit the will of sinful human beings to misdirect or erroneously record His message. Rather, "God *moved* and the prophet *mouthed* these truths; God *revealed* and man *recorded* His word."[1]

Interestingly, the Greek word for "carried along" in 2 Peter 1:21 is the same as that found in Acts 27:15-17. In this passage the experienced sailors could not navigate the ship because the wind was so strong. The ship was being *driven, directed,* and *carried along* by the wind. This is similar to the Spirit's driving, directing, and carrying the human authors of the Bible as He wished. The word is a strong one, indicating the Spirit's complete superintendence of the human authors. Yet, just as the sailors were active on the ship (though the wind, not the sailors, ultimately controlled the ship's movement), so the human authors were active in writing as the Spirit directed.

Were the New Testament writers aware that their writings were inspired by God and therefore authoritative?

Yes, I believe so. In 1 Corinthians 2:13 the apostle Paul said he spoke "not in words taught us by human wisdom but in words taught by the Spirit, expressing spiritual truths in spiritual words." In this passage Paul (who wrote over half the New Testament) affirmed that his words were authoritative because they were rooted not in fallible men but infallible God (the Holy Spirit). The Holy Spirit is the Spirit of *truth* who was promised to the apostles to teach and guide them into all the *truth* (see John 16:13).

Later, in 1 Corinthians 14:37, Paul said, "If anybody thinks he is a prophet or spiritually gifted, let him acknowledge that what I am writing to you is the Lord's command." In 1 Thessalonians 2:13 Paul likewise said, "And we also thank God continually because, when you received the word of God, which you heard from us, you accepted it not as the word of men, but as it actually is, the word of God, which is at work in you who believe." Again, the reason Paul's words were authoritative is because they were rooted in God, not in man. God used Paul as His instrument to communicate *His* word to man.

What are some of the incorrect views of the inspiration of Scripture?

There are at least seven incorrect views of inspiration that are circulating today. Briefly:

The "Dictation Theory" says that God raised up men, prepared the men *and* their vocabularies, and then dictated to them the very words which they would put down in the Scriptures.

The "Natural Inspiration Theory" says that the writers of Scripture were simply men of great genius. There was nothing supernatural involved. These were men with talent similar to that of Shakespeare.

The "Mystical Theory" says that the writers of Scripture were simply Spirit-filled and Spirit-guided believers, like any believer may be today.

The "Neoorthodox Theory" says that the Bible is a fallible and often unreliable "witness" to the Word of God. In a fallible way, it points to Christ.

The "Concept Inspiration Theory" holds that the concepts, but not the very words of Scripture, were inspired. So, for example, the concept of salvation in Christ may be inspired, but the words used to communicate this concept are not inspired and therefore may have mistakes.

The "Inspired Purpose Theory" says that although the Bible contains many factual errors and insoluble discrepancies, it still has "doctrinal integrity" and thus accomplishes God's purpose for it. The Bible's infallibility is carefully limited to the main purpose or principle emphasis of the Bible—that is, salvation.

The "Partial Inspiration Theory" says that certain parts of the Bible are inspired—that is, the portions that would otherwise have been unknowable (creation, prophecy, salvation by faith in Christ, and so forth).

The correct view of inspiration involves God's superintendence of the human writers of Scripture so that, while allowing for their own personalities and writing styles, they recorded without error, in the words of the original manuscripts, God's word to humankind.

OBJECTIONS TO INSPIRATION AND INERRANCY

Some critics question the Bible's reliability by arguing that the gospel writers were biased. How can we respond to this?

Some critics say the four gospel writers were biased in the sense that they had theological "motives." Their intent was to convince readers of Jesus' deity, we are told, and hence their historical testimony is untrustworthy.

The fallacy here is to imagine that to give an account of something one believes in passionately necessarily forces one to distort history. This is simply not true. In modern times some of the most reliable reports of the Nazi Holocaust were written by Jews who were passionately committed to seeing such genocide never repeated.[2]

The New Testament is not made up of fairy tales but rather is based on eyewitness testimony. In 2 Peter 1:16 we read, "We did not follow cleverly invented stories when we told you about the power and coming of our Lord Jesus Christ, but we were eyewitnesses of his majesty." First John 1:1 affirms, "That which was from the beginning, which we have heard, which we have seen with our eyes, which we have looked at and our hands have touched—this we proclaim concerning the Word of life."

Why did God allow four Gospels into the Bible that have apparent contradictions?

First of all, while the Gospels may have some *apparent* contradictions, I do not believe they have *genuine* contradictions. There are differences, yes, but actual contradictions, no.

Second, foundationally, it is important to keep in mind that inspiration and inerrancy are, strictly speaking, ascribed only to the original autographs of Scripture. Certainly I believe that the copies we have of the original autographs are extremely accurate. But theologians have been very careful to say that the Scriptures, in their *original autographs* and *properly interpreted*, will be shown to be *wholly true* in everything they teach.

Third, if all four Gospels were the same, with no differences, critics would be screaming "collusion" all over the place. The fact that the Gospels have differences show there was no collusion but rather represent four different (but inspired) accounts of the same events.

One should not assume that a *partial* account in a gospel is a *faulty* account. In Matthew 27:5, for example, we are told that Judas died by hanging himself. In Acts 1:18 we are told that Judas burst open in the middle and all his entrails gushed out. These are both partial accounts. Neither account gives us the full picture. But taken together we can easily reconstruct how Judas died. He hanged himself, and sometime later the rope loosened and Judas fell to the rocks below, thereby causing his intestines to gush out. As one probes into alleged contradictions, one consistently sees that they are all explainable in a reasonable way.

How can we respond to those who claim that science disproves the miracles of the Bible?

Science depends upon observation and replication. Miracles, such as the Incarnation and the Resurrection, are by their very nature unprecedented events. No one can replicate these events in a laboratory. Hence, science simply cannot be the judge and jury as to whether or not these events occurred.

The scientific method is useful for studying nature but not *super*-nature. Just as football stars are speaking outside their field of expertise when they appear on television to tell you what razor you should buy, so scientists are speaking outside their field when they address theological issues like miracles or the Resurrection.

Actually, there is good reason to believe in the biblical miracles. One highly pertinent factor is the brief time that elapsed between Jesus' miraculous public ministry and the publication of the Gospels. It was insufficient for the development of miracle legends. Many eyewitnesses to Jesus' miracles would have still been alive to refute any untrue miracle accounts (see 1 Corinthians 15:6).

One must also recognize the noble character of the men who witnessed these miracles (Peter, James, and John, for example). Such men were not prone to misrepresentation, and they were willing to give up their lives rather than deny their beliefs.

There were also hostile witnesses to the miracles of Christ. When Jesus raised Lazarus from the dead, for example, none of the chief priests or Pharisees disputed the miracle (John 11:45-48). (If they could have disputed it, they would have.) Rather, their goal was simply to stop Jesus (verses 47, 48). Because there were so many hostile witnesses who observed and scrutinized Christ, successful "fabrication" of miracle stories in His ministry would have been impossible.

I believe that nature and Scripture, properly interpreted, do not conflict. God has communicated to humankind both by *general* revelation (nature, or the observable universe) and *special* revelation (the Bible). Since both of these revelations come from God—and since God does not contradict Himself—we must conclude that these two revelations are in agreement with each other. While there may be conflicts between one's *interpretation* of the observable universe and one's *interpretation* of the Bible, there is no ultimate contradiction.

We might say that *science* is a fallible human interpretation of the observable universe while *theology* is a fallible human interpretation of the Scriptures. If the secularist challenges the idea that science can be fallible, remind him or her of what science historian Thomas Kuhn proved in his book *The Structure of Scientific Revolutions*—that is, science is in a constant state of change. New discoveries have consistently caused old scientific paradigms to be discarded in favor of newer paradigms.

Here is the point: it is not *nature* and *Scripture* that contradict; rather, it is *science* (man's fallible interpretation of nature) and *theology* (man's fallible interpretation of Scripture) that sometimes fall into conflict. Hence the secularist cannot simply dismiss certain parts of the Bible because "science and the Bible contradict."

How can we respond to the claim that some language in the Bible is scientifically incorrect?

Some critics allege that the Bible is not scientifically accurate in view of its frequent use of "phenomenological" language—that is, the language of appearances. Ecclesiastes 1:5, for example, refers to the sun "rising" and "setting." From a scientific perspective, the sun does not actually rise or set. But let's be fair. This is the same kind of language weather forecasters use today. "Rising" and "setting" are accepted ways of describing what the sun *appears* to be doing from an earthly perspective. So, the Bible's use of such language does not prove there are scientific errors in it.

2

~

The Reliability of Scripture

Does good archaeological support exist for the Bible?

Yes! Unlike other books that claim to be Scripture (such as the Book of Mormon), the Bible's accuracy and reliability have been proved and verified over and over again by archeological finds produced by both believing *and* nonbelieving scholars and scientists. This includes verification for numerous customs, places, names, and events mentioned in the Bible.

One among many examples is the fact that for many years the existence of the Hittites (a powerful people who lived during the time of Abraham) was questioned because no archeological digs had uncovered anything about them. Critics claimed the Hittites were pure myth. But today the critics are silenced. Abundant archeological evidence for the existence of the Hittites during the time of Abraham has been uncovered.

Bible scholar Donald J. Wiseman notes, "The geography of Bible lands and visible remains of antiquity were gradually recorded until today more than 25,000 sites within this region and dating to Old Testament times, in their broadest sense, have been located."[1] Nelson Glueck, a specialist in ancient literature, did an exhaustive study and concluded: "It can be stated categorically that no archaeological discovery has ever controverted a biblical reference."[2] Well-known scholar William F. Albright, following a comprehensive study, wrote: "Discovery after discovery has established the accuracy of innumerable details, and has brought increased recognition of the value of the Bible as a source of history."[3]

Does strong manuscript evidence exist for the New Testament? What about all the "variants" the critics talk about?

There are more than 24,000 partial and complete manuscript copies of the New Testament. These manuscript copies are very ancient and they are available for inspection *now*. There are also some 86,000 quotations from the early church fathers and several thousand lectionaries (church-service books containing Scripture quotations used in the early centuries of Christianity). In fact, there are enough quotations from the early church fathers that even if we did not have a single copy of the Bible, scholars could still reconstruct all but 11 verses of the entire New Testament from material written within 150 to 200 years from the time of Christ. Bottom line: *the New Testament has an overwhelming amount of evidence supporting its reliability.*

Now, in the many thousands of manuscript copies we possess of the New Testament, scholars have discovered that there are some 200,000 "variants." This may seem like a staggering figure to the uninformed mind. But to those who study the issue, the numbers are not as serious as it may initially appear. Indeed, a look at the hard evidence shows that the New Testament manuscripts are amazingly accurate and trustworthy.

To begin, we must emphasize that out of these 200,000 variants, 99 percent hold virtually no significance whatsoever. Many of these variants simply involve a missing letter in a word; some involve reversing the order of two words (such as "Christ Jesus" instead of "Jesus Christ"); some may involve the absence of one or more insignificant words.

Really, when all the facts are put on the table, only about 40 of the variants have any *real* significance—and even then, no doctrine of the Christian faith or any moral commandment is affected by them. For more than 99 percent of the cases the original text can be reconstructed to a practical certainty.

By practicing the science of textual criticism—comparing all the available manuscripts with each other—we can come to an assurance regarding what the original document must have said. Perhaps an illustration might be helpful.

Let us suppose we have five manuscript copies of an original document that no longer exists. Each of the manuscript copies are different. Our goal is to compare the manuscript copies and ascertain what the original must have said. Here are the five copies:

MANUSCRIPT #1: Jesus Christ is the Savior of the whole world.

MANUSCRIPT #2: Christ Jesus is the Savior of the whole world.

MANUSCRIPT #3: Jesus Christ s the Savior of the whole worl.

MANUSCRIPT #4: Jesus Christ is th Savior of the whle world.

MANUSCRIPT #5: Jesus Christ is the Savor of the whole wrld.

Could you, by comparing the manuscript copies, ascertain what the original document said with a high degree of certainty that you are correct? Of course you could.

This illustration may be extremely simplistic, but a great majority of the 200,000 variants are solved by the above methodology. By comparing the various manuscripts, all of which contain *very minor* differences like the illustration, it becomes fairly clear what the original must have said. Further, I must emphasize that the sheer volume of manuscripts we possess greatly narrows the margin of doubt regarding what the original biblical documents said.

Does good manuscript support exist for the Old Testament?

Yes! The Dead Sea Scrolls prove the accuracy of the transmission of the Old Testament books of the Bible. In fact, in these scrolls discovered at Qumran in 1947, we have Old Testament manuscripts that date about a thousand years earlier (150 B.C.) than the other Old Testament manuscripts previously in our possession (which dated to A.D. 980). The significant thing is that when one compares the two sets of manuscripts, it is clear that they are essentially the same, with very few changes. The fact that manuscripts separated by a thousand years are essentially the same indicates the incredible accuracy of the Old Testament's manuscript transmission.

The copy of the Book of Isaiah discovered at Qumran illustrates this accuracy. Dr. Gleason Archer, who personally examined both the A.D. 980 and 150 B.C. copies of Isaiah, comments:

> Even though the two copies of Isaiah discovered in Qumran Cave 1 near the Dead Sea in 1947 were a thousand years earlier than the oldest dated manuscript previously known (A.D. 980), they proved to be *word for word identical* with our standard Hebrew Bible in more than 95 percent of the text. The 5 percent of variation consisted chiefly of obvious slips of the pen and variations in spelling.[4] (italics mine)

The Dead Sea Scrolls *prove* that the copyists of biblical manuscripts took great care in going about their work. These copyists knew they were duplicating God's Word. Hence they went to incredible lengths to insure that no error crept into their work. The scribes carefully counted every line, word, syllable, and letter to guarantee accuracy.[5]

Does any biblical basis exist for the idea that God preserves Scripture through the ages?

Yes. I believe that the God who had the power and sovereign control to *inspire* the Scriptures in the first place is surely going to continue to exercise His power and sovereign control in the *preservation* of Scripture.

Actually, God's preservational work is illustrated in the text of the Bible. By examining how Christ viewed the Old Testament (keeping in mind that Jesus did not have in His possession the *original* books penned by the Old Testament writers, but possessed only copies), we see that He had full confidence that the Scriptures He used had been faithfully preserved through the centuries.

> Because Christ raised no doubts about the adequacy of the Scriptures as His contemporaries knew them, we can safely assume that the first-century text of the Old Testament was a wholly adequate representation of the divine word originally given. Jesus regarded the extant copies of His day as so approximate to the originals in their message that He appealed to those copies as authoritative.[6]

The respect that Jesus and His apostles held for the extant Old Testament text is an expression of their confidence that God providentially preserved these copies and translations so that they were substantially identical with the inspired originals.

Some people believe the King James Version is the only legitimate Bible. How can we respond to this claim?

To begin, the King James Version we universally accept today is not an exact copy of the edition released in 1611. The Bible that circulates today as the "Authorized" King James Version is actually the fourth revision of 1769.

A simple way to verify this is by reading John 3:7 in today's King James Version. The spelling of the individual words in this sentence is entirely different from that of the original 1611 version. I must also point out that the punctuation, capitalization, and use of italics have been changed as each respective edition came out. So, I must ask, *which* King James Version is inspired?

Moreover, if the King James Version is the only legitimate Bible, then what was God's inspired Word prior to 1611? It is highly revealing that some of the translators of the King James Version continued to use earlier English versions long after the publication of the King James Version. They even approvingly quoted from one of these Bibles (the Geneva Bible) in the original preface to the King James Version.

Also relevant to this discussion is the question of whether English is the *only* language that has God's inspired Word. What about people living in France or Spain or Russia?

Finally, it is a historical fact that the 1611 King James Version included the Apocrypha. Yet few if any who claim exclusive inspiration for the King James Version's English text would accept the Apocrypha as God's Word.

I say all this not to malign the King James Version. I say this only to stress the point that it is not the only legitimate version.

~

3

The Canon of Scripture

What is the "canon" of Scripture?

The word *canon* comes from a Greek word that means "measuring stick." Over time, the word eventually came to be used metaphorically of books that were "measured" and thereby *recognized* as being God's Word. When we talk about the "canon of Scripture" today, we are referring to all the biblical books that collectively constitute God's Word.

Were any of the biblical books written during New Testament times recognized as belonging in the canon at that time, or was it only centuries later that they were recognized as God's Word?

Many books written during New Testament times were recognized as being the Word of God at that time. It is highly revealing that in 1 Timothy 5:18, the apostle Paul joined an Old Testament reference and a New Testament reference and called them *both* (collectively) "Scripture" (Deuteronomy 25:4 and Luke 10:7). It would not have been unusual in the context of first-century Judaism for an Old Testament passage to be called "Scripture." But for a New Testament book to be called "Scripture" so soon after it was written says volumes about Paul's view of the authority of contemporary New Testament books.

To be more specific, only three years had elapsed between the writing of the Gospel of Luke and the writing of 1 Timothy (Luke was written around A.D. 60; 1 Timothy was written around A.D. 63). Yet, despite this, Paul (himself a Jew—a "Hebrew of Hebrews") does not hesitate to place Luke on the *same level of authority* as the Old Testament Book of Deuteronomy.

Further, the writings of the apostle Paul were recognized as Scripture by the apostle Peter (2 Peter 3:16). Paul, too, understood that his own writings were inspired by God and therefore authoritative (1 Corinthians 14:37; 1 Thessalonians 2:13). Paul, of course, wrote over half the New Testament.

How did the early church recognize which books were canonical?

As noted above, certain books were recognized as canonical during the time when the books were being written (1 Timothy 5:18; 2 Peter 3:16). When the church *formally* recognized what books belonged in the canon, there were five primary tests that were applied. Here they are, listed in question format:

1. *Was the book written or backed by a prophet or apostle of God?* The reasoning here is that the Word of God which is inspired by the Spirit of God for the people of God must be communicated through a man of God. Deuteronomy 18:18 informs us that only a prophet of God will speak the Word of God. Second Peter 1:20, 21 assures us that Scripture is only written by men of God. In Galatians 1:1-24 the apostle Paul argued support for the gospel he preached by appealing to the fact that he was an authorized messenger of God, an apostle.

2. *Is the book authoritative?* In other words, can it be said of this book as it was said of Jesus, "The people were amazed at his teaching, because he taught them as one who had authority, not as the teachers of the law" (Mark 1:22)?

Put another way, does this book ring with the sense of, "Thus saith the Lord"?

3. *Does the book tell the truth about God as it is already known by previous revelation?* The Bereans searched the Old Testament Scriptures to see whether Paul's teaching was true (Acts 17:11). They knew that if Paul's teaching did not accord with the Old Testament canon, it couldn't be of God. Agreement with all earlier revelation is essential. Paul certainly recognized this, for he said to the Galatians: "But even if we or an angel from heaven should preach a gospel other than the one we preached to you, let him be eternally condemned!" (Galatians 1:8)

4. *Does the book give evidence of having the power of God?* The reasoning here is that any writing that does not exhibit the transforming power of God in the lives of its readers could not have come from God. Scripture says that the Word of God is "living and active" (Hebrews 4:12). Second Timothy 3:16 indicates that God's Word has a transforming effect. If the book in question did not have the power to change a life, then, it was reasoned, the book couldn't have come from God.

5. *Was the book accepted by the people of God?* In Old Testament times, Moses' scrolls were placed immediately into the ark of the covenant (Deuteronomy 31:24-26). Joshua's writings were added in the same fashion (Joshua 24:26). In the New Testament, Paul thanked the Thessalonians for receiving the apostle's message as the Word of God (1 Thessalonians 2:13). Paul's letters were circulated among the churches (Colossians 4:16; 1 Thessalonians 5:27). It is the norm that God's people—that is, the majority of them and not simply a faction—will initially receive God's Word as such.

Why were certain New Testament books doubted as belonging in the canon?

The books that were doubted for a time were Hebrews, James, 2 Peter, 2 and 3 John, Jude, and Revelation.

Hebrews was doubted because the author of the book was unknown. However, the book eventually came to be viewed as having apostolic authority, if not apostolic authorship.

James was doubted because of its apparent conflict with Paul's teaching about salvation by faith alone. The conflict was resolved by seeing the *works* James speaks of as an *outgrowth* of real faith.

Second Peter was doubted because the style of this book differs from that of 1 Peter. It seems clear, however, that Peter used a scribe to write 1 Peter (see 1 Peter 5:12). So a style conflict is not really a problem.

Second and 3 John were doubted because the author of these books is called "elder," not "apostle." However, Peter (an apostle) is also called "elder" in 1 Peter 5:1. So it seems clear that the same person can be both an elder and an apostle.

Jude was doubted because it refers to two noncanonical books—the Book of Enoch and the Assumption of Moses. This objection was eventually overcome because even Paul quoted from pagan poets (see Acts 17:28 and Titus 1:12). Moreover, Jude enjoyed early acceptance by most of the early believers.

The Book of Revelation was doubted because it teaches a thousand-year reign of Christ. Since there was a local contemporary cult that taught the same, it was reasoned that Revelation must not be true Scripture. However, because many of the earliest church fathers believed in a thousand-year reign of Christ, too, this objection was eventually seen as being without merit.

What is the Apocrypha? And why do Roman Catholic Bibles have it while Protestant Bibles do not?

The Apocrypha refers to 14 or 15 books of doubtful authenticity and authority that the Roman Catholics decided belonged in the Bible sometime following the Protestant Reformation. The Catholic Council of Trent (1545-1563) canonized these books. This canonization took place largely as a result of the Protestant Reformation. Indeed, Luther had criticized the Catholics for not having scriptural support for such doctrines as praying for the dead. By canonizing the Apocrypha (which offers support for praying for the dead in 2 Maccabees 12:45, 46), the Catholics suddenly had "scriptural" support for this and other distinctively Catholic doctrines.

Roman Catholics argue that the Septuagint (the Greek translation of the Hebrew Old Testament) contained the Apocrypha. As well, church fathers like Iraneaus, Tertullian, and Clement of Alexandria used the Apocryphal books in public worship and accepted them as Scripture. Further, it is argued, St. Augustine viewed these books as inspired.

Protestants respond by pointing out that even though some of the Apocryphal books may have been alluded to in the New Testament, no New Testament writer *ever* quoted from *any* of these books as holy Scripture or gave them the slightest authority as inspired books. Jesus and the disciples virtually ignored these books, something that wouldn't have been the case if they had considered them to be inspired.

Moreover, even though certain church fathers spoke approvingly of the Apocrypha, there were other early church fathers—notably Origen and Jerome—who denied their inspiration. Further, even though the early Augustine acknowledged the Apocrypha, in his later years he rejected these books as being outside the canon and considered them inferior to the Hebrew Scriptures.[1]

The Jewish Council of Jamnia, which met in A.D. 90, rejected the Apocrypha as Scripture. Combine all this with the fact that there are clear historical errors in the Apocrypha (especially those relating to Tobit) and the fact that it contains unbiblical doctrines (like praying for the dead), and it is clear that these books do not belong in the Bible. In addition, unlike many of the biblical books, *there is no claim in any Apocryphal book in regard to divine inspiration.*

Is it true that Mark 16:9-20 does not belong in the Bible?

Mark 16:9-20 is absent from the two oldest Greek manuscripts in our possession—Codex Alexandrinus and Codex Sinaiticus. As well, these verses are absent from the Old Latin manuscripts, the Sinaitic Syriac manuscript, about 100 Armenian manuscripts, and the two oldest Georgian manuscripts. Further, Clement of Alexandria and Origen show no knowledge of the existence of these verses. Eusebius and Jerome attest that the passage was absent from almost all the Greek copies of Mark known to them. Understandably, then, many scholars believe that Mark 16:9-20 does not belong in the Bible. Fortunately, Mark 16:9-20 does not affect a single major doctrine of Christianity.

4

~

Interpreting Scripture

Why is it that Spirit-filled Christians have different interpretations regarding what specific Bible verses mean?

Scripture is clear that one of the ministries of the Holy Spirit is to illumine the minds of Christians so they can understand Scripture (1 Corinthians 2:13,14). This being the case, why do Spirit-filled Christians have different understandings as to what certain Bible verses mean?

In answering this question, you might liken the Holy Spirit to a radio station that is transmitting a perfect signal. Even though that radio signal is transmitted perfectly, there are all kinds of different quality radio receivers out there. Some have good reception; some have poor reception. Some have a good antennae; others have a broken antennae. Some have good batteries; others are low on energy. The point is, different radio receivers have varying degrees of success in receiving that perfect signal.

Christians are much the same way. The Holy Spirit's "signal" (that is, His illumination) is always perfect. But because of varying circumstances (perhaps sin, or not fully walking in the Spirit, or being overly concerned about the affairs of the world, or being blinded by Satan), Christians have varying degrees of success in receiving the Spirit's illumination.

One caricature people often have of Christians is that we interpret the Bible with wooden literalism. How can we respond to this claim?

Evangelicals do not hold to a "wooden literalism"—the kind that interprets biblical figures of speech literally. What is understood to be symbolic and what is taken literally should be based on the biblical context itself—such as when Jesus used obviously figurative parables to communicate spiritual truth.

A literal approach to Scripture recognizes that the Bible contains a variety of literary genres, each of which have certain peculiar characteristics that must be identified in order to interpret the text properly. Biblical genres include the historical (for example, Acts), the dramatic epic (Job), poetry (Psalms), wise sayings (Proverbs), and apocalyptic writings (Revelation). An incorrect genre judgment will lead one far astray in interpreting Scripture.

Even though the Bible contains a variety of literary genres and many figures of speech, the biblical authors most often employed literal statements to convey their ideas. And where they use a literal means to express their ideas, the Bible expositor must employ a corresponding means to explain these ideas—namely, a literal approach. Such an approach gives to each word in the text the same basic meaning it would have in normal, ordinary, customary usage—whether employed in writing, speaking, or thinking. Without such a method, communication between God and humankind is impossible.

What is the difference between exegesis and eisogesis?

Exegesis refers to drawing the meaning *out of* the text of Scripture, while eisogesis refers to superimposing a meaning *onto* the text. By using eisogesis instead of exegesis, a Marxist interpreter could, for example, so skew the meaning of the U.S. Constitution that it came out reading like a communistic document. Cultists have done the same type of thing with Holy Scripture. They so skew the meaning of the biblical text that it comes out saying something entirely different than what was intended by the author.

Instead of superimposing a meaning onto the biblical text, the objective interpreter seeks to discover the author's intended meaning (the only *true* meaning). One must recognize that what a passage means is fixed by the author and is not subject to alteration by readers. Meaning is *determined* by the author; it is *discovered* by readers.

What do you mean when you say that "Scripture interprets Scripture"?

Every word in the Bible is part of a verse, and every verse is part of a paragraph, and every paragraph is part of a book, and every book is part of the whole of Scripture. No verse of Scripture can be divorced from the verses around it.

In interpreting Scripture, there is both an immediate context and a broader context. The immediate context of a verse is the paragraph (or paragraphs) of the biblical book in question. The immediate context should always be consulted in interpreting Bible verses.

The broader context is the whole of Scripture. The entire Holy Scripture is the context and guide for understanding the particular passages of Scripture. We must keep in mind that the interpretation of a specific passage must not contradict the total teaching of Scripture on a point. Individual verses do not exist as isolated fragments, but as parts of a whole. The exposition of these verses, therefore, must involve exhibiting them in right relation both to the whole and to each other. *Scripture interprets Scripture.* If we would understand the parts, our wisest course is to get to know the whole.

Do you have any tips on how to interpret the Old Testament?

Yes—always interpret the Old Testament in view of the greater light of the New Testament. As theologian Benjamin Warfield put it,

> The Old Testament may be likened to a chamber richly furnished but dimly lighted; the introduction of light [from the New Testament] brings into it nothing which was not in it before; but it brings out into clearer view much of what is in it but was only dimly or even not at all perceived before.[1]

Christ's activities in Old Testament times provide a good example. In Isaiah 6:1-5 we are told that Isaiah witnessed the incredible glory of God. The greater light of the New Testament, however, tells us that Isaiah actually saw Jesus' glory (John 12:41). Likewise, in the Exodus account we are told that God Almighty sustained His people in the wilderness sojourn. But the greater light of the New Testament tells us that Christ was most definitely involved in sustaining His people in the wilderness (1 Corinthians 10:1-4). So, by approaching the Old Testament through the greater light of the New Testament, we see things in the Old Testament we wouldn't otherwise see.

Was Jesus in Matthew 13 supporting the idea that we should seek a hidden, secondary meaning in Scripture passages?

By no means! In Matthew 13, Jesus is portrayed as being in front of a mixed multitude comprised of both believers and unbelievers. He did not attempt to separate the believers from the unbelievers and then instruct only the believers. Rather, He constructed His teaching so that believers would come to understand what He said but unbelievers *would not*—and He did this by using parables.

After teaching one such parable, the disciples asked Jesus: "Why do you speak to the people in parables?" (Matthew 13:10). Jesus answered: "The knowledge of *the secrets* of the kingdom of heaven has been given to you [believers], but not to them [unbelievers]" (verse 11, italics added). Some New Agers have concluded that in view of this verse, there must be secrets in the words of Jesus that only true "believers" can discern. Hence, they say, we should approach the Bible with a view to finding the secret, hidden meanings in each verse.

Such an understanding of Matthew 13 is untenable. It is true that Jesus said, "The knowledge of *the secrets* of the kingdom of heaven has been given to you [believers], but not to them [unbelievers]" (italics added). However, the Greek word for *secret* in this passage simply means "mystery." A mystery in the biblical sense is a truth that cannot be discerned simply by human investigation, but requires special revelation from God. Generally, this word refers to a truth that was unknown to people living in Old Testament times, but is now revealed to humankind by God (Matthew 13:17; Colossians 1:26). In Matthew 13, Jesus provides information to believers about the kingdom of heaven that has never been revealed before.

One might legitimately ask why Jesus engineered His parabolic teaching so that *believers* could understand His teaching but *unbelievers* could not. The backdrop to this is that the disciples, having responded favorably to Jesus' teaching and having placed their faith in Him, already knew much truth about the Messiah. Careful reflection on Jesus' parables would enlighten them even further.

Hardened unbelievers, however, who had willfully and persistently refused Jesus' previous teachings, were prevented from understanding the parables. Jesus was apparently following an injunction He provided earlier in the

Sermon on the Mount: "Do not give dogs what is sacred; do not throw your pearls to pigs" (Matthew 7:6). Yet there is grace even here. For it is possible that Jesus may have prevented unbelievers from understanding the parables because He did not want to add more responsibility to them by imparting new truth for which they would be held responsible.

One should not miss the fact that the parables of the Sower (Matthew 13:3-9) and the Weeds (13:24-30) show that Jesus wanted His parables to be clear to those who were receptive. Jesus Himself provided the interpretation of these parables for His disciples. He did this not only so there would be no uncertainty as to their meaning, but to guide believers as to the proper method to use in interpreting the other parables. The fact that Christ did not interpret His subsequent parables shows that He fully expected believers to understand what He taught by following the methodology He illustrated for them. Clearly, then, Matthew 13 does not support but rather *argues against* seeking a hidden meaning in Scripture.

Does the Bible teach "sola scriptura"?

Yes. The Bible teaches that Scripture alone is the supreme and infallible authority for the church and the individual believer. This is not to say that creeds and tradition are unimportant, but the Bible alone is our final authority. Creeds and tradition are man-made.

Jesus said, "Scripture cannot be broken" (John 10:35). He said, "I tell you the truth, until heaven and earth disappear, not the smallest letter, not the least stroke of a pen, will by any means disappear from the Law until everything is accomplished" (Matthew 5:18). He said, "It is easier for heaven and earth to disappear than for the least stroke of a pen to drop out of the Law" (Luke 16:17).

Jesus used Scripture as the final court of appeal in every matter under dispute. He said to some Pharisees, "You nullify the word of God by your tradition that you have handed down" (Mark 7:13). To the Sadducees He said, "You are in error because you do not know the Scriptures or the power of God" (Matthew 22:29). To the devil, Jesus consistently responded, "It is written..." (Matthew 4:4-10). So, following Jesus' lead, the Scriptures alone are our supreme and final authority.

PART 2

~

COMMON QUESTIONS
FROM THE BIBLE

Common Questions from the Old Testament

Common Questions from the New Testament

5

~

Common Questions
from the Old Testament

Is there any merit to the so-called "gap theory" regarding God's work of creation (Genesis 1:1,2)?

The gap theory teaches that there was an original creation (Genesis 1:1), and that as a result of Lucifer's rebellion and fall, the earth became chaos. The picture of formlessness, emptiness, and darkness in Genesis 1:2 is allegedly a picture of divine judgment, for God could not have originally created the earth this way. Millions of years are said to have taken place between verses 1 and 2.

There are a number of problems with the gap theory. For one thing, the grammar of Genesis 1:1,2 does not allow for a gap. Verse 1 is an independent clause; verse 2 is composed of three circumstantial clauses (explaining the condition of the earth when God began to create), and it is directly connected to verse 3. There is no break between verses 1 and 2. Grammatically, then, the gap theory just doesn't fit.

The gap theory also depends on the phrase "formless and void" meaning *evil* or the *result of a judgment*; however, its usage in Job 26:7 and Isaiah 45:18 does not support this idea. Gap theorists also draw an artificial distinction between the Hebrew verbs *bara* (which they define as "creating out of nothing"—Genesis 1:1) and *asa* (which they define as "refashioning"—Genesis 1:7,16,25). A careful study of these two verbs reveals that they are used *interchangeably*;

asa does not mean "to refashion." In view of these and other factors, I don't give much credence to the gap theory.

Were the days mentioned in the creation account literal 24-hour days (Genesis 1:3–2:3)?

Theologians have debated this issue back and forth for centuries. There are four primary views:

1. Some theologians believe the days in the creation account were simply revelatory days—that is, they were days during which God *revealed* the creation scene to Moses. (Exodus 20:11, however, clearly contradicts this view.)

2. Other theologians believe each day in the creation account represents an age. Justification for this view is found in Joel 2:31, which portrays a day as a long period of time.

3. Other theologians believe the days in Genesis are literal solar days, but each day was separated by a huge time gap. This allegedly accounts for the apparent long geological ages that science has discovered.

4. Still other theologians believe the days of Genesis are literal solar days with no time gap between them. This is my view.

In support of this latter view, the Genesis account makes reference to evening and morning, indicating that literal days are meant (Genesis 1:5). Further, we read that God created the sun to rule the day and the moon to rule the night, thus indicating solar days (verse 16). Solar days also seem to be implied in Exodus 20:11 where we are told that "in six days the LORD made the heavens and the earth, the sea, and all that is in them, but he rested on the seventh day."

Moreover, Hebrew scholars tell us that whenever a number is used with the Hebrew word for day *(yom)*, it always refers to a literal solar day (no exceptions). Since God is said to have created the universe in *six* days, literal solar days must be meant.

Genesis 2:17 indicates that Adam and Eve would die the day they ate of the forbidden fruit. But they didn't die, did they?

Actually, they did die. They didn't die that day *physically*, but they did die *spiritually*.

The word "death" carries the idea of separation. Physical death involves the separation of the soul or spirit from the body. Spiritual death involves the separation of the human being from God. When Adam and Eve partook of the forbidden fruit, they were immediately separated from God in a spiritual sense. (Their consequent action of trying to hide from God in the Garden of Eden indicates their awareness of this spiritual separation.) The moment of their sin, they became "dead in...transgressions and sins" (Ephesians 2:1-3). Their separation and isolation from God eventually led to their physical deaths.

Why was Abel's offering accepted by God when Cain's was rejected (Genesis 4:3-5)?

I think the answer to this question is found in the attitude that each displayed in regard to their respective offerings. The biblical text says that Abel gave not only the firstborn of his flock, but the *choicest* of the firstborn (Genesis 4:4). In other words, Abel gave the "best of the best" that was in his possession. By contrast, we read that Cain brought "some of the fruits of the soil" (verse 3). One gets the feeling that Cain routinely gathered some fruit and offered it to the Lord to fulfill his obligation.

Abel's faith was apparently another factor. In Hebrews 11:4 we read, "By faith Abel offered God a better sacrifice than Cain did. By faith he was commended as a righteous man, when God spoke well of his offerings. And by faith he still speaks, even though he is dead." In contrast to Abel's faith and righteousness, Cain was apparently characterized by unbelief and unrighteousness.

Where did Cain get his wife (Genesis 4:17)?

Genesis 4:17 says, "Cain lay with his wife, and she became pregnant and gave birth to Enoch." Who was his wife? It is implied in the biblical text that Cain married one of his sisters. Several facts lead us to this conclusion.

First, it is clear that Adam and Eve had a number of children. Genesis 5:4 says, "After Seth was born, Adam lived 800 years and had other sons and daughters." Since Adam and Eve were the first man and woman, and since God had commanded them (and their descendants) to be fruitful and multiply (Genesis 1:28), it seems reasonable to conclude that Cain married one of his many sisters. It is also possible that he married a niece or even a grandniece.

One must keep in mind that in the early years of the human race there were no genetic defects that had yet developed as a result of the fall of man. By the time of Abraham, God had not yet declared this kind of marriage to be contrary to His will (see Genesis 20:12). Laws governing incest apparently did not become enacted until the time of Moses (Leviticus 18:7-17; 20:11,12,14,17,20,21). Hence, there was no prohibition regarding marrying a sister (or a niece or grandniece) in the days of Cain.

Are the "sons of God" mentioned in Genesis 6:2 evil angels?

This is a much-debated issue. A common view is that some evil angels cohabited with human women. In support of this position are the following facts:

1. Some of the Septuagint manuscripts (that is, manuscripts of early Greek translations of the Hebrew Old Testament) have the phrase "angels of God" instead of "sons of

God." This reveals that some of the early Jews understood this phrase to be referring to angels.

2. The Hebrew phrase for "sons of God" (or, more literally, "sons of Elohim") is a phrase that always refers to angels when used elsewhere in the Old Testament (see Job 1:6; 2:1; 38:7).

3. The "evil angel" interpretation of Genesis 6 may give us a clue as to why some angels are presently bound in prison and others are not (2 Peter 2:4).

4. It is argued that if the holy angels can appear as human beings and even participate in eating meals and doing good deeds (Genesis 18; Hebrews 13:2), is it not possible that at one time some fallen angels took on a human appearance and engaged in evil deeds?

Another view held by many is that some fallen angels possessed human men who then cohabited with "the daughters of men." This view has the merit of providing a good explanation of how angels who are bodiless (Hebrews 1:14) and sexless (Matthew 22:30) could cohabit with humans.

Still another common interpretation is that the phrase "sons of God" refers to the godly line of Seth (the Redeemer's line—Genesis 4:26) who intermingled with the godless line of Cain. Gleason Archer argues, "Instead of remaining true to God and loyal to their spiritual heritage, they allowed themselves to be enticed by the beauty of ungodly women who were 'daughters of men'—that is, of the tradition and example of Cain."[1] In support of this view is the fact that human beings are sometimes called "sons" (Isaiah 43:6).

Was the flood of Genesis 6–8 a universal flood or a local flood?

I believe the flood was universal. The waters climbed so high on the earth that "all the high mountains under the entire heavens were covered" (Genesis 7:19). They rose so greatly on the earth that they "covered the mountains to a depth of more than twenty feet" (verse 20). The flood lasted some 377 days (nearly 54 weeks), indicating more than just local flooding. The Bible also says that every living thing that moved on the earth perished, "all the creatures that swarm over the earth, and all mankind. Everything on dry land that had the breath of life in its nostrils died. Every living thing on the face of the earth was wiped out. . . . Only Noah was left, and those with him in the ark" (verses 21-23). The language of Genesis 6–8 is surely that of a universal flood.

Furthermore, the universal view best explains the fact that there is a worldwide distribution of diluvia deposits. A universal flood would also explain the sudden death of many woolly mammoths frozen in Alaskan and Siberian ice. Investigation shows that these animals died suddenly by choking or drowning and not by freezing.[2]

Finally, there is supportive evidence in the fact that there are many universal flood legends (more than 270) among people of various religions and cultural backgrounds all over the world. These people attribute the descent of all races to Noah.[3]

Why did God command Abraham to sacrifice his son as a burnt offering (Genesis 22:2)?

The context of Genesis 22 makes it quite clear that, ultimately, God never intended for this command to be executed. God restrained Abraham's hand just in the nick of time: "'Do not lay a hand on the boy,' he said. 'Do not do anything to him. Now I know that you fear God, because you have not withheld from me your son, your only son'" (Genesis 22:12). Scholars agree that God was only testing Abraham's faith. The test served to show that Abraham loved God more than he loved his own son.

What are we to make of Joshua 10:12-14, which speaks of Joshua bidding the sun to "stand still"?

Scholars have two primary suggestions as to how to interpret this passage. Some believe God may have just slowed down or stopped the normal rotation of the earth so that Joshua's forces were able to complete their victory over the Amorites. Others suggest that God prolonged the daylight by some sort of unusual refraction of the sun's rays. This would have given Joshua and his men more daylight hours but not necessarily more hours in the day.

Personally, I think God stopped the earth's rotation on its axis. Such a miracle poses no problem for the Almighty God of the universe. Performing a mighty miracle (stopping the earth's rotation) is no more difficult for Him than performing a minor miracle (withering a fig tree).

It is highly revealing that the Amorites worshiped the sun and the moon as deities. It would appear, then, that the true God brought about the defeat of the Amorites through the agency of their own supposed deities. This showed the utter futility of their belief in false gods.

Did Jephthah sacrifice his daughter to God (Judges 11:30-39)?

Scholars have dealt with this difficult passage in several different ways. One view is that Jephthah actually did offer his own daughter as a burnt sacrifice to the Lord. If this is the case, this does not in any way mean that God endorsed what Jephthah did. He was certainly not under orders from God to do this. God had earlier revealed that human sacrifice was absolutely forbidden (Leviticus 18:21; 20:2-5; Deuteronomy 12:31; 18:10).

We must keep in mind that simply because something is recounted in the Bible does not mean that God agrees with it. God certainly doesn't agree with the words or actions of Satan, but the Bible nevertheless accurately reports on his words and actions. In the present case, the author of Judges may have just provided an objective account of the event without passing judgment.

One must also remember that the Book of Judges deals with a period in human history when everyone was doing what was right in his or her own eyes. Judges 21:25 says, "In those days Israel had no king; everyone did as he saw fit." It is very possible that Jephthah was simply doing what was right in his own eyes, thereby victimizing his own daughter. If Jephthah actually committed this act, we can only conclude that he was acting in great folly and was going against the will of God, despite his good motives and apparent desire to please the Lord.

Another way to interpret this passage is that Jephthah offered up his daughter in the sense of consecrating her for service at the tabernacle for the rest of her life and devoting her to celibacy. This would involve offering up his daughter in a *spiritual* way instead of *physically* offering her as a burnt offering. As the apostle Paul said in Romans 12:1, people can be offered to God as "a living sacrifice."

If his daughter was indeed offered as a living sacrifice, this necessarily would involve a life of perpetual virginity, which was a tremendous sacrifice in the Jewish context of the day. She would not be able to bring up children to continue her father's lineage.

This may explain why his daughter responded by saying, "'Grant me this one request,' she said. 'Give me two months to roam the hills and weep with my friends, because I will never marry'" (Judges 11:37). Note that she didn't weep because of an impending death. She wept because she would never marry and hence would remain a virgin.

What actually happened at Endor? Was the prophet Samuel actually summoned from the dead by a witch (1 Samuel 28:3-25)?

Scholars have suggested several explanations. Some believe the witch worked a miracle by demonic powers and actually brought Samuel back from the dead. In support of this view, there are certain passages that seem to indicate that demons have the power to perform lying signs and wonders (Matthew 7:22; 2 Corinthians 11:14; 2 Thessalonians 2:9,10; Revelation 16:14). This view is unlikely, however, since Scripture also reveals that death is final (Hebrews 9:27), the dead cannot return (2 Samuel 12:23 cf. Luke 16:24-27), and demons cannot usurp or overpower God's authority over life and death (Job 1:10-12).

A second view is that the witch did not really bring up Samuel from the dead, but a demonic spirit simply impersonated the prophet. Those who hold to this view say that certain verses indicate that demons can deceive people who try to contact the dead (Leviticus 19:31; Deuteronomy 18:11; 1 Chronicles 10:13). This view is unlikely, however, because the passage seems to say that Samuel did in fact return from the dead, and that he provided a prophecy that actually came to pass. Further, it is unlikely that demons would have uttered God's truth, since the devil is the father of lies (John 8:44).

A third view is that God sovereignly and miraculously allowed Samuel's spirit to appear in order to rebuke Saul for his sin. Samuel's spirit did not appear as a result of the woman's powers (for indeed, no human has this power), but only because God sovereignly brought it about. The fact that Samuel actually seemed to return from the dead supports this view (1 Samuel 28:14), and this caused the witch to shriek with fear (see verse 12). The witch's cry of astonishment indicates that this appearance of Samuel was not the result of her usual tricks. That God allowed Samuel's spirit to appear on this one occasion should not be taken to mean that witches have any real power to summon the dead. God had a one-time purpose for this one-time special occasion.

Why did Solomon have so many wives (1 Kings 11:1-3)?

First Kings 11:1-3 indicates that King Solomon had hundreds of wives and hundreds of concubines, many from lands with which God had previously instructed the Israelites to avoid intermarrying. God knew that such intermarrying would lead to the worship of false gods. Why, then, did Solomon do this?

History reveals that Solomon was very aggressive in his foreign policy. In sealing treaties in ancient days, it was customary for a lesser king to give his daughter in marriage to the greater king (in this case, Solomon). Every time a new treaty was sealed, Solomon ended up with yet another wife. These wives were considered tokens of friendship and "sealed" the relationship between the two kings. It may be that Solomon was not even personally acquainted with some of these wives, even though he was married to them.

In the process of doing all this, Solomon was utterly disobedient to the Lord. He was apparently so obsessed with power and wealth that it overshadowed his spiritual life and he ended up falling into apostasy. He worshiped some of the false gods of the women who became married to him.

Moreover, in marrying more than one woman Solomon was going against God's revealed will regarding monogamy. From the very beginning God created one woman for one man (see Genesis 1:27; 2:21-24). Deuteronomy 17:17 explicitly instructs the king not to "take many wives." So Solomon sinned in two ways: (1) he engaged in polygamy, and (2) he violated God's commandment against marrying pagans, which ultimately led to his own apostasy.

In one verse we are told that Satan incited David to take a census of Israel (1 Chronicles 21:1). In another verse we are told that the Lord incited David to take this census (2 Samuel 24:1). Which account are we to believe?

Both! These are not *contradictory* accounts; they are *complementary* accounts. Both are true, but both reflect different aspects of a larger truth. Taken together, we can construct a fuller picture of what happened.

Satan was the actual instrument used to incite David to number Israel (1 Chronicles 21:1), but God permitted Satan to do this. In the Hebrew mindset, whatever God *permits*, God *commits*. By allowing this census taking, God is viewed as having brought about the act Himself (2 Samuel 24:1). (Keep in mind that the Hebrews were not too concerned about "first causes" and "secondary causes.") Satan did what he did because he wanted to destroy David and the people of God. God's purpose, however, was simply to humble David and teach him and his people a valuable spiritual lesson.

Is it true that "where there is no vision [for the future], the people perish" (Proverbs 29:18 KJV) ?

This verse has been grossly misunderstood by many Christians. It has often been twisted to say that unless we have long-range plans and a well thought-out strategy, we will perish. But such an idea is completely foreign to the context.

The New International Version correctly renders this verse: "Where there is no revelation, the people cast off restraint; but blessed is he who keeps the law." This verse simply means that when God's Word is suppressed or silenced, people lose restraint and become ungovernable. Instead of doing God's will, they allow their own baser appetites to take over and they indulge in all kinds of sinful activities.

We find this illustrated in the Book of Exodus. Moses had left the Israelites alone for a mere 40 days when he was on Mount Sinai receiving God's law. During that time, the people lost all restraint and ended up making an idol in the form of a golden calf (Exodus 32:25).

6

~

Common Questions
from the New Testament

Why would God give special revelation concerning Christ's birth to astrologers—the Magi (Matthew 2:1,2)?

Occultic astrologers seek to gain paranormal knowledge based on the movement and position of the stars. The Magi were *not* involved in this type of thing. They were not occultic seers and sorcerers in the sense that today's astrologers often are. These men were basically experts in the study of the stars. We might loosely equate them today to specialists in astronomy. Tradition tells us that there were three Magi who visited Christ, and they are said to be kings. But we do not know this for certain.

Matthew 20:29-34 says Jesus healed two blind men as He left Jericho. Mark 10:46-52 and Luke 18:35-43 say Jesus healed one man as He entered Jericho. How can we reconcile this apparent contradiction?

There are several possible explanations. One is that the healing took place as Jesus was leaving *old* Jericho and was nearing *new* Jericho (there were two Jerichos in those days). If Jesus were at a place between the two Jerichos, then, depending on one's perspective, He could be viewed as "leaving" one Jericho or "entering" the other Jericho. Now, there were apparently two blind men in need of healing, but Bartimaeus was the more aggressive of the two, and hence two of the gospel accounts (Mark and Luke) mention only him. If the blind men were healed between the two Jerichos, this would clear up the apparent contradiction between the gospel accounts.

Another possible explanation is that the blind men pleaded with Jesus as He entered (either the old or new) Jericho, but they didn't receive their actual healings until Jesus was leaving Jericho. It's also possible that Jesus healed one blind man as He was entering Jericho, and healed two other blind men as he was leaving Jericho. Clearly, there are a number of ways of reconciling the gospel accounts.

Did Judas die by hanging or by falling onto some rocks (Matthew 27:5; Acts 1:18)?

Matthew 27:5 tells us that Judas died by hanging himself. Acts 1:18 tells us that Judas fell onto some rocks and his body burst open. Is there a contradiction here?

No. Both accounts are true. Apparently Judas first hanged himself. Then, at some point, the rope either broke or loosened so that his body slipped from it and fell to the rocks below and burst open. (Some have suggested that Judas didn't do a very good job of tying the noose.) Neither account alone is complete. Taken together, we have a full picture of what happened to Judas.

Does Jesus advocate hating one's mother, father, spouse, and children for His sake (Luke 14:26)?

No, not when you understand Jesus' words correctly. In Luke 14:26 Jesus said, "If anyone comes to me and does not hate his father and mother, his wife and children, his brothers and sisters—yes, even his own life—he cannot be my disciple." In the Hebrew mindset, to "hate" simply means to "love less." Jesus is simply communicating that our supreme love must be for Him alone. Everything else (and everyone else) must take second place. This is in keeping with what Jesus said in Matthew 10:37: "Anyone who loves his father or mother more than me is not worthy of me; anyone who loves his son or daughter more than me is not worthy of me." Measuring our supreme love for Christ against all other lesser loves may make these lesser loves *seem* like hate by comparison.

Who are the "other sheep" mentioned in John 10:16?

The context indicates that the "other sheep" mentioned in John 10:16 are *Gentile* believers as opposed to *Jewish* believers. As a backdrop, the Jews in the Gospels were called "the lost sheep of Israel" (Matthew 10:6; 15:24), and those Jews who followed Christ were called His "sheep" (John 10).

Jesus often referred to His Jewish disciples as sheep in His flock. For example, when Jesus was giving the 12 disciples instructions for their future service, He said: "Behold, I send you out *as sheep* in the midst of wolves; therefore be shrewd as serpents, and innocent as doves" (Matthew 10:16 NASB, italics added). Later, Jesus told the disciples that His crucifixion would cause them to scatter: "You will all fall away because of Me this night, for it is written, 'I will strike down the shepherd, and *the sheep of the flock* shall be scattered'" (Matthew 26:31 NASB, italics added).

Now, when Jesus said, "I have *other* sheep, which are not of this fold" (NASB), He was clearly referring to non-Jewish, Gentile believers. The Gentile believers, along with the Jewish believers, "shall become *one flock* with *one shepherd*" (John 10:16 NASB). This is in perfect accord with Ephesians 2:11-22, where we are told that in Christ, Jews and Gentiles are reconciled in *one body*. Galatians 3:28 tells us that "there is neither Jew nor Greek [Gentile], there is neither slave nor free man, there is neither male nor female; for *you are all one in Christ Jesus*" (NASB, italics added). Likewise, Colossians 3:11 speaks of "a renewal in which there is no distinction between Greek [Gentiles] and Jew, circumcised and uncircumcised, barbarian, Scythian, slave and freeman, but Christ is all, and in all" (NASB).

Did Jesus teach that human beings are gods in John 10:34?

No. In John 10:34 Jesus said to some Jewish critics, "Is it not written in your Law, 'I have said you are gods'?" This verse does not teach that human beings are gods, but rather must be understood in light of Psalm 82, which Jesus was quoting.

In Psalm 82 we find God's judgment against the evil Israelite judges. The judges were called "gods" because they pronounced life and death judgments against people.[1] But they became corrupt and unjust in their dealings.

In verse 6, Asaph, speaking of these unjust human judges, said: "I said, 'You are "gods"; you are all sons of the Most High.' But you will die like mere men; you will fall like every other ruler." Asaph is clearly speaking in irony. He is saying in effect: "I have called you 'gods,' but in fact you will die like the men that you really are." When Jesus alluded to this psalm in John 10, He was saying that what the Israelite judges were called in irony and in judgment, *He is in reality.*

What did Jesus mean when He said we would do greater miracles than He did (John 14:12)?

In John 14:12 we read, "I tell you the truth, anyone who has faith in me will do what I have been doing. He will do even greater things than these, because I am going to the Father." Does this mean you and I can do even more incredible miracles than Jesus performed while He was on earth? *No way!*

In this verse Jesus is simply saying that His many followers would do things greater *in extent* (all over the world) and greater *in effect* (multitudes being touched by the power of God). Jesus was referring to the whole scope of the impact of God's people and the church on the entire world throughout all history. In other words, Jesus was speaking *quantitatively*, not *qualitatively*.

What does Scripture mean when it says an elder of the church must be "the husband of but one wife" (1 Timothy 3:12)?

This verse has been debated by Christians since the first century. There are four basic suggestions as to what it means:

1. The elder must be married only once. No remarriage is allowed, even if the wife dies.

2. The elder must be married to one wife *at a time* (that is, no polygamy is allowed).

3. A single person cannot be an elder in the church.

4. The elder must be faithful to his wife (that is, he must be a "one-woman man"). I believe this is probably the correct view.

Does Revelation 7:4 teach that there will be only 144,000 "anointed" believers who go to heaven, with all other believers being assigned to live forever on a paradise earth?

No. This is a false teaching of the Watchtower Society (the Jehovah's Witnesses).

The Watchtower Society says that even though the 144,000 are said to be of the 12 tribes of Israel, these cannot literally be the tribes of natural Israel because there never was a tribe of Joseph in the Old Testament, even though one is mentioned in Revelation 7:4-8. As well, the tribes of Ephraim and Dan—which were tribes of Israel in the Old Testament—are not included in the list in Revelation 7. Further, the Levites—who are mentioned as being a tribe in Revelation 7—were set aside for service in connection with the temple in the Old Testament but were not ever reckoned as one of the 12 tribes. It is thus concluded that the 144,000 are actually anointed believers who will live forever with Christ in heaven. All other believers will spend eternity on a paradise earth.[2]

Contrary to the Watchtower view, it is the clear testimony of Scripture that a heavenly destiny awaits *all* who believe in Jesus Christ, not just a select group of 144,000 anointed believers (see Ephesians 2:19; Philippians 3:20; Colossians 3:1; Hebrews 3:1; 12:22; 2 Peter 1:10, 11). Drawing a dichotomy between those with a heavenly destiny and those with an earthly destiny has absolutely no warrant in Scripture. All who believe in Christ are "heirs" of the eternal kingdom (Galatians 3:29; 4:28-31; Titus 3:7; James 2:5). The righteousness of God that leads to life in heaven is available "through faith in Jesus Christ *for all those who believe; for there is no distinction*" (Romans 3:22 NASB, italics added).

Jesus Himself promised, "If anyone serves Me, let him follow Me; and where I am, there shall My servant also be [that is, heaven]" (John 12:26 NASB). Jesus clearly affirmed that all believers will be together in "one flock" under "one shepherd" (John 10:16). There will not be two "flocks"—one on earth and one in heaven. Scripture is clear: one flock, one Shepherd!

What about the Watchtower contention that the tribes mentioned in Revelation 7 cannot be literal tribes of Israel? One must first point out that the very fact that specific tribes are mentioned along with specific numbers for those tribes removes all possibility that this is a figure of speech.

Nowhere else in the Bible does a reference to 12 tribes of Israel mean anything but 12 tribes of Israel.

Why, then, are the Old Testament tribes of Dan and Ephraim omitted in Revelation 7? As a backdrop, it must first be pointed out that the Old Testament has no fewer than 20 variant lists of the tribes, and these lists include anywhere from ten to 13 tribes, though the number 12 is predominant (cf. Genesis 49; Deuteronomy 33; Ezekiel 48). Hence, no list of the 12 tribes of Israel must be identical. However, since 12 seems to be the ideal number in terms of listing Israel's tribes, it is clear that John in Revelation 7 and 14 wanted to maintain this ideal number.

Most scholars today agree that the reason Dan's tribe was omitted was because that tribe was guilty of idolatry on many occasions and, as a result, was largely obliterated (Leviticus 24:11; Judges 18:1,30; cf. 1 Kings 12:28,29). To engage in unrepentant idolatry is to be cut off from God's blessing. As well, there was an early tradition that the Antichrist would come from the tribe of Dan.

Ephraim's tribe, too, was involved in idolatry and paganized worship (Judges 17; Hosea 4:17), and was hence omitted from the list in Revelation 7. The readjustment of the list to include Joseph and Manasseh to complete the 12 thus makes good sense.

Why was the tribe of Levi included in the listing of tribes in Revelation 7, rather than maintaining its special status as a priestly tribe under the Mosaic Law? It is probable that the tribe of Levi is included here because the priestly functions of the tribe of Levi ceased with the coming of Christ—the ultimate High Priest. Indeed, the Levitical priesthood was fulfilled in the person of Christ (Hebrews 7–10). Because there was no further need for the services of the tribe of Levi as priests, there was no further reason for keeping this tribe distinct and separate from the others; hence, they were properly included in the tribal listing in the Book of Revelation.

PART 3

~

KNOWING GOD

The Triune God
Errors Relating to the Doctrine of God
God the Holy Spirit

~

The Triune God

Was God lonely before He created the universe and the world of humankind?

No. God contains within Himself three centers of personal activity, each denoted by personal pronouns ("I," "Me"). This means that there is an incomprehensible richness in the inner life of God. During this precreation eternity past, the Father, Son, and Holy Spirit existed in a state of uninterrupted, completely fulfilling fellowship. The Father and the Holy Spirit enjoyed an eternal loving interaction with each other and with the Son. Recall that near the close of His three-year ministry on earth, Jesus, in His prayer to the Father, spoke of eternity past as a matter of memory: "Thou didst love Me before the foundation of the world" (John 17:24 NASB).

Does the fact that the word "Trinity" is not in the Bible mean the doctrine is unbiblical?

By no means! Though the *word* Trinity is not mentioned in the Bible, the *concept* is clearly derived from Scripture (see the discussion later in the chapter).

It is generally the Jehovah's Witnesses who say the Trinity is an unbiblical doctrine because the word is not in the Bible. A good response to them is to point out that the word *Jehovah* does not appear as such in the Bible. In fact, the word *Jehovah* does not appear in any legitimate Hebrew or Greek manuscripts of the Bible. The word was originally formed by superstitious Jewish scribes who joined the consonants YHWH (which *is* a biblical word) with the vowels from Adonai. The result was Yahowah, or Jehovah. The point, of course, is that if you reject the doctrine of the Trinity because the word "Trinity" does not appear in the Bible, then by that same logic the doctrine of Jehovah must be considered false since this term does not appear in the Bible. In any event, Matthew 28:19 and 2 Corinthians 13:14 are great passages to cite in proving that the doctrine of the Trinity *is*, in fact, a biblical doctrine.

Does the fact that God is not a God of confusion (1 Corinthians 14:33) prove that the doctrine of the Trinity cannot be true, since this doctrine is hard to understand?

This is an absurd suggestion. Simply because one is unable to fully comprehend a doctrine does not mean the doctrine is false. For human beings to be able to understand everything about God, they would need to have the very mind of God. Scripture affirms:

✓ "Oh, the depth of the riches both of the wisdom and knowledge of God! How unsearchable are His judgments and unfathomable His ways!" (Romans 11:33 NASB).

✓ " 'For My thoughts are not your thoughts, neither are your ways My ways,' declares the LORD. 'For as the heavens are higher than the earth, so are My ways higher than your ways, and My thoughts than your thoughts' " (Isaiah 55:8, 9 NASB).

✓ "For now we see in a mirror dimly, but then face to face; now I know in part, but then I shall know fully just as I also have been fully known" (1 Corinthians 13:12 NASB).

Such verses make it clear that human reasoning has limitations. Finite minds cannot possibly understand everything there is to know about an infinite being. Creatures cannot know everything there is to know about the sovereign Creator. Just as a young child cannot understand everything his father says, so we as God's children cannot understand everything about our heavenly Father.

What, then, did the apostle Paul mean when he said, "God is not a God of confusion but of peace"? Consulting the context of 1 Corinthians makes everything clear. The Corinthian church was plagued by internal divisions and disorder, especially in regard to the exercise of spiritual gifts (1 Corinthians 1:11). Since God is a God of peace and not a God of confusion, Paul says, the church itself must seek to model itself after God by seeking peace and avoiding disharmony in its services. By so doing, the church honors God.

How can we respond to those who claim that the doctrine of the Trinity is rooted in Babylonian and Assyrian paganism?

The Babylonians and Assyrians believed in *triads* of gods who headed up a pantheon of many other gods. But these triads constituted three separate gods (polytheism), which is utterly different from the doctrine of the Trinity which maintains that there is *only one God* (monotheism) with three persons within the one Godhead.

Moreover, such pagan ideas predate Christianity by some 2,000 years and were geographically far removed from the part of the world where Christianity developed.[1] From a historical and geographical perspective, then, the suggestion that Christianity borrowed the Trinitarian concept from pagans is quite infeasible. Cultists such as the Jehovah's Witnesses (who teach this idea) are rewriting history in an attempt to make their own doctrine (which denies the Trinity) appear more feasible.

It is interesting to note that pagans taught the concept of a great flood that killed much of humankind. The pagans also taught the idea of a messiah-like figure (named Tammuz) who was resurrected. Hence, as Bible scholar Paul G. Weathers argues, "if the Watchtower uses the same method of reasoning, it follows that the Christian belief in the flood, the Messiah (Jesus), and his resurrection are pagan. After all, the pagans believed these things before the Christians!"[2]

The point is, simply because pagans spoke of a concept remotely resembling something found in Scripture does not mean that the concept was stolen from pagans.

Does good biblical support exist for the doctrine of the Trinity?

Yes. The doctrine of the Trinity is based on three lines of evidence: (1) evidence that there is only one true God; (2) evidence that there are three persons who are God; and (3) evidence that indicates three-in-oneness within the Godhead.

Before we examine these three lines of evidence, it is important that we clarify what we do not mean by the word "Trinity." We must avoid two errors: (1) that the Godhead is composed of three utterly distinct persons such as Peter, James, and John, a concept that would lead to what is known as tritheism (belief in three different gods); and (2) that the Godhead is one person only and the triune aspect of His being is no more than three fields of interest, activities, and manifestations, which is referred to in theology as modalism. The fallacy of these errors will become clearer as we examine the biblical evidence for the Trinity.

Evidence for one God. The fact that there is only one true God is the consistent testimony of Scripture from Genesis to Revelation. It is like a thread that runs through every page of the Bible. God positively affirmed through Isaiah the prophet: "This is what the LORD says—Israel's King and Redeemer, the LORD Almighty: I am the first and I am the last; apart from me there is no God" (Isaiah 44:6). God also said, "I am God, and there is no other; I am God, and there is none like me" (46:9).

The oneness of God is also often emphasized in the New Testament. In 1 Corinthians 8:4, for example, the apostle Paul asserted that "an idol is nothing at all in the world and that there is no God but one." James 2:19 says, "You believe that there is one God. Good! Even the demons believe that—and shudder." These and a multitude of other verses (including John 5:44; 17:3; Romans 3:29, 30; 16:27; Galatians 3:20; Ephesians 4:6; and 1 Timothy 2:5) make it absolutely clear that there is one and only one God.

Evidence for three persons who are called God. On the one hand, Scripture is absolutely clear that there is only one God. Yet, in the unfolding of God's revelation to humankind, it also becomes clear that there are three distinct persons who are called God in Scripture.

> ✓ *The Father Is God:* Peter refers to the saints "who have been chosen according to the foreknowledge of God the Father" (1 Peter 1:2).

> ✓ *Jesus Is God:* When Jesus made a post-resurrection appearance to doubting Thomas, Thomas said: "My Lord and my God" (John 20:28). As well, the Father said of the Son, "Your throne, O God, will last for ever and ever, and righteousness will be the scepter of your kingdom" (Hebrews 1:8).

> ✓ *The Holy Spirit Is God:* In Acts 5:3, 4, we are told that lying to the Holy Spirit is equivalent to lying to God.

Moreover, each of the three persons on different occasions is seen to possess the attributes of deity.

✓ For example, all three are said to be *omnipresent* (everywhere present): the Father (John 4:19-24), the Son (Matthew 28:20), and the Holy Spirit (Psalm 139:7).

✓ All three are *omniscient* (all-knowing): the Father (Psalm 139:1,2), the Son (Matthew 9:4), and the Holy Spirit (1 Corinthians 2:10).

✓ All three are *omnipotent* (all-powerful): the Father (1 Peter 1:5), the Son (Matthew 28:18), and the Holy Spirit (Romans 15:19).

✓ Furthermore, *holiness* is ascribed to each person: the Father (Revelation 15:4), the Son (Acts 3:14), and the Holy Spirit (John 16:7-14).

✓ *Eternity* is ascribed to each person: the Father (Psalm 90:2), the Son (Micah 5:2; John 1:2; Revelation 1:8,17), and the Holy Spirit (Hebrews 9:14).

✓ And each of the three is individually described as the *truth*: the Father (John 14:6,7), the Son (Revelation 3:7), and the Holy Spirit (1 John 5:6).

Three-in-oneness in the Godhead. In the New American Standard Bible, Matthew 28:19 reads: "Go therefore and make disciples of all the nations, baptizing them in the name of *the* Father and *the* Son and *the* Holy Spirit" (italics added). It is highly revealing that the word "name" is singular in the Greek, indicating that there is one God, but there are three distinct persons within the Godhead—*the* Father, *the* Son, and *the* Holy Spirit.[3] Theologian Robert Reymond draws our attention to the importance of this verse for the doctrine of the Trinity:

> Jesus does not say, (1) "into the names [plural] of the Father and of the Son and of the Holy Spirit," or

what is its virtual equivalent, (2) "into the name of the Father, and into the name of the Son, and into the name of the Holy Spirit," as if we had to deal with three separate Beings. Nor does He say, (3) "into the name of the Father, Son, and Holy Spirit," (omitting the three recurring articles), as if "the Father, Son, and Holy Ghost" might be taken as merely three designations of a single person. What He does say is this: (4) "into the name [singular] of *the* Father, and of *the* Son, and of *the* Holy Spirit," first asserting the unity of the three by combining them all within the bounds of the single Name, and then throwing into emphasis the distinctness of each by introducing them in turn with the repeated article.[4]

Very clearly, then, the Scriptures affirm that there is one God, but within the unity of the Godhead, there are three coequal and coeternal persons—the Father, the Son, and the Holy Spirit.

How can three "persons" be in one God?

Most theologians acknowledge today that the term "person" is an imperfect expression of what the Bible communicates. Some believe the word tends to distract from the unity of the Trinity. Certainly, in God there are not three separate individuals such as Peter, John, and Matthew who have different characteristics, but only *personal self-distinctions* within the Godhead. Theologian Lewis Sperry Chafer explains that

in applying the term "person" to God, the word is used in a distinctive sense from its normal use in relation to human beings. Though each member of the Godhead manifests the qualities of personality, such as intellect, sensibility, and will, they do not act independently as three separate human individuals would act. Nevertheless, the personalities involved

in the Trinity are expressed in such terms as "I,"
"Thou," "He," and the Persons of the Godhead
address each other as individuals and manifest their
individuality in some personal acts.[5]

Hence, the Father, Son, and Holy Spirit are "persons" in
the sense that each has the personal attributes of mind, emotions, and will, and each of the three is aware of the others,
speaks to the others, and carries on a loving relationship
with the others.

If you find it difficult to comprehend all this, you are in
good company. One day while puzzling over the doctrine of
the Trinity, the great theologian Augustine was walking
along the beach when he observed a young boy with a
bucket, running back and forth to pour water into a little
hole. Augustine asked, "What are you doing?"

The boy replied, "I'm trying to put the ocean into this
hole."

Augustine smiled, recognizing the utter futility of what
the boy was attempting to do.

After pondering the boy's words for a few moments,
however, Augustine came to a sudden realization. He realized that he had been trying to put an infinite God into his
finite mind. It can't be done. We can accept God's revelation
to us that He is triune in nature and that He has infinite perfections. But with our finite minds we cannot fully understand everything about God. Our God is an awesome God.

Some verses say God the Father is the Creator; some say the Son is the Creator; and some say the Holy Spirit is the Creator. How do we reconcile these?

It is true that different passages ascribe the work of creation differently. Many Old Testament references to the
creation attribute it simply to *God* or *Lord* rather than to the
individual persons of the Father, Son, or Holy Spirit (Genesis

1:1; Psalm 96:5; Isaiah 37:16; 44:24; 45:12; Jeremiah 10:11,12). Other passages relate the creation specifically to the Father (Revelation 4:11), to the Son (Colossians 1:16; Hebrews 1:2; John 1:3), or to the Holy Spirit (Job 33:4; Psalm 104:30).

How do we put all these passages together into a coherent whole? A passage that has bearing on this issue is 1 Corinthians 8:6, which describes the Father as the one *"from whom* all things came" and the Son as the one *"through whom* all things came." Based on this, many have concluded that while the Father may be considered Creator in a broad, general sense, the Son is the actual agent or mediating *cause* of creation. Through the Son, all things came into being. Creation is viewed as being "in" the Holy Spirit in the sense that the life of creation is found in the Holy Spirit.

Though breaking down the creative roles of the persons of the Trinity may be helpful in some ways, we must be careful not to make these distinctions absolute. For example, though the Holy Spirit's role may have involved the bestowing of life, we are told elsewhere in Scripture that life is in Christ (John 1:4). Moreover, we must be careful to avoid thinking that the Son as a mediating agent ("through whom" the creation came into being) means that the Son had a lesser role than the Father. Indeed, the same Greek word for "through" [*diá*] that is used of Christ's work of creation in 1 Corinthians 8:6 is used elsewhere in Scripture of the Father's role in creation (Romans 11:36; Hebrews 2:10).

The King James Version rendering of 1 John 5:7 provides clear proof for the Trinity. However, scholars now say the words in this verse are not in the earliest Greek manuscripts. Does this mean the doctrine of the Trinity is not true?

No. Simply because this one verse has no manuscript support does not mean the doctrine of the Trinity is not true.

Numerous other passages—for example, Matthew 28:19 and 2 Corinthians 13:14—have undeniably strong manuscript support, and they establish that (1) there is only one true God; (2) there are three persons who are God; and (3) there is three-in-oneness within the Godhead.

Regarding 1 John 5:7, it is true that this verse has no support among the early Greek manuscripts, though it is found in some Latin manuscripts. Its appearance in late Greek manuscripts is explained by the fact that Erasmus was placed under pressure by church authorities to include it in his Greek New Testament of A.D. 1522. (He had omitted it in his two earlier editions of 1516 and 1519 because he could not find any Greek manuscripts that contained it.) The inclusion of the verse in the Latin Bible was probably due to a scribe incorporating a marginal comment (gloss) into the text as he copied the manuscript of 1 John.

~

Errors Relating to the Doctrine of God

Is "Jehovah" God's true name?

This name is not found in the Hebrew and Greek manuscripts from which English translations of the Bible are derived. The Old Testament contains the name *Yahweh*—or, more literally, *YHWH* (the original Hebrew had only consonants).

Regarding the term "Jehovah," the ancient Jews had a superstitious dread of pronouncing the name *YHWH*. They felt that if they uttered this name, they might violate the third commandment, which deals with taking God's name in vain (Exodus 20:7). So, to avoid the possibility of breaking this commandment, the Jews for centuries substituted the name *Adonai* (Lord) or some other name in its place whenever they came across it in public readings of Scripture. Eventually, the fearful Hebrew scribes decided to form a new word (Jehovah) by inserting the vowels from Adonai (a-o-a) into the consonants, YHWH.

Though there is no biblical justification for the term "Jehovah," it is important to recognize that scholars are not precisely clear as to the correct way to pronounce the Hebrew word *YHWH*. Though most modern scholars believe *Yahweh* is the correct rendering (as I do), we can't be sure about that. Perhaps this is one reason why some legitimate translations—such as the American Standard Version

of 1901 and even the King James Version (in four verses)—
used the term *Jehovah*. Other translations use the word LORD
(all caps) to render the word *Yahweh*.

Does the fact that God had to rest after six days of creation mean He is not all-powerful (Genesis 2:2)?

No. God didn't have to rest in the sense that His physical energy had become depleted and He needed to recu-
perate. Rather, the Hebrew word for *rest* communicates the
idea of "ceasing from activity." Hence, Genesis 2:2 is simply
saying that God completed His work of creation and then
stopped. There was nothing further to do. The job was
done.

Is it true that the God of the Old Testament is a God of judgment and wrath while the God of the New Testament is a God of love?

No. This is a common misconception propagated by
critics of Christianity. Both the Old and New Testaments
point to one and the same God. And this God is a God of
both love *and* judgment.

On the one hand, God did judge people in Old Testament times when the circumstances called for it. This was
the case when He sent ten horrible plagues against the
Egyptians (Exodus 7–11). But He is also seen displaying
love and grace throughout the Old Testament. Following
Adam and Eve's sin, God's promise of a coming Redeemer
was an act of love and grace (Genesis 3:15). God's provision
of an ark for Noah and his family was an act of love and
grace (Genesis 6:9-22). God's provision of the covenants
was an act of love and grace (Genesis 12:1-3; 2 Samuel 7:12-
16). God's sending of the prophets to give special revelation
to Israel was an act of love and grace.

In the New Testament, the love of God was continually manifested to the people through the person of Jesus Christ. In fact, we might even say that Jesus is "love incarnate." But it is also true that some of the most scathing denouncements from God—especially in regard to the Jewish leaders—came from the mouth of Jesus (see Matthew 23:27,28,33).

So, again, the God of the Old *and* New Testaments is a God of love *and* judgment.

What is modalism?

Modalism views the Father, Son, and Holy Spirit as modes of manifestation of the one God. Sabellius, a third-century heretic, taught that the Father was God's mode of manifestation in the work of creation and the giving of the law. The Son was God's mode of manifestation in the Incarnation and work as the Redeemer. The Holy Spirit is God's mode of manifestation in regeneration, sanctification, and the giving of grace.

This heresy is easily refuted by the fact that all three persons in the New Testament are portrayed together (2 Corinthians 13:14; Matthew 28:19). Moreover, we read that the Father *sent* the Son (John 3:17). The Father and Son *love* each other (John 14:31). The Father *speaks* to the Son, and the Son *speaks* to the Father (John 11:41,42). The Holy Spirit *comes upon* Jesus at the baptism (Matthew 3). Jesus and the Father are viewed as having *sent* the Holy Spirit (John 15:26). Clearly these are distinct persons who interact with each other.

What is pantheism?

Pantheism is the view that *God is all* and *all is God*. The word pantheism comes from two Greek words—*pan* ("all") and *theos* ("God"). In pantheism, all reality is viewed as being infused with divinity. The god of pantheism is an impersonal, amoral "it" as opposed to the personal, moral

"He" of Christianity. The distinction between the Creator
and the creation is completely obliterated in this view.

A major problem of pantheism is that it fails to ade-
quately deal with the existence of real evil in the world. If
God is the essence of *all* life forms in creation, then one must
conclude that both good *and* evil stem from the same
essence (God). The Bible, on the other hand, teaches that
God is good and not evil. The God of the Bible is light, and
"in him is no darkness at all" (1 John 1:5; cf. Habakkuk 1:13;
Matthew 5:48). First John 1:5 is particularly cogent in the
Greek, which translates literally: "And darkness there is not
in him, not in any way." John could not have said it more
forcefully.

Jeff Amano and Norman Geisler provide an excellent
example of how evil is problematic for the pantheistic view
of God:

> When Francis Schaeffer spoke to a group of students
> at Cambridge University, there was a [pantheistic]
> Hindu who began criticizing Christianity. Schaeffer
> said, "Am I not correct in saying that on the basis of
> your system, cruelty and noncruelty are ultimately
> equal, that there is no intrinsic difference between
> them?"
>
> The Hindu agreed. One of the students immediately
> caught on to what Schaeffer was driving at. He
> picked up a kettle of boiling water that he was going
> to use to make tea and held the steaming pot over
> the Indian's head.
>
> This young Hindu looked up and asked the student
> what he was doing.
>
> The student said with a cold yet gentle finality,
> "There is no difference between cruelty and non-
> cruelty." Thereupon the Hindu walked out into the
> night.[1]

Some cultists teach that in the Old Testament Jesus is "Yahweh" and the Father is "Elohim." How can we disprove this idea from the Bible?

There are a number of verses in the Bible which demonstrate that Elohim and Yahweh are one and the same God. For example, in Genesis 27:20 Isaac's son said, "The LORD [Yahweh] your God [Elohim] gave me success." In this verse, then, we find reference to "Yahweh your Elohim" (the Lord your God).

Likewise, in Jeremiah 32:18 we find reference to the "great and powerful God [Elohim], whose name is the LORD [Yahweh] Almighty." Clearly, Elohim and Yahweh are one and the same God.

There are also clear passages in the Bible where Jesus is individually referred to as Elohim, thereby disproving the claim that only the Father is Elohim and Jesus is only Yahweh. In Isaiah 40:3 we read, "A voice of one calling: 'In the desert prepare the way for the LORD [Yahweh]; make straight in the wilderness a highway for our God [Elohim].'" This verse was written in reference to the future ministry of Christ, according to John 1:23. Within the confines of a single verse Christ is called both Yahweh *and* Elohim.

Does Genesis 1:26,27 teach that there is more than one God?

No. It is true that the word used of God in Genesis 1:26-27 is *Elohim,* and it has a plural ending ("im"). But this is actually a "plural of majesty," pointing to the majesty, dignity, and greatness of God. The plural ending gives a fuller, more majestic sense to God's name.[2]

What about the plural pronouns in Genesis 1 ("Let *us* make man in *our* image")? Biblical grammarians tell us that the plural pronouns in the passage are a grammatical necessity. The plural pronoun "us" is required by the plural ending of Elohim: "Then God [*Elohim*, plural] said, 'Let us [*plural*] make man in our [*plural*] image.'"[3] In other words, the plural pronoun "us" corresponds grammatically with the plural form of the Hebrew word Elohim. One demands the other.

Notice the words I've italicized in Genesis 1:26, 27:

> Then God said, "Let us make man in *our image*, in *our likeness*, and let them rule over the fish of the sea and the birds of the air, over the livestock, over all the earth, and over all the creatures that move along the ground." So God created man in *his own image*, in the *image of God he* created him; male and female he created them.

The phrases "*our* image" and "*our* likeness" in verse 26 are explained in verse 27 as "the *image of God*" and "in *his own* image." This supports the idea that even though plural pronouns are used in reference to God, only one God is meant.

Does Psalm 82:1, 6 indicate that there are many gods in the universe?

No. In this passage we find God's judgment against the evil Israelite judges. These judges were, of course, intended to act righteously and be His representatives on earth. They were to administer God's justice. They were called gods (with a little g) *not* because they were actual deity but because they pronounced life and death judgments over the people.[4]

These judges soon became corrupt in their dealings with men. God's charge against them was that they administered justice *unjustly*, showing favor to the wicked instead of upholding the rights of the helpless and oppressed.[5]

So, in verse 6, we find the psalmist Asaph communicating God's judgment on them. He is saying in effect: "I have called you 'gods,' but in fact you will die like the men you really are."

This Psalm helps us to understand what Jesus was saying in John 10:34. When Jesus alluded to this Psalm, He was saying that what the unjust Israelite judges were called in irony and judgment, *He is in reality.* "He does what they could not do, and is what they could never be."[6]

Does 1 Corinthians 8:5 indicate that there are many gods in the universe?

No. First Corinthians 8:5 reads, "For even if there are so-called gods, whether in heaven or on earth (as indeed there are many 'gods' and many 'lords')...." Taken alone, this verse might *seem* to teach that there are many gods. But the context of 1 Corinthians 8 is clearly monotheistic. The context is set for us in verse 4: "We know that an idol is nothing in the world, and that there is none other God but one" (KJV). Then, in verse 6, we read: "But to us there is but *one* God, the Father, of whom are all things, and we in him; and one Lord Jesus Christ, by whom are all things, and we by him" (KJV, italics added).

In verse 5 Paul is not saying that there actually are many true "gods" and "lords." Rather he refers to false pagan entities who are "called" gods and lords. There is a world of difference between being "called" a god and actually being God. Shirley MacLaine, in her book *Out on a Limb,* said, "I am God," but that doesn't mean she *is* God. Similarly, just because Paul acknowledges that there are pagan entities "called" gods doesn't mean they actually *are* gods.

Apparently, in the context of the city of Corinth, these "gods" were the idols of Greek and Roman mythology. Paul in this verse is simply recognizing that in New Testament days many false gods were worshiped—though, in fact, such gods do not really exist. Paul, as a Hebrew of Hebrews,

was monotheistic to the core and believed in only one God
(1 Timothy 2:5; cf. Deuteronomy 6:4).

How can we respond to the claim that Christianity sets forth a "Father" concept of God and is therefore sexist?

To begin, God equally values both men and women.
God created both men *and* women in the image of God
(Genesis 1:26). Christian men and women are positionally
equal before God (Galatians 3:28). The four Gospels indicate
that Jesus exalted women in a very anti-woman Jewish
environment (see John 4). So, Christianity cannot be said to
be sexist; rather, Jesus, the head of Christianity, vigorously
fought the sexism of His day.

It is interesting to observe that while God is referred to
in the Bible as "Father" (and never "Mother"), some of His
actions are occasionally described in feminine terms. For
example, Jesus likened Himself to a loving and saddened
mother hen crying over the waywardness of her children
(Matthew 23:37-39). God is also said to have "given birth"
to Israel (Deuteronomy 32:18).

It is important to understand that God is not a gender
being as humans are. He is not of the male *sex* per se. The
primary emphasis in God being called "Father" is that He is
personal. Unlike the dead and impersonal idols of
paganism, the true God is a personal being with whom we
can relate. In fact, we can even call Him *Abba* (which loosely
means "daddy"). That's how intimate a relationship we can
have with Him.

Does the fact that Moses spoke to God "face to face" mean that God has a physical body (Exodus 33:11)?

No. Foundationally, Scripture informs us that God is
spirit (John 4:24). And a spirit does not have flesh and
bones (Luke 24:39). Hence, the description of Moses

speaking to God "face to face" cannot be taken to mean that God actually has a physical face. Rather, the phrase is simply a Hebrew way of indicating "personally," "directly," or "intimately." Moses was in the direct presence of God and interacted with Him on a personal and intimate basis. The word *face*, when used of God, is an anthropomorphism—that is, it is a word used to describe God in humanlike terms.

Does the fact that Moses saw God's "back" mean God has a physical body (Exodus 33:21-23)?

No. As a backdrop, humble and meek Moses requested of God, "Show me your glory" (Exodus 33:18). But God warned Moses, "You cannot see my face, for no one may see me and live" (verse 20). So the Lord said to Moses, "There is a place near me where you may stand on a rock. When my glory passes by, I will put you in a cleft in the rock and cover you with my hand until I have passed by. Then I will remove my hand and you will see my back; but my face must not be seen" (verses 21-23).

We know from other passages that God is spirit and He is formless (see Isaiah 31:3; John 4:24). Just as the word "hand" is an anthropomorphism, so the word "back" is an anthropomorphism. And what does the word "back" indicate? The Hebrew word for *back* can easily be rendered "aftereffects."[7] Moses did not see the glory of God directly, but once it had gone past, God did allow him to view the results, or the afterglow, that His glorious presence had produced.[8]

Does the fact that human beings are created in the image of God mean that God has a physical body like we do (Genesis 1:26,27)?

No. Genesis 1:26, 27 is not referring to man being created in the *physical* image of God. Indeed, God is spirit

(John 4:24), and a spirit does not have flesh and bones (Luke 24:39). God is portrayed as being invisible throughout Scripture (See John 1:18; 1 Timothy 1:17; Colossians 1:15). So whatever is meant by "image of God" must be consistent with the fact that God is an invisible spirit.

In context, being created in God's image means that human beings share, though imperfectly and finitely, in God's communicable attributes such as life, personality, truth, wisdom, love, holiness, and justice. In view of being created in God's "image," man has the capacity for spiritual fellowship with Him.

Does the fact that Jesus said, "Anyone who has seen me has seen the Father," mean that the Father has a physical body like Jesus does (John 14:9)?

No. Remember, God is by nature spirit (John 4:24). John 14:9 simply means that Jesus is the perfect revelation of God. Jesus became a man specifically to reveal the Father to humankind: "No one has ever seen God, but God the One and Only [Jesus], who is at the Father's side, has made him known" (John 1:18). That's why Jesus could say, "When [a person] looks at me, he sees the one who sent me" (John 12:45). And that's why Jesus could affirm, "Whoever accepts me accepts the one who sent me" (13:20).

What are some of the ways Jesus revealed the Father?

✓ Jesus revealed God's awesome power (John 3:2).

✓ Jesus revealed God's incredible wisdom (1 Corinthians 1:24).

✓ Jesus revealed and demonstrated God's boundless love (1 John 3:16).

✓ Jesus revealed God's unfathomable grace (2 Thessalonians 1:12).

It is against this backdrop that Jesus said, "Anyone who has seen me has seen the Father" in John 14:9. Jesus came as the ultimate revelation of the Father.

God the Holy Spirit

Does the Holy Spirit's lack of a name indicate that the Spirit is not a person?

No. Spiritual beings are not always named in Scripture. For example, evil spirits are rarely named in Scripture, but rather are identified by their particular character (that is, "unclean," "wicked," and so forth—see Matthew 12:45). In the same way, by contrast, the Holy Spirit is identified by His primary character—which is holiness. To say that the Holy Spirit is not a person because a name is not ascribed to Him is simply fallacious reasoning.

Related to this issue, we must point out that the Holy Spirit is in fact related to the name of the other persons of the Trinity in Matthew 28:19: "Therefore go and make disciples of all nations, baptizing them in *the name* of the Father and of the Son and of the Holy Spirit." Just as the Father and the Son are persons, so the Holy Spirit is a person. And all three are related by the same name.

Does the fact that the Holy Spirit fills many people at the same time indicate that the Holy Spirit is not a person but is rather a force (Acts 2:4)?

No! We know this to be untrue because Ephesians 3:19 speaks of God filling all the Ephesian believers. Likewise,

Ephesians 4:10 speaks of Christ filling all things, and Ephesians 1:23 speaks of Christ as the one who "fills all in all" (NASB). The fact that God and Christ can fill all things does not mean that the Father and Jesus are not persons. In the same way, the fact that the Holy Spirit can "fill" numerous people does not prove that He is not a person.

What biblical evidence exists to prove that the Holy Spirit is a person?

It has long been recognized that the three primary attributes of personality are mind, emotions, and will. A force does not have these attributes. If it can be demonstrated that the Holy Spirit has mind, emotions, and will, the idea that the Holy Spirit is merely a "force" crumbles like a house of cards.

The Holy Spirit has a mind. The Holy Spirit's intellect is seen in 1 Corinthians 2:10 where we are told that "the Spirit searches all things" (cf. Isaiah 11:2; Ephesians 1:17). The Greek word for *search* means "to thoroughly investigate a matter." We are also told in 1 Corinthians 2:11 that the Holy Spirit "knows" the thoughts of God. How can the Spirit "know" the thoughts of God if the Spirit does not have a mind? A force does not know things. Thought processes require the presence of a mind.

Romans 8:27 tells us that just as the Holy Spirit knows the things of God, so God the Father knows "what the mind of the Spirit is" (NASB). The word translated *mind* in this verse literally means "way of thinking, mindset, aim, aspiration, striving."[1] A mere force—electricity, for example—does not have a way of thinking or a mindset.

The Holy Spirit has emotions. In Ephesians 4:30 we are admonished, "Do not grieve the Holy Spirit of God." Grief is an emotion and is not something that can be experienced by a force. Grief is something one *feels*. The Holy Spirit feels the emotion of grief when believers sin. In the context of

Ephesians, such sins include lying (verse 25), anger that leads to sin (verse 26), stealing (verse 28), laziness (verse 28), and speaking unkind words (verse 29).

The Holy Spirit has a will. We are told in 1 Corinthians 12:11 that the Holy Spirit distributes spiritual gifts "to each one individually just as He wills" (NASB). The phrase *He wills* translates the Greek word *bouletai*, which refers to "decisions of the will after previous deliberation."[2] The Holy Spirit makes a sovereign choice regarding what spiritual gifts each respective Christian receives. A force does not have such a will.

The Holy Spirit's works confirm His personality. Besides having the above attributes of personality, the Holy Spirit is seen doing many things in Scripture that only a person can do. For example, the Holy Spirit *teaches* believers (John 14:26), He *testifies* (John 15:26), He *guides* believers (Romans 8:14), He *commissions* people to service (Acts 13:4), He *issues commands* to believers (Acts 8:29), He *restrains sin* (2 Thessalonians 2:7), He *intercedes* (prays) for believers (Romans 8:26), and He *speaks* to people (John 15:26; 2 Peter 1:21).

In view of the evidence above, it is beyond doubt that the Holy Spirit is a person and not a "force."

Did the disciples receive the Holy Spirit before the Day of Pentecost (John 20:22)?

Following His resurrection from the dead, Jesus appeared to His disciples and said to them: "'Peace be with you! As the Father has sent me, I am sending you.' And with that he breathed on them and said, 'Receive the Holy Spirit'" (John 20:21, 22). Does this mean that the disciples received the Holy Spirit *prior* to the Day of Pentecost?

Some scholars have suggested that this was a prophetic utterance that would ultimately be fulfilled 50 days later on the Day of Pentecost. However, this viewpoint doesn't seem to do justice to the sense of immediacy that is communicated in Jesus' words. I believe that in this passage we witness Jesus giving the disciples a temporary empowerment from the Holy Spirit to carry on their work of ministry until they would be fully empowered on the Day of Pentecost. Since Christ had called them to a unique work, He gave them a unique empowerment for that work.

Was the prophecy of Joel 2:28-32 completely fulfilled on the Day of Pentecost (Acts 2:16)?

No, I don't think so. What we see in Acts 2 is simply an example of prophetic foreshadowing. Peter, who cited Joel 2:28-32, never said this prophecy was completely fulfilled on that day. He was saying, however, that the events that occurred on Pentecost in association with the Holy Spirit were not a result of intoxication but rather were in harmony with Old Testament revelation. It is common in prophetic literature to witness foreshadowing. Hence, the ultimate fulfillment of Joel's prophecy is yet future.

Is the baptism of the Holy Spirit the same thing as the filling of the Holy Spirit?

No. These are two separate ministries of the Holy Spirit. I believe baptism is a one-time event that takes place at the moment of conversion (1 Corinthians 12:13). If baptism did not happen at the moment of conversion, there would be some believers who, even though saved, didn't belong to the body of Christ. I say this because it is the baptism of the Holy Spirit that joins a believer to the body of Christ.

By contrast, the filling of the Holy Spirit is not a one-time event. In fact, God desires that the filling be a continual and ongoing experience for us. In Ephesians 5:18 we are instructed, "Do not get drunk on wine, which leads to debauchery. Instead, be filled with the Spirit." The word *filled* in this verse is a present-tense imperative in the Greek.

The present tense means that it should be a perpetual, ongoing experience. The imperative means it is a command from God. Being "filled" with the Spirit is not presented as a simple option but is a divine imperative for Christians.

Being "filled" with the Spirit involves being *controlled* by the Spirit. Instead of being controlled by wine and the things of this world, we are to be under the control of the Spirit.

What does the Bible say about speaking in tongues? Is this a gift I should be seeking?

The Holy Spirit is the one who bestows spiritual gifts on believers (1 Corinthians 12:11). Not every Christian has every gift. So I think Christians should be happy with whatever gift the Holy Spirit has sovereignly decided to give them.

There are a number of facts about speaking in tongues that we can derive from Scripture:

1. Speaking in tongues is not the definitive evidence of the baptism of the Holy Spirit. Not all the Corinthians spoke in tongues (1 Corinthians 14:5), but they had all been baptized (12:13).

2. The fruit of the Holy Spirit (Galatians 5:22, 23) does not include speaking in tongues. Therefore, Christlikeness does not require speaking in tongues.

3. Most of the New Testament writers are silent on tongues. Only three books (Acts, 1 Corinthians, and Mark) mention it. (Note: Mark 16:17 is not in the two best Greek manuscripts.) Significantly, many of the other New Testament books speak a great deal about the Holy Spirit, but fail to even mention speaking in tongues.

4. There are more important gifts than tongues, and these are to be sought (1 Corinthians 12:28, 31).

Personally, I think much too big a deal is often made about speaking in tongues.

What is the difference between natural talents and spiritual gifts?

There are a number of key differences. Natural talents are from God but are transmitted through parents; spiritual gifts come directly from God (1 Corinthians 12:4; Romans 12:3, 6). Natural talents are possessed from the moment of birth; spiritual gifts are received when one becomes a Christian. Natural talents are generally used to benefit human beings on the natural level; spiritual gifts bring spiritual blessing to people (1 Corinthians 12:11; Ephesians 4:11-13).

There are similarities as well. Both talents and spiritual gifts must be developed and exercised. Otherwise one will not become proficient in their use. As well, both natural talents and spiritual gifts can be used for God's glory. For example, a Christian might have the spiritual gift of teaching. He might also have the natural talent of being able to play the guitar. It is feasible that this person could exercise his spiritual gift of teaching by writing and performing songs that teach about God.

Is the practice of being "slain in the spirit" a biblical practice?

No, I don't think it is. In fact, not only is the term not in the Bible, the experience is not in the Bible either.

I'm not saying that there are no examples in Scripture of human beings falling to their knees as they witness the incredible glory of God. This is what happened to the apostle John (Revelation 1). But this idea of being touched by a human being who is "anointed" by the Spirit and then being knocked cold is not a biblical phenomena.

How are we to explain such experiences? It may be a psychological or emotional phenomena. Someone may so strongly expect to be knocked cold by the Spirit thought to be present in the anointed preacher that when the preacher touches him or her, down he or she goes. (Sociologists have noted that this type of experience is actually common to many religions.) There's also the possibility that the powers of darkness may be involved in this experience (2 Thessalonians 2:9).

Many who believe in this phenomena like to cite certain passages in its support, such as Genesis 15:12-21, Numbers 24:4, 1 Samuel 19:20, and Matthew 17:6. But in every case they are reading their own meaning *into* the text instead of drawing the meaning *out of* the text. These passages in context offer virtually no support for the idea of being slain in the spirit.

What is the sin against the Holy Spirit (Matthew 12:31,32)?

Matthew 12:31,32 says, "Every sin and blasphemy will be forgiven men, but the blasphemy against the Spirit will not be forgiven. Anyone who speaks a word against the Son of Man will be forgiven, but anyone who speaks against the Holy Spirit will not be forgiven, either in this age or in the age to come."

The backdrop to this passage is that the Jews who had just witnessed a mighty miracle of Christ should have recognized that Jesus performed this miracle in the power of the Holy Spirit. After all, the Hebrew Scriptures, with which the Jews were well familiar, prophesied that when the Messiah came He would perform many mighty miracles in the power of the Spirit (see Isaiah 35:5-6). Instead, these Jewish leaders claimed that Christ did this and other miracles in the power of the devil, the *unholy* spirit. This was a sin against the Holy Spirit. This shows that these Jewish leaders had hardened themselves against the things of God.

I believe that Matthew 12 describes a unique situation among the Jews, and that the actual committing of this sin requires the presence of the Messiah on earth doing His messianic miracles. In view of this, I don't think this sin can be duplicated today exactly as described in Matthew 12.

I think it's also important to realize that a human being can repent of his or her personal sins (whatever they are) and turn to God as long as there is breath still left in his or her lungs. Until the moment of death, every human being has the opportunity to turn to God and receive the free gift of salvation (Ephesians 2:8,9).

PART 4

∾

JESUS CHRIST:
THE DIVINE MESSIAH

The Incarnation of Jesus Christ

Is Jesus Lesser than the Father?

The Deity of Christ

Christ in the Old Testament

The Resurrection

Errors Regarding the Person of Christ

10

~

The Incarnation of Jesus Christ

What does the name "Jesus" mean?

The angel's pronouncement that Mary's child would be called Jesus (Luke 1:31) is full of meaning. *Jesus* means "the Lord saves" or "the Lord is salvation" (or, more literally, "Yahweh saves" or "Yahweh is salvation"). This name is the counterpart of the Old Testament name "Joshua," who led Israel out of the wilderness experience into a new land and a new life. Jesus the Savior leads us out of our spiritual wilderness experience into a new sphere of existence and a new life of fellowship with God.

What is the theological significance of the two genealogies of Christ (Matthew 1:1-16; Luke 3:23-38)?

Up to David, the two genealogies are very similar, practically the same. In fact, they share some 18 or 19 common names, depending on whether Matthan and Matthat are the same person. From David on, they are very different. Almost none of the names from David to Joseph coincide. (In fact, only two of the names—Shealtiel and Zerubbabel—coincide.) Why are they different?

Matthew's genealogy traces Joseph's line of descendants, and deals with the passing of the legal title to the throne of David (David ➡ Solomon ➡ Jehoikim ➡ Coniah ➡ Joseph ➡ Jesus). As Joseph's adopted son, Jesus became his legal heir so far as his inheritance was concerned. The "of whom was born Jesus" (Matthew 1:16) is a feminine relative pronoun, clearly indicating that Jesus was the physical child of Mary and that Joseph was not His physical father.

Matthew traced the line from Abraham and David in 39 links to Joseph. Matthew obviously did not list every individual in the genealogy. Jewish reckoning did not require every name in order to satisfy a genealogy.

Abraham and David were the two unconditional covenants pertaining to the Messiah. Matthew's Gospel was written to Jews, so Matthew wanted to prove to Jews that Jesus was the promised Messiah. This would demand a fulfillment of the Abrahamic Covenant (Genesis 12) and the Davidic Covenant (2 Samuel 7). Matthew was calling attention to the fact that Jesus came to fulfill the covenants made with Israel's forefathers.

Luke's genealogy traces Mary's lineage and carries all the way back beyond the time of Abraham to Adam and the commencement of the human race. Whereas Matthew's genealogy pointed to Jesus as the Jewish Messiah, Luke's genealogy points to Jesus as the Son of Man, a name often used of Jesus in Luke's Gospel. Whereas Matthew's genealogy was concerned with the Messiah as related to the Jews, Luke's genealogy was concerned with the Messiah as related to the entire human race.

Did Jesus, who is eternal God, become fully man?

Yes. To deny either the undiminished deity *or* the perfect humanity of Christ is to put oneself outside the pale of orthodoxy (see 1 John 4:2, 3). Actually, there are innumerable passages in the New Testament that confirm Christ's full humanity. For example, Hebrews 2:14 tells us that "since the children have flesh and blood, *he too shared in their humanity* so that by his death he might destroy him who holds the power of death—that is, the devil." Romans 8:3

says that God sent Jesus "in the likeness of sinful man to be a sin offering." The apostle Paul affirms that "in Christ all the fullness of the Deity lives *in bodily form*" (Colossians 2:9).

Scripture is clear that though Jesus never surrendered any aspect of His deity in the Incarnation, He experienced normal human development through infancy, childhood, adolescence, and into adulthood. According to Luke 2:40, Jesus "grew," "became strong," and was "filled with wisdom." These are things that could never be said of His divine nature. It was in His humanity that He grew, became strong, and became filled with wisdom.

Likewise, Luke 2:52 tells us that "Jesus grew in wisdom and stature, and in favor with God and men." Again, Jesus' growth in wisdom and stature is something that can only be said of His humanity.

Christ's development as a human being was normal in every respect, with two major exceptions: Christ always did the will of God and He never sinned. As Hebrews 4:15 puts it, in Christ "we do not have a high priest who is unable to sympathize with our weaknesses, but we have one who has been tempted in every way, just as we are—*yet was without sin*." Christ is "holy," "blameless," and "pure" (Hebrews 7:26). Hence, though Christ is utterly sinless, His human nature was exactly the same as ours in every other respect.

Why was the virgin birth necessary?

I can think of at least five reasons why the virgin birth was absolutely necessary:

1. The doctrine of the virgin birth determines whether you have a natural or supernatural Jesus.

2. By the virgin birth, God kept Jesus from possessing a sin nature from Joseph (see 2 Corinthians 5:21; 1 Peter 2:22-24; Hebrews 4:15; 7:26).

3. The Old Testament makes clear that Jesus had to be both God *and* man as the Messiah (see Isaiah 7:14; 9:6). This could only be fulfilled through the virgin birth.

4. Related to the above, Jesus is our Kinsman-Redeemer. In Old Testament times the next of kin (one related *by blood*) always functioned as the kinsman-redeemer of a family member who needed redemption from jail. Jesus became related to us *by blood* so He could function as our Kinsman-Redeemer and rescue us from sin. This required the virgin birth.

5. The virgin birth was necessary in view of the prediction in Genesis 3:15 (Jesus was predicted to come from the "seed of the woman").

What was the "star" the Magi saw when Christ was born (Matthew 2:2,7,9)?

Many scholars have debated what this "star" was. I think a good argument could be made that it was a manifestation of the Shekinah glory of God. Recall that this same glory had led the children of Israel through the wilderness for 40 years as a pillar of fire and a cloud (Exodus 13:21). Perhaps this "fire," manifest high in the earth's atmosphere, having the appearance of a large star from the vantage point of the earth's surface, led the Magi to Christ.

The likelihood of the "star" being the Shekinah glory is supported by the fact that it would have been impossible for a single star or a confluence of stars in the stellar heavens to single out an individual dwelling in the village of Bethlehem. Only if the light of the "star" were similar to the pillar of fire that led Israel in the desert could the house be positively identified. Upon entering the house specified by the "star," the Magi "saw the child with his mother Mary" (Matthew 2:11).

In what sense did Christ "make himself nothing" in the Incarnation (Philippians 2:6-9)? Did He give up some or all of His divine attributes?

Christ did not give up any attributes. His "making Himself nothing" (Philippians 2:6-9) ultimately boils down to three things: a veiling of His preincarnate glory, a voluntary nonuse of some of His divine attributes on some occasions, and the condescension involved in taking on a human nature. Let's look at these three elements in a little more detail.

A veiling of Jesus' preincarnate glory. Part of Christ's "making Himself nothing" involved veiling the glory that was His for all eternity as God. This was necessary in order for Him to take on the appearance of a man. Christ never *surrendered* His glory. (Recall that on the Mount of Transfiguration, Jesus allowed His intrinsic glory to shine forth for a brief time, illuminating the whole mountainside—Matthew 17.) Rather, Jesus *veiled* His glory in order to dwell among mortal human beings.

Had Christ *not* veiled His preincarnate glory, humankind would not have been able to behold Him. It would have been the same as when the apostle John beheld the exalted Christ in His glory: "I fell at his feet as though dead" (Revelation 1:17); or as when Isaiah beheld the glory of Christ in his vision in the temple and Isaiah said, "Woe to me ... I am ruined" (Isaiah 6:5; John 12:41).

A voluntary nonuse of some divine attributes on some occasions. Christ's "making Himself nothing" also involved a voluntary nonuse of some of His divine attributes on some occasions in order for Him to accomplish His objectives. Christ could never have actually surrendered any of His attributes, for then He would have ceased to be God. But He could (and did) voluntarily choose not to use some of them on some occasions during His time on earth in order to live among human beings and their limitations (for example, see Matthew 24:36).

It is critical to recognize that during His three-year ministry, Jesus did in fact use the divine attributes of *omniscience* (all-knowingness—John 2:24; 16:30), *omnipresence* (He was everywhere present—John 1:48), and *omnipotence* (He was all-powerful, as evidenced by His many miracles such as raising people from the dead—John 11). Hence, whatever limitations Christ may have suffered when He "made himself nothing" (Philippians 2:7), He did not subtract a single divine attribute or in any sense make Himself less than God.

Condescension to take on a human nature. Third, most important, Christ's "making Himself nothing" involved condescending by taking on the likeness (literally "form" or "appearance") of a man, and taking on the form ("very nature") of a bondservant. Christ was thus truly human. This humanity was one that was subject to temptation, distress, weakness, pain, sorrow, and limitation. Yet, at the same time, it must be noted that the word "likeness" suggests *similarity but difference.* "Though His humanity was genuine, He was different from all other humans in that He was sinless."[1] Nevertheless, this represented a great *condescension* on the part of the second person of the Trinity.

How can two natures—a divine nature and a human nature—be united in the one person of Jesus Christ?

To answer this, we must first understand what a "nature" is. The word "nature," when used of Christ's divinity, refers to all that belongs to deity, including all the attributes of deity. When used of Christ's humanity, "nature" refers to all that belongs to humanity, including all the attributes of humanity.

One person. Though Jesus in the Incarnation had both a human and a divine nature, He was only one person—as indicated by His consistent use of "I," "Me," and "Mine" in reference to Himself. Jesus never used the words "us," "we," or "ours" in reference to His human-divine person. The divine nature of Christ never carried on a verbal conversation with His human nature.

Two natures. One of the most complex aspects of the relationship of Christ's two natures is that, while the attributes of one nature are never attributed to the other, the attributes of both natures are properly attributed to His one person. Thus Christ at the same moment in time had what seem to be contradictory qualities. He was finite and yet infinite, weak and yet omnipotent, increasing in knowledge and yet omniscient, limited to being in one place at one time and yet omnipresent. In the Incarnation, the person of Christ is the partaker of the attributes of both natures, so that whatever may be affirmed of either nature—human or divine—may be affirmed of the one person.

Though Christ sometimes operated in the sphere of His humanity and in other cases in the sphere of His deity, in all cases what He did and what He was could be attributed to His one person. Thus, though Christ in His human nature knew hunger (Luke 4:2), weariness (John 4:6), and the need for sleep (Luke 8:23), just as Christ in His divine nature was omniscient (John 2:24), omnipresent (John 1:48), and omnipotent (John 11), *all of this was experienced by the one person of Jesus Christ.*

The human-divine union lasts forever. When Christ became a man in the Incarnation, He did not enter into a temporary union of the human and divine natures in one person that ended at His death and resurrection. Rather, the Scriptures make clear that Christ's human nature continues forever.

Christ's human body that died on the cross was transformed into a *resurrected* human body suited to His glorious existence in heaven. When Christ ascended into heaven, He ascended in His glorified human body, as witnessed by several of His disciples (Acts 1:9). When Christ returns, He will return as the "Son of Man"—a title which points to His humanity (Matthew 26:64). In the Incarnation, then, Jesus permanently became the God-man.

Could Christ have sinned as a human being?

No, I don't believe so. This is known as the impeccability of Christ. As the God-man Christ could not have sinned because:

(1) In His divine nature, He is immutable and does not change.

(2) In His divine nature, He is omniscient, knowing all the consequences of sin.

(3) In His divine nature, He is omnipotent in His ability to resist sin.

(4) Hebrews 4 tells us that He was tempted yet was *without* sin.

(5) Christ had no sin nature like all other human beings and was perfectly holy from birth (Luke 1:35).

(6) There is an analogy between the written Word of God (the Bible) and the living Word of God (Christ). Just as the Bible has a human element and a divine element and is completely without error, so Christ is fully divine and fully human and is completely without (and unable to) sin.

Does this mean that Christ's temptations were unreal? No. Christ was genuinely tempted but the temptations stood no chance of luring Christ to sin. It is much like a canoe trying to attack a U.S. battleship. The attack is genuine, but it stands no chance of success.

I believe the reason Christ went through the temptation experience with the devil (Matthew 4) was not to see whether He could be made to sin, but to *prove* that He *could not* be made to sin. In fact, some theologians have suggested that Christ was the aggressor in this encounter. The devil may have hoped to avoid the encounter altogether. After 40 days in the wilderness, at the height of Christ's weakness from a human standpoint, the devil gave it His best shot in tempting Christ. The devil was unsuccessful.

11

~

Is Jesus Lesser than the Father?

Is Proverbs 8:22,23 referring to Jesus, and if so, does this mean Jesus is a created being?

Proverbs 8:22,23 says, "The LORD brought me forth as the first of his works, before his deeds of old; I was appointed from eternity, from the beginning, before the world began." This passage does not refer to Jesus. Such an interpretation not only violates the context of the Book of Proverbs, it also violates the whole of Scripture.

Note that the first nine chapters of Proverbs deal with wisdom personified. A personification is a rhetorical figure of speech in which inanimate objects or abstractions are endowed with human qualities or are represented as possessing human form. In Proverbs 1–9, wisdom is figuratively endowed with human qualities.

With this backdrop in mind, it is critical to recognize that there is no indication in the text that Proverbs 8 is to be taken any differently than chapters 1 through 7 and 9. This being so, if we take Proverbs 8:22 to be speaking literally about Christ, we must also assume that Christ is a woman crying in the streets (1:20,21) who lives with someone named "Prudence" (8:12).[1] Proverbs 1–9 makes no sense if one tries to read Christ into the text.

Proverbs 8:22,23 is simply speaking metaphorically of God's eternal wisdom and how it was "brought forth" (verse 24) to take part in the creation of the universe. Proverbs 8 is not saying that wisdom came into being at a point in time (for God has always had wisdom). And it certainly is not saying that Jesus is a created being since the passage is not dealing with Jesus but with wisdom personified.

Does the fact that Jesus is called a "Mighty God" in Isaiah 9:6 mean He is a lesser God than "God Almighty" (the Father)?

No. It is true that Jesus is called "Mighty God" in Isaiah 9:6. But in the very next chapter in Isaiah (10:21) Yahweh Himself is called "Mighty God" (using the same Hebrew word). The fact that Yahweh is called "Mighty God" completely obliterates any suggestion that the expression must refer to a lesser deity as opposed to "Almighty God." Because Yahweh is called "Mighty God," the fact that Jesus too is called "Mighty God" points to His equality with God the Father.

To emphasize that there is not more than *one* Mighty God in heaven, the following verses are important to keep in mind:

> ✓ Isaiah 44:6b: "I am the first and I am the last, and there is no God besides Me" (NASB).

> ✓ Isaiah 44:8b: "Is there any God besides Me, or is there any other Rock? I know of none" (NASB).

> ✓ Isaiah 45:5a: "I am the LORD, and there is no other; besides Me there is no God" (NASB).

It is highly revealing to note that in Isaiah 40:3, Jesus is called both *Yahweh* and *Elohim* in the same verse: "In the desert prepare the way for the LORD [*Yahweh*]; make straight in the wilderness a highway for our God [*Elohim*]." This verse was written in reference to the future ministry of Jesus Christ (John 1:23), and represents one of the strongest affirmations of Christ's deity in the Old Testament.

Was Jesus implying that He was not good in Mark 10:17,18? Is this an argument against His deity?

In Mark 10:17,18 we read, "As Jesus started on his way, a man ran up to him and fell on his knees before him. 'Good teacher,' he asked, 'what must I do to inherit eternal life?' 'Why do you call me good?' Jesus answered. 'No one is good—except God alone.'"

In this passage, Jesus was not claiming that He wasn't "good." Nor was He denying that He was God to the young ruler asking the question. Rather, Jesus was asking the man to examine the implications of what he was saying. In effect, Jesus said: "Do you realize what you are saying when you call Me 'good'? Are you saying I am God?" Jesus' response was not a denial of His deity but was rather a veiled claim to it.

Does the fact that Jesus said no one knows the day or hour of His return except the Father mean that He is less than God Almighty (Mark 13:32)?

No. But explaining this issue requires a little theological background. Though a bit complex, the eternal Son of God was, prior to the Incarnation, *one* in person and nature (wholly divine). In the Incarnation, He became *two* in nature (divine and human) while remaining *one person*.

Thus Christ at the same moment in time had what seem to be contradictory qualities. He was finite and yet infinite, weak and yet omnipotent, increasing in knowledge and yet omniscient, limited to being in one place at one time and yet omnipresent. It was only from His humanity that Christ could say that He didn't know the day or hour of His return. In His humanity, Jesus was not omniscient but was limited in understanding just as all human beings are. If

Jesus had been speaking from the perspective of His divinity, He wouldn't have said the same thing.

Scripture is abundantly clear that in His divine nature, Jesus is omniscient—just as omniscient as the Father is. The apostle John said that Jesus "did not need man's testimony about man, for he knew what was in a man" (John 2:25). Jesus' disciples said, "Now we can see that you know all things" (16:30). After the Resurrection, when Jesus asked Peter for the third time if Peter loved Him, Peter responded: "Lord, you know all things; you know that I love you" (21:17). Jesus knew just where the fish were in the water (Luke 5:4-6; John 21:6-11), and He knew just which fish contained the coin (Matthew 17:27). He knows the Father as the Father knows Him (Matthew 11:27; John 7:29; 8:55; 10:15; 17:25).

So, again, Christ in His deity is omniscient. It is only from the perspective of His humanity that He was ignorant of the time of the Second Coming.

Does John 1:1 in the Greek say Jesus is God or does it say He is merely "a god"?

This verse teaches that Jesus is God. It is the worst kind of error to translate this verse "The Word [Christ] was *a* god," so as to deny the full deity of Christ. (This is how the Jehovah's Witnesses translate the verse.)[2] First of all, the full deity of Christ is supported by other references in John (for example, 8:58; 10:30; 20:28) as well as the rest of the New Testament (Colossians 1:15,16; 2:9; Titus 2:13; Hebrews 1:8).

Moreover, for those interested in Greek, it is not necessary to translate Greek nouns that have no definite article with an indefinite article (there is no indefinite article in Greek). In other words, *theos* ("God") without the definite article *ho* ("the") (as is the case in John 1:1) does not need to be translated as "a God" as the Jehovah's Witnesses have done in reference to Christ. It is significant that *theos* without the definite article *ho* is used of Jehovah-God in the New Testament (Luke 20:38). Because the lack of the definite article in Luke 20:38 in reference to Jehovah does not mean He is a lesser God, neither does the lack of the definite article in John 1:1 in reference to Jesus mean He is a lesser God. The fact is, the presence or absence of the definite article does not alter the fundamental meaning of *theos*.

It is noteworthy that if John had intended an adjectival sense ("godlike" or "divine"), he had an adjective (*theios*) ready at hand that he could have used. Instead, John emphatically said that Jesus is God (*theos*)!

As if this weren't enough, it is significant that there are New Testament texts that *do* use the definite article and speak of Christ as "the God" (*ho theos*). One example of this is John 20:28, where Thomas said to Jesus, "My Lord and my God." The verse reads literally from the Greek: "The Lord of me and the God [*ho theos*] of me" (see also Matthew 1:23 and Hebrews 1:8). So it does not matter whether John did or did not use the definite article in John 1:1—the Bible clearly teaches that Jesus is God, not just *a* god.

Does that fact that Jesus is called God's "only begotten Son" prove that Jesus is not God (John 3:16 KJV)?

No. The words "only begotten" do not mean that Christ was *created* (as the ancient heretic Arius taught), but rather means "unique" or "one of a kind." Reformed scholar Benjamin Warfield comments: "The adjective 'only begotten' conveys the idea, not of derivation and subordination, but of uniqueness and consubstantiality: Jesus is all that God is, and He alone is this."[3] Jesus is the "Son of God" in the sense that He has the same nature as the Father—a *divine* nature. Whenever Christ claimed to be the Son of God in the New Testament, His Jewish critics tried to stone Him because they correctly understood Him as claiming to be God (see John 5:18).

What did Jesus mean when He said the Father is "greater" than He (John 14:28)?

In John 14:28 Jesus said, "If you loved me, you would be glad that I am going to the Father, for the Father is greater than I." Jesus is not speaking in this verse about His nature or His essential being (Christ had earlier said "I and the Father are one" in this regard—John 10:30) but is rather speaking of His lowly position in the Incarnation.[4] The Athanasian Creed affirms that Christ is "equal to the Father as touching his Godhood and inferior to the Father as touching his manhood."[5]

The Father was seated upon the throne of highest majesty in heaven; the brightness of His glory was uneclipsed as He was surrounded by hosts of holy beings perpetually worshiping Him with uninterrupted praise. Far different was it with His incarnate Son—despised and rejected of men, surrounded by implacable enemies, and soon to be nailed to a criminal's cross. It is from this perspective that Jesus could say that the Father is "greater" than Him.

Does the fact that Jesus made reference to "my God" (John 20:17) prove that He Himself is not God?

By no means! Prior to the Incarnation, Christ, the second person of the Trinity, had only a divine nature. But in the Incarnation Christ took on a human nature. It is thus *in His humanity* that Christ acknowledged the Father as "my God." Positionally speaking as a man, as a Jew, and as our high priest ("made like his brothers in every way," Hebrews 2:17), Jesus could address the Father as "God." However, in His divine nature He could never refer to the Father as "my God," for Jesus was fully equal to the Father in every way regarding His divine nature.

In what sense is God the "head" of Christ (1 Corinthians 11:3)?

In 1 Corinthians 11:3 we read, "Now I want you to realize that the head of every man is Christ, and the head of the woman is man, and the head of Christ is God." A close examination of this verse shows that it has nothing to do with inferiority or superiority of one person over another; rather, it has to do with patterns of authority.

Notice that Paul says the man is the head of the woman, even though men and women are utterly equal in their essential nature. Men and women are both human and both are created in God's image (Genesis 1:26-28). As well, they are said to be "one" in Christ (Galatians 3:28). These verses, taken with 1 Corinthians 11:3, show us that *equality of being* and *social hierarchy* are not mutually exclusive. Even though men and women are completely equal in terms of their nature, there is nevertheless a functional hierarchy that exists between them.

In the same way, Christ and the Father are utterly equal in their divine being (Jesus said "I and the Father are one"— John 10:30), though Jesus is functionally under the Father's headship (1 Corinthians 11:3). There is no contradiction in affirming both an *equality of being* and a *functional subordination* among the persons in the Godhead. Christ in His divine nature is fully equal to the Father, though relationally (or functionally) He is subordinate or submissive to the Father. This verse in no way implies that Jesus is less than God.

Does the fact that Jesus is called the "firstborn" mean He is a created being (Colossians 1:15)?

No. The word *firstborn* does not mean "first created." Rather, as Greek scholars agree, the word (Greek: *prototokos*) means "first in rank, preeminent one, heir."[6] The word carries the idea of positional preeminence and supremacy.

Christ is the "firstborn of creation" in the sense that He is positionally preeminent over creation and is supreme over all things. He is also the "heir" of all creation in the sense that all that is the Father's is also the Son's.

It is critical that we interpret words according to how those words were *intended* to be interpreted by the speaker or writer of those words. We *cannot* and *must not* superimpose meanings onto words that are foreign to the author's intended meaning.

Among the ancient Hebrews, the word *firstborn* referred to the son in the family who was in the preeminent position, regardless of whether or not that son was literally the first son born to the parents. This "firstborn" son would not only be the preeminent one in the family, he would also be the heir to a double portion of the family inheritance.

The life of David illustrates this meaning of *firstborn*. David was the youngest (*last*-born) son of Jesse. Nevertheless, Psalm 89:27 says of him: "I also shall make him My first-born, the highest of the kings of the earth" (NASB). Though David was the *last* one born in Jesse's family, David is called the "firstborn" because of the preeminent position God was placing him in.[7]

For Colossians 1:15 to mean "first created," Paul would not have called Christ the "firstborn" (*prototokos*) but the "first-created" (*protoktisis*)—a term that is *never* used of Christ in the New Testament.[8] Indeed, as scholar J. B. Lightfoot notes, "The fathers of the fourth century rightly called attention to the fact that the Apostle writes not *protoktisis* ['first-created'], but *prototokos* ['firstborn']."[9] Christ is preeminent over all creation!

Some say Christ is a created being because He is called "the Beginning of God's creation" in Revelation 3:14

(NASB). How can we respond to this idea?

There is a wide range of meanings for the Greek word *arche*, translated "beginning" in Revelation 3:14 in the Jehovah's Witnesses' *New World Translation*. Though *arche* can mean "beginning," the word is truly unique and also carries the important active meaning of "one who begins," "origin," "source," "creator," or "first cause." Evangelical scholars agree that this is the intended meaning of the word in Revelation 3:14.[10]

The authoritative *Greek-English Lexicon of the New Testament and Other Early Christian Literature* says the meaning of *arche* in Revelation 3:14 is "first cause."[11] Indeed, in Revelation 3:14 *arche* is used to refer to "the active beginning of the creation, the One who caused the creation, referring to Jesus Christ not as a created being, but the One who created all things (John 1:3)."[12] The English word *architect* is derived from *arche*. We might say that Jesus is the architect of all creation (John 1:3; Colossians 1:16; Hebrews 1:2).

It is noteworthy that the only other three times *arche* is used in the Book of Revelation, it is used of God as "the *beginning* and the end" (Revelation 21:6; 22:13).[13] Certainly the use of *arche* with God Almighty does not mean that He had a created beginning. Instead, these verses communicate the idea that God is both the *beginner* and the *consummation* of creation. He is the *first cause* of creation; He is its *final goal.*[14] The word *arche* is used in the same sense in Revelation 3:14. Christ is the *beginner* of God's creation (cf. John 1:3; Hebrews 1:2; Colossians 1:16).

∼

The Deity of Christ

What biblical evidences exist to prove that Jesus is Yahweh?

A comparison of the Old and New Testaments provides powerful testimony to Jesus' identity as Yahweh. Support for this is found, for example, in Christ's crucifixion. In Zechariah 12:10, Yahweh is speaking prophetically: "They will look on me, the one they have pierced." Though Yahweh is speaking, this is obviously a reference to Christ's future crucifixion. We know that "the one they have pierced" is Jesus, for He is described this same way by the apostle John in Revelation 1:7.

The Septuagint provides us with additional insights on Christ's identity as Yahweh. (The Septuagint is a Greek translation of the Hebrew Old Testament that predates Christ.) It renders the Hebrew phrase for "I AM" (God's name) in Exodus 3:14 as *ego eimi*. On a number of occasions in the Greek New Testament, Jesus used this term as a way of identifying Himself as God. For example, in John 8:24 (NASB) Jesus declared: "Unless you believe that I am [*ego eimi*] He, you shall die in your sins." The original Greek for this verse does not have the word *He*. The verse literally reads: "If you do not believe that I AM, you shall die in your sins."

Then, according to verse 28, Jesus told the Jews: "When you lift up the Son of Man, then you will know that I am [*ego eimi*] He." Again, the original Greek reads: "When you lift up the Son of Man, then you will know that I AM" (there is no *He*). Jesus purposefully used the phrase as a means of pointing to His identity as Yahweh.

It is also highly revealing that Old Testament passages about Yahweh were directly applied to Jesus in the New Testament. For instance, Isaiah 40:3 says: "In the desert prepare the way for the LORD [*Yahweh*]; make straight in the wilderness a highway for our God [*Elohim*]." Mark's Gospel tells us that Isaiah's words were fulfilled in the ministry of John the Baptist preparing the way for Jesus Christ (Mark 1:2-4).

Still another illustration is Isaiah 6:1-5, where the prophet recounts his vision of Yahweh "seated on a throne, high and exalted" (verse 1). The seraphs sang to one another, "Holy, holy, holy is the LORD [*Yahweh*] Almighty; the whole earth is full of his glory" (verse 3). Isaiah also quotes Yahweh as saying: "I am the LORD; that is my name! I will not give my glory to another" (42:8). Later, the apostle John—under the inspiration of the Holy Spirit—wrote that Isaiah "saw Jesus' glory" (John 12:41). Yahweh's glory and Jesus' glory are equated.

Christ's deity is further confirmed for us in that many of the actions of Yahweh in the Old Testament are performed by Christ in the New Testament. For example, in Psalm 119 we are told about a dozen times that it is Yahweh who gives and preserves life. But in the New Testament, Jesus claims this power for Himself: "For just as the Father raises the dead and gives them life, even so the Son gives life to whom he is pleased to give it" (John 5:21).

In the Old Testament the voice of Yahweh was said to be "like the roar of rushing waters" (Ezekiel 43:2). Likewise, we read of the glorified Jesus in heaven: "His feet were like bronze glowing in a furnace, and his voice was like the sound of rushing waters" (Revelation 1:15). What is true of Yahweh is just as true of Jesus.

It is also significant that in the Old Testament, Yahweh is described as "an everlasting light," one that would make the sun, moon, and stars obsolete (Isaiah 60:19,20). Jesus will do the same for the future eternal city in which the saints will dwell forever: "The city does not need the sun or the moon to shine on it, for the glory of God gives it light, and the Lamb is its lamp" (Revelation 21:23).

Clearly, then, Jesus is Yahweh and is eternally self-existent—coequal and coeternal with God the Father and God the Holy Spirit. Before time began, Christ was "I AM." He was before all things. Like the Father and the Holy Spirit, He is everlastingly the Living One.

Did Jesus become the Son of God, or was He eternally the Son of God?

I believe Jesus is *eternally* the Son of God. Perhaps no name or title of Christ has been so misunderstood as this one. Some have taken the term to mean that Christ came into existence at a point in time and that He is in some way inferior to the Father. Some believe that since Christ is the Son of God, He cannot possibly be God in the same sense as the Father.

Such an understanding is based on a faulty conception of what *son of* meant among the ancients. Though the term *can* refer to "offspring of," it carries the more important meaning "of the order of."[1] The phrase is often used this way in the Old Testament. For example, *sons of the prophets* meant "of the order of prophets" (1 Kings 20:35). *Sons of the singers* meant "of the order of singers" (Nehemiah 12:28 NASB). Likewise, the phrase *Son of God* means "of the order of God," and represents a claim to undiminished deity.

Ancient Semitics and Orientals used the phrase *son of* to indicate likeness or sameness of nature and equality of being.[2] Hence, when Jesus claimed to be the Son of God, His Jewish contemporaries fully understood that He was making a claim to be God in an unqualified sense. Indeed, the Jews insisted, "We have a law, and according to that law he [Christ] must die, because he claimed to be the Son of God" (John 19:7; see also 5:18). Recognizing that Jesus was identifying Himself *as* God, the Jews wanted to kill Him for committing blasphemy.

Scripture indicates that Christ's Sonship is an *eternal* Sonship (see Psalm 2:7).[3] It is one thing to say that Jesus *became* the Son of God; it is another thing altogether to say that He was *always* the Son of God. We must recognize that if there was a time when the Son was not the Son, then—to be consistent—there was also a time when the Father was not the Father. If the first person's designation as "Father" is an eternal title, then the second person's designation as "Son" must be so regarded.

Clear evidence for Christ's eternal Sonship is found in the fact that Christ is represented as *already being* the Son of God before His birth in Bethlehem. For instance, recall Jesus' discussion with Nicodemus in John 3. Jesus said, "For God so loved the world that he *gave* his one and only Son, that whoever believes in him shall not perish but have eternal life. For God did not *send* his Son *into* the world to condemn the world, but to save the world through him" (John 3:16,17, emphasis added). That Christ—as the Son of God—was *sent into* the world implies that He was the Son of God *before* the Incarnation.

Further evidence for Christ's eternal Sonship is found in the fact that Hebrews 1:2 says God created the universe through His "Son"—implying that Christ was the Son of God prior to the Creation. Moreover, Christ as the Son is explicitly said to have existed "before all things" (Colossians 1:17; see especially verses 13,14). As well, Jesus, speaking as the Son of God (John 8:54-56), asserts His eternal preexistence before Abraham (verse 58).

What is the significance of Jesus pronouncing peoples' sins forgiven?

This act shows that Christ perceived of Himself as God. We see this illustrated in Mark 2 where a paralytic was lowered through a roof by his friends in order to get close to Jesus in hopes of a healing. The first thing Jesus said to the paralytic was, "Son, your sins are forgiven" (Mark 2:5).

Upon first reading, such words seem out of place. But further investigation indicates that Jesus was making an important statement. Jesus knew that all those present were aware that only God could pronounce someone's sins as being forgiven. (In Isaiah 43:25, God said, "I, even I, am he who blots out your transgressions, for my own sake, and remembers your sins no more.") Hence, when Jesus said "your sins are forgiven," He was clearly placing Himself in the position of God.

The scribes that were present understood Jesus' words this way, for they reasoned, "Why does this man speak that way? He is blaspheming; who can forgive sins but God alone?" (Mark 2:7 NASB). Of course, Jesus' subsequent healing of the paralytic served to substantiate His claim to be God.

Why did Jesus always say "Verily, verily, I say unto you" instead of "Thus saith the Lord," as the Old Testament prophets did?

Jesus' teachings were always presented as being ultimate and final. He never wavered in this. He unflinchingly placed His teachings above those of Moses and the prophets—and in a Jewish culture at that! He always spoke in His own authority. He never said, "Thus saith the Lord," as did the prophets; He always said, "Verily, verily, *I say* unto you...." He never retracted anything He said, never guessed or spoke with uncertainty, never made revisions, never contradicted Himself, and never apologized for what He said. He even asserted that "heaven and earth will pass away, but my words will never pass away" (Mark 13:31), hence elevating His words directly to the realm of heaven.

Jesus' teachings had a profound effect on people. His listeners always seemed to surmise that these were not the words of an ordinary man. When Jesus taught in Capernaum on the Sabbath, the people "were amazed at his teaching, because his message had authority" (Luke 4:32). After the Sermon on the Mount, "the crowds were amazed at his teaching, because he taught as one who had authority, and not as their teachers of the law" (Matthew 7:28,29). When some Jewish leaders asked the temple guards why they hadn't arrested Jesus when He spoke, they responded: "No one ever spoke the way this man does" (John 7:46).

One cannot read the Gospels long before recognizing that Jesus regarded Himself and His message as inseparable. The reason Jesus' teachings had ultimate authority was because He was (is) God. The words of Jesus were the very words of God!

Was Jesus claiming deity when He said that He and the Father "are one" (John 10:30)?

Yes, I believe so. While the Greek word for "one" *(hen)* by itself does not have to refer to more than unity of purpose, the context of John 10 is clear that much more than this is meant in terms of Jesus and the Father. How do we know this? For one thing, the Jewish leaders immediately picked up stones to put Jesus to death. They understood Jesus to be claiming to be God in an unqualified sense. Indeed, according to verse 33, the Jews said: "For a good work we do not stone You, but for blasphemy; and because You, being a man, *make Yourself out to be God*" (NASB, italics added). The penalty for blasphemy, according to Old Testament law, is death by stoning.

Jesus didn't respond by saying, "Oh, no, you've got it all wrong. I wasn't claiming to be God. I was just claiming to have a unity of purpose." Even the Jews claimed to have a unity of purpose with God. They wouldn't have tried to stone Jesus for that. They understood Jesus as He *intended* to be understood—they understood Him to be claiming deity.

Some cultists say we shouldn't worship Jesus. What do the Scriptures say about this?

Jesus Christ *was* worshiped (Greek: *proskuneo*) as God many times according to the gospel accounts, and He always accepted such worship as perfectly appropriate. Jesus accepted worship from Thomas (John 20:28), the angels (Hebrews 1:6), some wise men (Matthew 2:11), a leper (Matthew 8:2), a ruler (Matthew 9:18), a blind man (John 9:38), an anonymous woman (Matthew 15:25), Mary Magdalene (Matthew 28:9), and the disciples (Matthew 28:17). All these verses contain the word *proskuneo*, the same word used of worshiping the Father in the New Testament.

Now, to draw a contrast, consider that when Paul and Barnabas were in Lystra and miraculously healed a man by God's mighty power, those in the crowd shouted, "The gods have come down to us in human form!" (Acts 14:11). When Paul and Barnabas perceived that the people were preparing to worship them, "they tore their clothes and rushed out into the crowd, shouting: 'Men, why are you doing this? We too are only men, human like you. We are bringing you good news, telling you to turn from these worthless things to the living God, who made heaven and earth and sea and everything in them'" (verses 14,15). As soon as they perceived what was happening, they immediately corrected the gross misconception that they were gods.

Unlike Paul and Barnabas, Jesus never sought to correct His followers when they bowed down and worshiped Him.

Indeed, Jesus considered such worship perfectly appropriate. Of course, we wouldn't expect Jesus to try to correct people in worshiping Him if He truly was God in the flesh, as He claimed to be. In keeping with this, it is highly revealing that in the Book of Revelation God the Father (Revelation 4:10) and Jesus Christ (5:11-14) are portrayed as receiving *the exact same worship*.

The fact that Jesus willingly received (and condoned) worship on various occasions says a lot about His true identity, for it is the consistent testimony of Scripture that *only God* can be worshiped. Exodus 34:14 tells us: "Do not worship any other god, for the LORD, whose name is Jealous, is a jealous God" (cf. Deuteronomy 6:13; Matthew 4:10). In view of this, the fact that Jesus was worshiped on numerous occasions shows that He is in fact God.

13

~

Christic in the Old Testament

Is there a reference to Jesus as the "Son of God" in the Old Testament?

I believe so. Proverbs 30 was authored by a man named Agur. In the first four verses of this chapter, Agur reflects on man's inability to comprehend the infinite God. Because of this inability, Agur abases himself and humbly acknowledges his ignorance. Agur effectively communicates the idea that reverence for God is the beginning of true wisdom.

In verse 4, Agur's reflections are couched in terms of a series of questions. He asks: "Who has gone up to heaven and come down? Who has gathered up the wind in the hollow of his hands? Who has wrapped up the waters in his cloak? Who has established all the ends of the earth? What is his name, and the name of his son? Tell me if you know!"

Many scholars concede to the likelihood of this being an Old Testament reference to the first and second persons of the Trinity, the eternal Father and the eternal Son of God.[1] And it is highly significant that this portion of Scripture is not predictive prophecy speaking about a *future* Son of God. Rather, it speaks of the Father and the Son of God in *present-tense terms* during *Old Testament times*, exercising sovereign control over the world.

Was Melchizedek a preincarnate appearance of Christ in the Old Testament?

I don't think so. Melchizedek is described in Scripture as *being like* the Son of God, not as *being* the Son of God Himself (Hebrews 7:3). It seems best to view Melchizedek as an actual historical person—a mere human being—who was a "type" of Christ. A type is someone (or something) that prophetically foreshadows someone (or something) else.

The reason some Old Testament persons or things foreshadow someone or something in the New Testament is that God planned it that way. In the revelatory process, God in His sovereignty so arranged the outworking of history that certain individuals, things, events, ceremonies, and institutions foreshadowed Christ in His person or ministry. This, I believe, is the case with Melchizedek.

Those who argue that Melchizedek was not just a type of Christ but was actually a preincarnate appearance of Christ usually cite Hebrews 7:3 in support of this view: "Without father or mother, without genealogy, without beginning of days or end of life, like the Son of God he remains a priest forever." No human being, it is argued, can be without father or mother, without genealogy, or without beginning of days or end of life.

In response, many scholars argue that this verse simply means that the Old Testament has *no record* of these events. Old Testament scholar Gleason Archer notes that "the context makes clear that Melchizedek was brought on the scene as a type of the Messiah, the Lord Jesus. In order to bring out this typical character of Melchizedek, the biblical record purposely omits all mention of his birth, parentage, or ancestors."[2] This is not to say that Melchizedek had no father or mother. Rather, "this verse simply means that none of those items of information was included in the Genesis 14 account and that they were purposely omitted in order to lay the stress on the divine nature and imperishability of the Messiah, the Antitype."[3]

In what way was Melchizedek a type of Christ? Melchizedek's name is made up of two words meaning "king" and "righteous." Melchizedek was also a priest. Thus, Melchizedek foreshadows Christ as a righteous king/priest. Melchizedek was also the king of "Salem" (which means peace). This points forward to Christ as the King of peace.

What is a "theophany"?

The word "theophany" comes from two Greek words: *theos* ("God") and *phaino* ("to appear"). We might define a theophany as an appearance or manifestation of God, usually in visible, bodily form. I believe that theophanies in the Old Testament were actually preincarnate appearances of Christ. The principal theophany of the Old Testament is the Angel of the Lord (or, more literally, *Angel of Yahweh*). (See my book, *Christ Before the Manger: The Life and Times of the Preincarnate Christ*, for more on this.)

Was the Angel of the Lord who appeared throughout the Old Testament actually a preincarnate appearance of Christ?

Yes, I believe so. There are three primary lines of evidence that support this view: (1) This Angel is identified as being Yahweh (or God). (2) Though the Angel is identified as being Yahweh, He is also seen to be distinct from another person called Yahweh—thus implying plurality within the Godhead. (3) The Angel of Yahweh must be Jesus Christ by virtue of what we learn from both the Old and New Testaments about the nature and function of each person in the Trinity. Let's look at these lines of evidence in more detail.

(1) The Angel of Yahweh is God. In the Old Testament the Angel of the Lord (or "Angel of Yahweh") makes very definite claims to deity. A well-known example is found in the account of Moses and the burning bush: "Moses was tending the flock of Jethro his father-in-law, the priest of Midian, and he led the flock to the far side of the desert and came to Horeb, the mountain of God. There the angel of the LORD appeared to him in flames of fire from within a bush" (Exodus 3:1, 2).

Now, notice how the "Angel" identified himself to Moses: "I am the God of your father, the God of Abraham, the God of Isaac and the God of Jacob" (Exodus 3:6a). Upon hearing the Angel's identity, "Moses hid his face, because he was afraid to look at God" (verse 6b). Clearly this "Angel" was a manifestation of God.

(2) The Angel of Yahweh is distinct from Yahweh. Though the Angel of Yahweh was recognized as being Yahweh (God), He is also recognized as being *distinct* from another person called Yahweh. In Zechariah 1:12 we find the Angel of Yahweh interceding to another person called Yahweh on behalf of the people of Jerusalem and Judah: "The angel of the LORD [Yahweh] said, 'LORD [Yahweh] Almighty, how long will you withhold mercy from Jerusalem and from the towns of Judah, which you have been angry with these seventy years?'"

What we have here, I believe, is *one* person of the Trinity (the second person—the preincarnate Christ as the Angel of Yahweh) interceding before *another* person of the Trinity (the first person—God the Father). As a result of this intercession, the Father reaffirmed His intentions to bless and prosper the chosen people.

Some might be tempted to argue that since the Angel of Yahweh is portrayed as interceding to or calling upon Yahweh, He must be less than deity. However, the Angel's intercessory prayer to Yahweh on behalf of Judah is no more a disproof of His essential unity with Yahweh than the intercessory prayer of Christ to the Father in John 17 is a dis-proof of His divinity.

(3) The Angel of the Lord is the preincarnate Christ. How can one person who is clearly identified as God (the Angel of Yahweh) address *another* person who is just as clearly God (Yahweh)? Since there is *only one God*, the answer must lie in the personal distinctions of the Trinity. More specifi-cally, the answer lies in recognizing the Angel of Yahweh as the second person of the Trinity, Jesus Christ.

I believe there are a number of fundamental considera-tions which, when combined, collectively present a strong case for the idea that the Angel of Yahweh was actually a preincarnate appearance of Jesus Christ. Let us briefly look at five of these considerations.

1. First, while Christ is the visible God of the New Tes-tament, neither the Father nor the Holy Spirit characteristi-cally manifest themselves visibly. Paul tells us that God the Father is invisible (Colossians 1:15; 1 Timothy 1:17) and "lives in unapproachable light, whom *no one has seen* or can see" (1 Timothy 6:16, italics added). John's Gospel likewise tells us that "no one has ever seen God [the Father], but God the One and Only [Jesus Christ], who is at the Father's side, has made him known" (John 1:18). John 5:37 similarly tells us that no one has ever seen God the Father's form.

Scripture also portrays the Holy Spirit as being invisible to the human eye. In the Upper Room Discourse, for example, Jesus said of the Holy Spirit: "The world cannot accept him, because it neither sees him nor knows him. But you know him, for he lives with you and will be in you" (John 14:17). The invisible Holy Spirit is known by believers because *He indwells them.*

The above facts about the Father and the Holy Spirit point to Christ as being the one who visibly appeared in Old Testament times as the Angel of Yahweh. This would seem to be the only interpretation that does full justice to the above Scripture passages.

2. Just as Christ was sent by the Father in the New Testament (John 3:17), so the Angel of Yahweh is sent by Yahweh in the Old Testament (Judges 13:8,9). The divine pattern in Scripture is that the Father is the *Sender* and the Son is the *Sent One*.

Of course, this implies no superiority of the Father or inferiority of the Son. This is simply the eternal relationship of the first and second persons of the Trinity. That the Angel and Jesus were both sent by the Father—one in the Old Testament, the other in the New—lends support to the idea that they are one and the same person.

3. As I noted earlier, the Angel of Yahweh in the Old Testament and Christ in the New Testament *interceded with* and *called upon* God the Father. The New Testament pattern is that the second person of the Trinity, Jesus, consistently intercedes with the first person, the Father (see John 17; Hebrews 7:25; 1 John 2:1). This pattern is never reversed in Scripture (that is, we never see the Father interceding with Jesus). The intercessory ministry of the Angel therefore points us to His identity as the preincarnate Christ.

4. The divine Angel and Christ engaged in amazingly similar ministries. Besides interceding for the people of God (Zechariah 1:12,13; 3:1,2; John 17; Romans 8:34; Hebrews 7:25), both the Angel and Christ were involved in *revealing truth* (Daniel 4:13,17,23; 8:16; 9:21,22; John 1:1,14,18), *commissioning individuals for service* (Exodus 3:7,8; Judges 6:11-23; 13:1-21; Matthew 4:18-20; 28:19,20; Acts 26:14-18), *delivering those enslaved* (Exodus 3; Galatians 1:4; 1 Thessalonians 1:10; 2 Timothy 4:18; Hebrews 2:14,15), *comforting the downcast* (Genesis 16:7-13; 1 Kings 19:4-8; Matthew 14:14; 15:32-39), *protecting God's servants* (Psalm 34:7; Daniel 3:15-30; 6:16-23; Matthew 8:24-26), *acting as judge* (1 Chronicles 21:1,14,15; John 5:22; Acts 10:42), among many other things. I believe that such parallel ministries point to the common identity of the Angel and Jesus Christ.

5. The Angel of Yahweh no longer appears after the Incarnation. In view of the extremely active role played by the Angel of Yahweh throughout Old Testament history, His sudden disappearance after the Incarnation would be strange indeed unless He was a preincarnate manifestation of Jesus Christ. There is no other way to explain the Angel's complete inactivity among human beings in New Testament times unless He is recognized as *continuing* His activity as *God incarnate*—that is, as Jesus Christ.

Some sharp readers may be thinking, *What about the references (albeit few) in the New Testament to an "angel of the Lord"?* Theologian Norman Geisler explains it this way:

> *An* angel of the Lord (Gabriel) appeared to Joseph (Matthew 1:20); *an* angel of the Lord spoke to Philip (Acts 8:26); and *an* angel of the Lord released Peter (Acts 12:7), but not *the* Angel of the Lord. Furthermore, the New Testament "angel of the Lord," unlike "*the* Angel of the Lord" in the Old Testament, did not permit worship of himself (cf. Revelation 22:8-9), but "*the* Angel of the Lord" in the Old Testament demanded worship (cf. Exodus 3:5; Joshua 5:15).[4]

It is exceedingly important to distinguish between *an* angel of the Lord in the New Testament (a created angel) and *the* Angel of the Lord in the Old Testament (the preincarnate Christ). The reader must be cautious not to get confused on this point.

If we are correct in saying that appearances of the Angel of Yahweh in Old Testament times were actually preincarnate appearances of Christ, then it is critical that we anchor in our minds the precise sense in which He can properly be called an angel. In accordance with its Hebrew root, the word *angel* was used of Christ in the sense of "Messenger," "One who is sent," or "Envoy."[5] This usage of the word indicates that Christ was acting on behalf of the Father. Christ, as the Angel of Yahweh, was a divine *Intermediary* between God the Father and man.

14

~

The Resurrection

How important an issue is the Resurrection?

Very important! The apostle Paul said, "If Christ has not been raised, then our preaching is vain" (1 Corinthians 15:14 NASB). If the Resurrection did not really happen, the apostles were false witnesses, our faith is futile, we're still lost in our sins, the dead in Christ have perished, and we're the most pitiful people on the face of the earth—to say nothing of the fact that there's no hope for any of us beyond the grave. Clearly, this is a transcendentally important issue.

What biblical evidence exists to prove that Jesus rose from the dead?

Jesus first attested to His resurrection by appearing to Mary, who then told the disciples the glorious news. That evening, the disciples had gathered in a room with the doors shut for fear of the Jews (John 20:19). This fear was well founded, for after Jesus had been arrested, Annas the high priest specifically asked Jesus about the disciples (18:19). Jesus had also previously warned the disciples in the upper room: "If they persecuted me, they will persecute you also" (15:20). These facts no doubt lingered in their minds after Jesus was brutally crucified.

But then their gloom turned to joy. The risen Christ appeared in their midst and said to them, "Peace be with you!" (John 20:19b) This phrase was a common Hebrew greeting (1 Samuel 25:6). But on this occasion there was added significance to Jesus' words. After their conduct on Good Friday (they all scattered like cowards after Jesus' arrest), the disciples may well have expected a rebuke from Jesus. Instead, He displayed compassion by pronouncing peace upon them.

Jesus immediately showed the disciples His hands and His side (John 20:20). The risen Lord wanted them to see that it was truly He. The wounds showed that He did not have another body but the *same* body. He was dead, but now He is alive forevermore.

Over the days that followed, Jesus made many appearances and proved that He had really resurrected from the dead. Acts 1:3 says, "He showed himself to these men and gave many convincing proofs that he was alive. He appeared to them over a period of forty days and spoke about the kingdom of God." Moreover, "He appeared to more than five hundred of the brothers at the same time, most of whom are still living, though some have fallen asleep" (1 Corinthians 15:6). The resurrection of Christ is perhaps the best-attested historical event of ancient times.

How can we respond to critics who claim the disciples just made up the story about Jesus' resurrection?

Point out how hard it is to believe that these followers— predominantly Jewish and therefore aware of God's stern commandments against lying and bearing false witness— would make up such a lie, and then suffer and *give up their own lives* in defense of it. Moreover, if Jesus' followers concocted events like the Resurrection, wouldn't Jesus' critics have then immediately come forward to debunk these lies and put an end to Christianity once and for all?

It is worth noting that the apostle Paul in 1 Corinthians 15:1-4 speaks of Christ's resurrection as part of a confession that had been handed down for years. First Corinthians was written around A.D. 55, a mere 20 years after Christ's resurrection. But many biblical scholars believe the confession in 1 Corinthians 15:1-4 was formulated within a few years of Jesus' death and resurrection.

As noted above, Paul said the resurrected Christ appeared to more than 500 people at a single time, "most of whom are still alive" (1 Corinthians 15:6). If Paul had misrepresented the facts, wouldn't one of these 500 have come forward to dispute his claims? But no one came forward to dispute anything because the Resurrection really occurred.

Was Jesus raised from the dead as a spirit being, or was He resurrected physically?

Christ was resurrected physically (Luke 24:39). I need to note, though, that there are two key passages in the New Testament that are sometimes misinterpreted by cultists to teach that Jesus raised from the dead as a spirit creature: 1 Corinthians 15:44-50 and 1 Peter 3:18. Let's take a brief look at these passages.

1 Corinthians 15:44-50. It is true that the resurrection body is called a "spiritual body" in 1 Corinthians 15:44. However, the primary meaning of "*spiritual* body" here is not an immaterial body but a supernatural, spirit-dominated body. The Greek words *soma pneumatikos* (translated "spiritual body" in this verse) refer to a body *directed by* the spirit, as opposed to one under the dominion of the flesh.

It is an indisputable fact that the Greek word for "body" (*soma*), when used of a person, always means *physical body* in the New Testament. There are no exceptions to this. Greek scholar Robert Gundry, in his authoritative book *Soma in Biblical Theology*, speaks of "Paul's exceptionless use of *soma* for a physical body."[1] Hence, all references to Jesus' resurrection "body" (*soma*) in the New Testament must be taken to mean a resurrected *physical* body. This supports the view that the phrase "spiritual body *[soma]*" in 1 Corinthians 15:44 refers to a spirit-dominated and supernatural *physical* body.

The context in 1 Corinthians 15 indicates that Paul intended the meaning of "supernatural" in verses 40-50. I say this because the contrasts in verses 40-50—"earthly" versus "heavenly," "perishable" versus "imperishable," "weak" versus "powerful," "mortal" versus "immortal"— show that the translation "supernatural" as a contrast to "natural" fits Paul's line of argumentation much better than the word "spiritual."

1 Peter 3:18. This verse says, "For Christ died for sins once for all, the righteous for the unrighteous, to bring you to God. He was put to death in the body but made alive by the Spirit."

This verse does not refer to a spiritual resurrection of Christ; rather, it refers to Christ's physical resurrection by the Holy Spirit. I believe this verse is saying that Jesus was raised from the dead—or "quickened"—*by* the Holy Spirit. Indeed, God did not raise Jesus *as* a spirit but raised Him *by* His Spirit. This is in keeping with Romans 1:4 which tells us that it was "through the Spirit of holiness" that Jesus was "declared with power to be the Son of God by his resurrection from the dead."

Of course, this is not to deny that the Father and Son were involved in the Resurrection as well. God the Father is often said to have raised Christ from the dead (Acts 2:32; 13:30; Romans 6:4; Ephesians 1:19,20). But without diminishing the Father's key role in the Resurrection, it is just as clear from Scripture that Jesus raised Himself from the dead (John 10:17,18). Hence, it is clear that *each* of the three persons in the Trinity—the Father, Son, *and* the Holy Spirit— was involved in Christ's resurrection.

A foundational principle of Bible interpretation is that *Scripture interprets Scripture.* This principle says that if one interprets a particular verse in such a way that it is clearly contradicted by other Bible verses, then one's interpretation is proven incorrect. *Scriptural harmony is essential.*

In view of this principle, 1 Peter 3:18 cannot possibly be taken to mean that Jesus was raised from the dead in a spiritual body. Note the following facts that are derived from other key Scriptures:

✓ The resurrected Christ Himself said: "See My hands and My feet, that it is I Myself; touch Me and see, for a spirit does not have flesh and bones as you see that I have" (Luke 24:39 NASB). Notice three things here: (1) The resurrected Christ indicates in this verse that He is not a spirit; (2) The resurrected Christ indicates that His resurrection body is made up of flesh and bones; (3) Christ's physical hands and feet represent physical proof of the materiality of His resurrection from the dead.

✓ Further support for the physical resurrection of Christ can be found in Christ's words recorded in John 2:19-21: "Jesus answered them, 'Destroy this temple, and I will raise it again in three days.' The Jews replied, 'It has taken forty-six years to build this temple, and you are going to raise it in three days?' But the temple he had spoken of was his body." Jesus here said that He would be *bodily* raised from the dead, not raised as a spirit creature.

✓ The resurrected Christ ate physical food on four different occasions. And He did this as a means of proving that He had a real physical body (Luke 24:42, 43; Acts 1:4). It would have been deception on Jesus' part to have offered His ability to eat physical food as a proof of His bodily resurrection if He had not been resurrected in a physical body.

✓ The physical body of the resurrected Christ was touched and handled by different people. For example, He was touched by Mary (John 20:17) and by some women (Matthew 28:9). He also challenged the disciples to physically touch Him so they could rest assured that His body was material in nature (Luke 24:39).

✓ The body that is "sown" in death is the *very same body* that is raised in life (1 Corinthians 15:35-44). That which goes into the grave is raised to life (see verse 42).

If Jesus' resurrection body was physical in nature, how could He get into closed rooms, apparently by materialization (John 20:19)?

In John 20:19 we read, "On the evening of that first day of the week, when the disciples were together, with the doors locked for fear of the Jews, Jesus came and stood among them and said, 'Peace be with you!'"

Jesus' resurrection body was *material* (see Luke 24:39). The fact that He could get into a room with a closed door does not prove He had to dematerialize in order to do it. One must keep in mind that if He had chosen to do so, Jesus could have performed this same miracle before His death in His preresurrection material body. As the Son of God, His miraculous powers were just as great before the Resurrection. Prior to His resurrection Jesus performed miracles with His physical body that transcended natural laws, such as walking on water (John 6:16-20). But this miracle did not prove that His preresurrection body was immaterial or even that it could dematerialize. Otherwise, Peter's preresurrection walk on water would mean his body dematerialized for a moment and then quickly rematerialized (Matthew 14:29)!

Scripture indicates that the resurrection body, although physical, is by its very nature a supernatural body (1 Corinthians 15:44). Hence, it should be expected that it can do supernatural things, such as appearing in a room with closed doors.

Is there any legitimacy to Hugh Schonfield's "Passover Plot" theory?

No. Schonfield argued that Jesus conspired with Joseph of Arimathea, Lazarus, and an anonymous young man to convince His disciples that He was the Messiah. He allegedly manipulated events to make it appear that He was the fulfillment of numerous prophecies. Regarding the Resurrection, Jesus allegedly took some drugs and feigned death, but was revived later. Unfortunately, the crucifixion wounds ultimately proved fatal and He died. The plotters then stole and disposed of Jesus' body, and the appearances of Christ were simply a case of mistaken identity.[2]

This theory is full of holes. First, Christ was of the highest moral character in the way He lived His life and in His teachings. It breaches all credulity to say that Jesus was deceitful and sought to fool people into believing He was the Messiah. Moreover, there are many prophecies fulfilled in the person of Jesus that He couldn't have conspired to fulfill, such as His birthplace (Micah 5:2), being born of a virgin (Isaiah 7:14), and the identity of His forerunner, John the Baptist (Malachi 3:1).

It is also highly unlikely that the plotters could have stolen Jesus' dead body in order to dispose of it. The tomb had a huge stone (weighing several tons) blocking it, it had a seal of the Roman government, and it was guarded by Roman guards trained in the art of defense and killing.

The idea that the appearances of Christ were simply a case of mistaken identity is ridiculous. Jesus appeared to *too many people* (including 500 at a single time—1 Corinthians 15:6), on *too many occasions* (12), over *too long a time* (40 days) for this to be the case.

How can we respond to the so-called "swoon theory" of the Resurrection?

This theory suggests that Jesus didn't really die on the cross. He was nailed to the cross and suffered from loss of blood and went into shock. But He didn't die. He merely fainted (or swooned) from exhaustion. The disciples mistook

Him for dead and buried Him alive in a tomb. They were easily fooled, living in the first century as they did.

Suddenly, the cold tomb woke Jesus from His state of shock. And when Jesus emerged from the tomb and was seen by the disciples, they knew He must have resurrected from the dead.

This theory is highly imaginative. In fact, I think it requires more faith to believe this theory than it does to believe that Jesus really resurrected. Consider the facts:

- ✓ Jesus went through six trials and was beaten beyond description.

- ✓ He was so weak that He couldn't even carry the wooden cross bar.

- ✓ Huge spikes were driven through His wrists and feet.

- ✓ A Roman soldier thrust a spear into His side so that blood and water came out.

- ✓ Four Roman executioners (who had many years of experience in their line of work) goofed and mistakenly pronounced Jesus dead.

- ✓ Over a hundred pounds of gummy spices were applied to Jesus' body, and during this process, no one saw Jesus breathing.

- ✓ A large stone weighing several tons was rolled against the tomb, Roman guards were placed there, and a seal wrapped across the entrance.

- ✓ Jesus awoke in the cool tomb, split off the garments, pushed the several-ton stone away, fought off the Roman guards, and appeared to the disciples.

This does not seem reasonable.

How can we respond to those who try to explain away Christ's resurrection by saying the women and the disciples went to the wrong tomb?

To believe in this theory, we'd have to conclude that the women went to the wrong tomb, that Peter and John ran to the wrong tomb, that the Jews then went to the wrong tomb, followed by the Jewish Sanhedrin and the Romans who went to the wrong tomb. We'd also have to say that Joseph of Arimathea, the *owner* of the tomb, also went to the wrong tomb. As well, the angel from heaven appeared at the wrong tomb.

I don't think so.

How could Jesus have remained in the tomb "three days and three nights" if He was crucified on Friday and rose on Sunday?

The gospel accounts are clear that Jesus was crucified and buried on Friday, sometime before sundown. (Sundown was considered the beginning of the next day for the Jews.) This means Jesus was in the grave for part of Friday, the entire Sabbath (Saturday), and part of Sunday. In other words, He was in the tomb for two full nights, one full day, and part of two days.

How do we reconcile this with Jesus' words in Matthew 12:40: "For as Jonah was three days and three nights in the belly of a huge fish, so the Son of Man will be three days and three nights in the heart of the earth"? This is not hard to explain. In the Jewish mindset, any *part* of a day was reckoned as a *complete* day. The Babylonian Talmud (a set of Jewish commentaries) tells us that "the portion of a day is as the whole of it." Hence, though Jesus was really in the tomb for part of Friday, all of Saturday, and part of Sunday, in Jewish reckoning He was in the tomb for "three days and three nights."

∾

Errors Regarding the Person of Christ

Some claim that Jesus was Michael the Archangel in the Old Testament. Is this view correct?

No. Jesus was most certainly not the Archangel Michael in the Old Testament. For one thing, Michael in Daniel 10:13 is specifically called *"one of* the chief princes." The fact that Michael is "one of" the chief princes indicates that he is *one among a group* of chief princes. How large that group is, we are not told. But the fact that Michael is one among equals proves that he is not unique. By contrast, the Greek word used to describe Jesus in John 3:16 ("God's *only begotten* son" KJV) is *monogenes*—meaning "unique" or "one of a kind." He is not a "chief prince" but is rather the unique "King of kings and Lord of lords" (Revelation 19:16).

Moreover, in Hebrews 1:5 we are told that no angel can ever be called God's son: "To which of the angels did He [God] ever say, 'Thou art My Son ... '"? Since Jesus *is* the Son of God, and since no angel can ever be called God's son, then Jesus cannot possibly be the Archangel Michael.

Further, we are explicitly told in Hebrews 2:5 that the world *is not* (and *will not be*) in subjection to an angel. The backdrop to this is that the Dead Sea Scrolls (discovered at Qumran in 1947) reflect an expectation that the Archangel Michael would be a supreme figure in the coming messianic kingdom. It may be that some of the recipients of the Book of Hebrews were tempted to assign angels a place above Christ. Whether or not this is true, Hebrews 2:5 makes it absolutely clear that *no* angel will rule in God's kingdom. This being so, Christ cannot be Michael since He is said to be the ruler of God's kingdom over and over again in Scripture (Genesis 49:10; 2 Samuel 7:16; Psalm 2:6; Daniel 7:13-14; Matthew 2:1,2; 9:35; Luke 1:32,33; Revelation 19:16).

Finally, we must note that the Archangel Michael does not have the authority in himself to rebuke Satan. In Jude 9 we read, "But Michael the archangel, when he disputed with the devil and argued about the body of Moses, did not dare pronounce against him a railing judgment, but said, 'The Lord rebuke you.'" By contrast, Jesus rebuked the devil on a number of occasions (e.g., Matthew 17:18 and Mark 9:25). Since Michael *could not* rebuke the devil in his own authority and Jesus *could* (and *did*) rebuke the devil in His own authority, Michael and Jesus cannot be the same person.

Was Jesus the spirit-brother of Lucifer, as Mormons claim?[1]

Absolutely not! Though we could cite many passages that refute this hideous doctrine, we will limit our attention to Colossians 1:16, where we are specifically told that the entire angelic realm—including the angel Lucifer—was personally created by Jesus Christ: "For by him all things were created: things in heaven and on earth, visible and invisible, whether thrones or powers or rulers or authorities; all things were created by him and for him."

The little phrase *all things* means that Christ created the whole universe of things. Everything—whether it be simple or complex, visible or invisible, heavenly or earthly, imminent or transcendent—is the product of Christ.

It is highly revealing that Paul says that Christ created "thrones," "powers," "rulers," and "authorities." In the rabbinical (Jewish) thought of the first century, these words were used to describe different orders of angels (Romans 8:38; Ephesians 1:21; 3:10; 6:12; Colossians 2:10,15; Titus 3:1). Apparently, there was a heresy flourishing in Colossae (to whom Paul wrote Colossians) that involved the worship of angels. In the process of worshiping angels, Christ had been degraded. So, to correct this grave error, Paul emphasizes in this verse that Christ is the one who created all things—including all the angels—and hence, He is supreme and is alone worthy to be worshiped.

We know from Scripture that Lucifer is a created angelic being—a "cherub" (Ezekiel 28:13-19; cf. Isaiah 14:12-15). Since Lucifer was an angel, and since Christ created all the angels, it is very clear that Christ is not a "spirit brother" of Lucifer. Christ is not of the created realm; rather, He is the Creator. Lucifer and Christ are of two entirely different classes—the *created* and the *Creator*.

New Agers say that Jesus and the Christ are two distinct persons or entities and argue that the human Jesus became the Christ as an adult.[2] How can we respond to this?

"Jesus" and "the Christ" are not two distinct persons or entities. Jesus and the Christ refer to one and the same person. Jesus did not "become" a Christ as an adult, but was rather the one and only Christ from the very beginning.

When the angel announced the birth of Jesus to the shepherds, he identified Jesus this way: "Today in the town of David a Savior has been born to you; *he is Christ* the Lord" (Luke 2:11, italics added). Simeon, who was filled with the Holy Spirit, recognized the babe Jesus as Christ, in fulfillment of God's promise to him that "he would not die before he had seen the Lord's Christ" (Luke 2:26). Clearly Jesus didn't just become the Christ as an adult.

The Greek word for Christ (*Christos*) means "anointed one" and is a direct parallel to the Hebrew word for Messiah. In other words, "Messiah" and "Christ" are words referring to the same person. Recall that Andrew went to his brother Simon and said to him, "'We have found *the Messiah*' (that is, *the Christ*)" (John 1:41). Hundreds of messianic prophecies in the Old Testament point to a *single Messiah* or Christ—Jesus Christ.

Jesus made His identity *as* the Christ the primary issue of faith. This is seen on two different occasions in the New Testament (Matthew 16:13-20 and John 11:25-27). Significantly, when Jesus was acknowledged as the Christ, He did not say to people, "You, too, have the Christ within." Instead He warned that others would come falsely claiming to be the Christ (Matthew 24:4,5,23,24).

Did Jesus go to India during His childhood years and study under Indian gurus, as New Agers claim?[3]

No. Though the Gospels do not directly address Jesus' childhood, there are strong and convincing indirect evidences that Jesus never traveled to India during this time. We begin with Luke 2:52, the only verse in the New Testament that summarizes Jesus' life from the age 12 up to the time of His ministry: "And Jesus grew in wisdom and stature, and in favor with God and men."

Jesus, of course, was both God *and* man. As God, He was omniscient and all-wise; He could never "grow in wisdom" from the divine perspective. In His humanity, however, He did grow in wisdom—and probably gained this wisdom like most Jewish boys His age: that is, by studying the Old Testament Scriptures. Jesus apparently spent the greater part of His childhood years studying and meditating on the Old Testament Scriptures, not wandering from city to city in India.

We find further evidence that Jesus never traveled to India in that He was well-known in His community as a long-standing carpenter (Mark 6:3) and as a carpenter's son (Matthew 13:55). (It was customary among the Jews for fathers to teach their sons a trade during their childhood years. Jesus' father, Joseph, taught Him the trade of carpentry.) That carpentry played a large role in Jesus' life up to the time of His ministry is clear from the fact that some of His parables and teachings drew upon His experience as a carpenter (for example, building a house on rock as opposed to sand—Matthew 7:24-27).

According to the Gospels, Jesus was raised in Nazareth, and the people in and around Nazareth displayed obvious familiarity with Him as if they had had regular contact with Him for a prolonged time. We read that at the beginning of His three-year ministry, Jesus "went to Nazareth, *where he had been brought up*, and on the Sabbath day he went into the synagogue, *as was his custom.* And he stood up to read" (Luke 4:16, emphasis added). After He finished reading, "all spoke well of him and were amazed at the gracious words that came from his lips. *'Isn't this Joseph's son?'* they asked" (Luke 4:22). This clearly implies that those in the synagogue recognized Jesus as a local resident.

Another argument can be found in the fact that while some in Nazareth were impressed at the graciousness of Jesus' words in the Temple, others were offended that He was attracting so much attention. These seemed to be treating Him with a contempt born of familiarity. We read in Matthew 13:54-57: "Coming to his hometown, he began teaching the people in their synagogue, and they were amazed.... 'Isn't this the carpenter's son? Isn't his mother's name Mary, and aren't his brothers James, Joseph, Simon and Judas?... Where then did this man get all these things?' And they took offense at him." It is as if they were thinking: *We've known Jesus since He was a child, and now He's standing before us claiming to be the Messiah. What nerve and audacity He has!* They wouldn't have responded this way if they hadn't had regular contact with Him for a prolonged time.

Among those who became angriest at Jesus were the Jewish leaders. They accused Him of many offenses, including breaking the Sabbath (Matthew 12:1-14), blasphemy (John 8:58,59; 10:31-33), and doing miracles in Satan's power (Matthew 12:24). But they *never* accused Him of teaching or practicing anything learned in the East. The Jews considered such teachings and practices to be idolatry and sorcery. Had Jesus *actually* gone to India to study under "the great Buddhas," this would have been excellent grounds for discrediting and disqualifying Him regarding His claim to be the promised Jewish Messiah. If the Jewish leaders *could* have accused Jesus of this, they certainly *would* have.

How can we respond to those who say that Jesus was just a good moral teacher?

No mere "example" or "moral teacher" would ever claim that the destiny of the world lay in His hands, or that people would spend eternity in heaven or hell depending on whether they believed in Him (John 6:26-40). The only "example" this would provide would be one of lunacy. And for Jesus to convince people that He was God (John 8:58) and the Savior of the world (Luke 19:10) when He really wasn't would be the ultimate *im*morality. Hence, to say that Jesus was just a good moral teacher *and nothing more* makes virtually no sense.

What is the "Gnostic" view of Christ?

Gnosticism (Greek: *gnosis,* meaning "knowledge") was a heresy that briefly flourished in the second century A.D., purporting to offer knowledge of otherwise hidden "truth" as the indispensable key to man's salvation.[4]

Gnostic speculation begins with a single eternal principle (that is, God) from which multiple aeons (that is, intermediate beings or manifestations) spring in a declining hierarchy.[5] Due to an error of one of the lower aeons (who was a subordinate god called the "Demiurge," usually considered to be Yahweh of the Old Testament), the material world was produced. This gave birth to a dualism between matter and spirit, or between the earthly and the heavenly.[6]

In this world of matter created by the "Demiurge," there is allegedly to be found a remnant of the spiritual world; namely, the soul of man—which is considered a spark of divinity from the upper world (though ignorant of its celestial origins). In some inexplicable way, man's soul became entangled in the world of matter, an unfortunate turn of events which then required intervention by the *good* God (that is, that single eternal principle from which all aeons spring).[7]

Deliverance was subsequently provided by the sending of a special emissary from the kingdom of light into the world of darkness. This emissary is most often identified with Christ. He is variously represented either as a celestial being appearing in a phantom-like body (a view labeled "Docetism"), or as a higher power or spirit (Christ) who temporarily associated himself with an earthly being (Jesus).[8]

The Gnostic Christ allegedly came to earth to provide a "Gnostic redemption" for humanity. For the Gnostics, "Christ came into the world, not in order to suffer and die, but in order to release the divine spark of light imprisoned in matter. The Gnostic Jesus was not a savior; he was a revealer. He came for the express purpose of communicating his secret gnosis."[9]

How can we respond to cults who teach that Jesus is God the Father and the Holy Spirit?

Scripture is clear that the Father, Son, and Holy Spirit are distinct persons. Scripture tells us that the Father *sent* the Son (John 3:16,17), the Father and Son *love* each other (John 5:20), and the Father and Son *speak* to each other (John 8:47; 11:41,42). Moreover, the Father *knows* the Son and the Son *knows* the Father (John 10:15), and Jesus is our *advocate with* the Father (1 John 2:1).

Further, it is clear that Jesus is not the Holy Spirit, for the Holy Spirit *descended* upon Jesus at His baptism (Luke 3:22). The Holy Spirit is said to be *another* comforter (John 14:16). Jesus *sent* the Holy Spirit (John 15:26). And the Holy Spirit seeks to *glorify* Jesus (John 16:13,14).

In view of these facts, it is impossible to argue that Jesus is the Father and the Holy Spirit. (See the chapter on the Trinity for more on how the Father, Son, and Holy Spirit relate to each other.)

Does the fact that Jesus is called "Everlasting Father" in Isaiah 9:6 mean that Jesus is the Father?

No, Jesus is not the Father. As we seek to interpret the meaning of the phrase "Everlasting Father" in reference to Christ (Isaiah 9:6), it is critical to keep in mind what other Scriptures have to say about the distinction between the Father and the Son. The Father is considered by Jesus as someone other than Himself more than 200 times in the New Testament. And over 50 times in the New Testament the Father and Son are seen to be distinct within the same verse (for example, Romans 15:6; 2 Corinthians 1:4; Galatians 1:2,3; Philippians 2:10,11; 1 John 2:1; 2 John 3).[10]

If the Father and the Son are distinct, then in what sense can Jesus be called "Everlasting Father" (Isaiah 9:6)? This phrase is better translated *Father of eternity*, and carries the meaning "possessor of eternity." *Father of eternity* is here used "in accordance with a custom usual in Hebrew and in Arabic, where he who possesses a thing is called the father of it. Thus, *the father of strength* means strong; *the father of knowledge*, intelligent; *the father of glory*, glorious."[11] According to this common usage, the meaning of *Father of eternity* in Isaiah 9:6 is "eternal." Christ as the "Father of eternity" is an eternal being.[12]

The Targum—a simplified paraphrase of the Old Testament Scriptures utilized by the ancient Jews—rendered Isaiah 9:6: "His name has been called from of old, Wonderful Counselor, Mighty God, *He who lives forever....*"[13] Clearly, the ancient Jews considered the phrase *Father of eternity* as indicating the eternality of the Messiah.

Does John 10:30 teach that Jesus and the Father are the same person?

No. In John 10:30 Jesus affirmed, "I and the Father are one" (John 10:30). This verse does not mean that Jesus and the Father are one and the same person. We know this to be true because in the phrase, "I and the Father are one," a first person plural—"we are" (*esmen* in the Greek)—is used. The verse literally reads from the Greek, "I and the Father *we are* one." If Jesus intended to say that He and the Father were one *person*, He certainly would not have used the first person plural, which clearly implies *two* persons.

Moreover, the Greek word for "one" (*hen*) in this verse refers *not* to personal unity (that is, the idea that the Father and Son are one person) but to unity of essence or nature (that is, that the Father and Son have the same divine nature). This is evident in the fact that the form of the word in the Greek is neuter, not masculine. Further, the verses that immediately precede *and* follow John 10:30 distinguish Jesus from the Father (John 10:25, 29, 36, 38).

Does John 14:6-11 prove that Jesus is God the Father, as some cultists claim?

No. In this extended passage Jesus said, "If you had known Me, you would have known My Father also.... He who has seen Me has seen the Father....Do you not believe that I am in the Father, and the Father is in Me?....Believe Me that I am in the Father, and the Father in Me..." (John 14:6-11 NASB). These verses prove only that the Father and the Son are one in *being*, not that they are one *person*.

Notice that in John 14:6 Jesus clearly distinguishes Himself from the Father when He says, "No one comes *to* the Father, but *through* Me" (emphasis added). The words "to" and "through" would not make any sense if Jesus and the Father were one and the same person. They only make sense if the Father and Jesus are distinct persons, with Jesus being the Mediator between the Father and humankind.

Further, when Jesus said, "He who has seen Me has seen the Father" (John 14:9), He wasn't saying He *was* the Father. Rather, Jesus is the perfect revelation of the Father (1:18). Jesus, the *second* person of the Trinity, is the perfect revelation of the Father, the *first* person of the Trinity.

Does 2 Corinthians 3:17 prove that Jesus is the Holy Spirit, as some cultists claim?

No. In 2 Corinthians 3:17 we read, "Now the Lord is the Spirit; and where the Spirit of the Lord is, there is liberty" (NASB). Many expositors view this verse as saying that the Holy Spirit is "Lord" not in the sense of being Jesus but in the sense of being Yahweh (the Lord God). We know the verse is not saying that Jesus is the Holy Spirit, for just earlier in 2 Corinthians 3 the apostle Paul clearly distinguishes between Jesus and the Holy Spirit (see verses 3-6).

Further, more broadly, the whole of Scripture indicates that Jesus is not the Holy Spirit. As noted earlier in the chapter, the Holy Spirit is said to be *another* comforter (John 14:16; cf. 1 John 2:1). Jesus *sent* the Holy Spirit (John 15:26; 16:7). The Holy Spirit seeks to *glorify* Jesus (John 16:13,14).

PART 5

~

HUMANITY AND THE SIN PROBLEM

The Origins of Humankind

Man Related to God

The Sin Problem

16

~

The Origins of Humankind

Was man created, or did he evolve from apes?

I believe in a literal creation and that the Genesis account gives us an accurate picture of humankind's beginnings (Genesis 1–2). I also believe that there are many problems in the evolutionary hypothesis. Following is a summary of just six:

1. Scientists by and large agree that the universe had a beginning. They may disagree as to how that beginning happened, but they largely agree there was a beginning. Now, in my view, the fact that there was a beginning implies the existence of a Beginner—a Creator. As Scripture says, "Every house is built by someone, but God is the builder of everything" (Hebrews 3:4).

2. By observing the world and universe around us, it becomes apparent that a Designer was involved. Everything is just perfect for life on earth—*so* perfect and so "fine tuned" that it gives every evidence of coming from the hands of an intelligent Designer (God). The earth's size, composition, distance from the sun, rotational period, and many other factors are all just right for life. The chances of there being even one planet where all of these factors converge by accident are almost nonexistent.

In keeping with the above, the genetic code of all biological life on earth gives evidence of intelligent design. In fact, the information contained in genetic code is comparable to the information stored in complex computer programs. The complex design implies the existence of a Designer (God).

3. As one examines the fossil records, one not only finds no evidence supporting evolution, one finds evidence against it. If the theory of evolution were true, one would expect to see in the fossil records progressively complex evolutionary forms, indicating transitions that took place. But there is no such evidence. *No* (I repeat, *no*) transitional links have been discovered in the fossil records.

4. The theory of evolution assumes a long series of positive and upward mutations. In almost all known cases, however, mutations are not beneficial but are harmful to living beings and often result in death. Deformities typically *lessen* the survival potential of an animal, not strengthen it. Even if there were a few good mutations that took place, the incredible number of damaging mutations would utterly overwhelm the good ones.

5. The first and second laws of thermodynamics are foundational to science and have never been contradicted in observable nature. The first law says that matter and energy are not created nor destroyed; they just change forms. The second law says that in an isolated system (like our universe), the natural course of things is to degenerate. The universe is running down, not evolving upward.

6. False claims are often made by evolutionists. Some have claimed that there is scientific evidence that evolution is true. These individuals generally appeal to the fact that mutations *within* a species are a proven scientific fact (microevolution). But it requires an incredible leap of logic to say that the existence of mutations *within* species proves the possibility of mutations or transformations into *entirely new* species (macroevolution). You can't breed two dogs and get a cat!

Is theistic evolution a biblical concept?

No, I don't think so. Theistic evolution involves the notion that God initially began creation and then used evolution to produce the universe as we know it. God allegedly entered into the process of time to modify what was developing. Those who hold to this view generally attempt to reconcile the findings of science with the Bible.

There are a number of serious problems with the doctrine of theistic evolution. For one thing, it must make a complete allegory out of Genesis 1:1–2:4, for which there is no warrant. Certainly the suggestion that humanity is derived from a nonhuman ancestor cannot be reconciled with the explicit statement of man's creation in Genesis 2:7. Man did not evolve but rather was created from the dust of the ground. Further, if Adam was not a real historical person, then the analogy between Christ and Adam in Romans 5:12-21 utterly breaks down.

Certainly Christ believed in a literal creation of Adam and Eve (Matthew 19:4; Mark 10:6). (Christ would know, for He is elsewhere portrayed as the Creator—John 1:3; Colossians 1:16; Hebrews 1:2,10.) If His words cannot be trusted in these particulars, how can anyone be sure His words can be trusted in other matters?

Is man composed of two aspects (body and soul/spirit) or three aspects (body, soul, and spirit)?

This has been a much-debated issue. The dichotomist view is that man is composed of two parts—material (body) and immaterial (soul/spirit). In this view, "soul" and "spirit" are seen as essentially the same. Man's entire immaterial part is called "soul" in 1 Peter 2:11 and "spirit" in James 2:26. Hence they must be equal.

In the trichotomist view, the soul and spirit are viewed as separate substantive entities. Hence, man is viewed as consisting of three realities—body, soul, *and* spirit. Tri-chotomists generally say that the body involves world-con-sciousness, the soul involves self-consciousness, and the spirit involves God-consciousness. Support for this view is found in Hebrews 4:12 and 1 Thessalonians 5:23.

Perhaps a few distinctions would be helpful. If we are talking about mere *substance*, then we must conclude that man has only a material and an immaterial aspect. How-ever, if we are talking about *function*, then we may say that within the sphere of man's immaterial aspect there are a number of functions—including that of soul and spirit.[1] Other components of man's immaterial nature include the heart (Hebrews 4:12; Matthew 22:37), the conscience (1 Peter 2:19; Hebrews 10:22), and the mind (Romans 12:2).

What does the Bible say about the equality of the races?

God created *all* races of man. All human beings are com-pletely equal—equal in terms of their creation (Genesis 1:28), the sin problem (Romans 3:23), God's love for them (John 3:16), and God's provision of salvation for them (Matthew 28:19). The apostle Paul affirmed, "From one man he made every nation of men, that they should inhabit the whole earth; and he determined the times set for them and the exact places where they should live" (Acts 17:26). More-over, Revelation 5:9 tells us that God's redeemed will be from "every tribe and tongue and people and nation" (NASB). There is thus no place for racial discrimination, for all men are equal in God's sight.

What does the Bible say about male-female equality?

Jesus had a very high view of women. In a Jewish cul-ture where women were discouraged from studying the law, Jesus taught women right alongside men as equals

(Matthew 14:21; 15:38). And when He taught, He often used women's activities to illustrate the character of the kingdom of God, such as baking bread (Luke 13:20f.), grinding corn (Luke 17:35), and sweeping the house to find a lost coin (Luke 15:8-10).

Some Jewish Rabbis taught that a man should not speak to a woman in a public place, but Jesus not only spoke to a woman (who, incidentally, was a Samaritan) but also drank from her cup in a public place (John 4:1-30). The first person He appeared to after resurrecting from the dead was Mary and not the male disciples (John 20). Clearly, Jesus had a very high view of women.

Galatians 3:28 tells us that there is neither male nor female in Jesus Christ. First Peter 3:7 says men and women are fellow heirs of grace. Ephesians 5:21 speaks of mutual submission between man and wife. In John 7:53—8:11 Jesus wouldn't permit the double standard of the woman being taken in adultery and letting the man go free. In Luke 10:39 Jesus let a woman sit at His feet, which was a place reserved for the male disciples. Verses such as these show that in God's eyes men and women are spiritually equal. Nevertheless, Scripture also speaks of male leadership in the family and in the church (Ephesians 5:22; 1 Corinthians 11:3; 14:34; 1 Timothy 2:11).

~

Man Related to God

How can man's free will be reconciled with God's sovereignty?

Scripture portrays God as being absolutely sovereign (Acts 15:8; Ephesians 1:11; Psalm 135:6). Scripture also portrays man as having a free will (Genesis 3:1-7). It is certainly inscrutable to man's finite understanding how both divine sovereignty and human free will can both be true, but both doctrines are taught in Scripture. In fact, both of these are often seen side by side in the span of a single Scripture verse.

For example, in Acts 2:23 we read of Jesus: "This man was handed over to you by God's set purpose and foreknowledge; and you, with the help of wicked men, put him to death by nailing him to the cross." Here we see *divine sovereignty* ("by God's set purpose and foreknowledge") and *human free will* ("you, with the help of wicked men, put him to death").

We also see both doctrines in Acts 13:48: "When the Gentiles heard this, they were glad and honored the word of the Lord; and all who were appointed for eternal life believed." God's *sovereignty* is clear ("all who were appointed for eternal life") as is man's *free will* ("believed").

It has been suggested that divine sovereignty and human free will are like parallel railroad tracks that are often found side by side in Scripture, and the tracks never come together on this side of eternity. When we enter glory, we will no doubt come to a fuller understanding of these biblical doctrines. Now we see as in a mirror darkly. Then we shall see clearly (1 Corinthians 13:12).

If it is true that God is sovereign in all things, then why should we pray?

It is true that God is sovereign over all things (Ephesians 1:18-23). But we must recognize that God has ordained not only the "ends" but also the "means" to those "ends." In other words, God has sovereignly ordained not only to bring certain things about, He has also ordained to accomplish certain things as a result of the individual prayers of His people. Hence, we should most definitely pray for specific needs (see Philippians 4:6). We must never forget the scriptural teaching that we do not have because we do not ask God (James 4:2).

What is the distinction between God's sovereignty and naturalistic determinism?

Determinism says that all events (including man's actions) occur by necessity, being caused by previous events (there is a perpetual outworking of cause-and-effect relationships). No deity need be involved. In God's sovereignty, God is in control of causes *and* effects, moving all things toward a purposeful end. He is in control of primary and secondary causes, and moves all things according to His will.

How can God say He loves Jacob but hates Esau (Romans 9:13)?

The word "hate" should not be taken to mean that God had the human emotional sense of disgust, disdain, and a desire for revenge against Esau. God did not have a negative psychological emotion that burned against Esau. Rather the word should be understood as the Hebrew idiom it is—a word that means "to love less" (cf. Genesis 29:30-33). We might loosely paraphrase Romans 9:13, "In comparison to my great love for Jacob, my feeling for Esau, whom I 'love less,' may *seem* like hatred, even though I don't really emotionally hate him."

It seems cruel that God hardened Pharaoh's heart (Exodus 4:21). Is that fair?

Ten times in the text of Scripture it is said that the Pharaoh hardened *his own* heart (Exodus 7:13,14,22; 8:15,19,32; 9:7,34,35; 13:15), and ten times that God hardened Pharaoh's heart (4:21; 7:3; 9:12; 10:1,20,27; 11:10; 14:4,8,17). In Romans 9:17,18 the apostle Paul uses this as an example of the inscrutable will of God and of His mercy toward human beings. The Pharaoh hardened his own heart seven times *before* God first hardened it, though the prediction that God would do it preceded all.

It is evident that God hardens on the same grounds as showing mercy. If men will accept mercy, He will give it to them. It they will not, thus hardening themselves, He is only just and righteous in judging them. Mercy is the effect of a right attitude, and hardening is the effect of stubbornness or a wrong attitude toward God. It is like the clay and the wax in the sun. The same sunshine hardens one and softens the other. The responsibility is with the materials, not with the sun. Scholars have suggested that the danger of resisting God is that He will eventually give us over to our own choices (see Romans 1:24-28).

Even so, it must be pointed out that God has always exercised His sovereign right of choice (Exodus 9:6-13). And we sinners can hardly call Him to task for it. The Maker has an indisputable right to do as He pleases with what He makes (verses 14-21). It is only by virtue of His patience and mercy that even a remnant of stubborn, rebellious Israel survived His judgment (verses 22-29).

Some Scriptures say that God does not change His mind (1 Samuel 15:29). Other Scriptures seem to portray God changing His mind (see verse 11). What are we to make of this?

On the one hand God is unchanging in His essence or nature (Malachi 3:6) and is unchanging in His eternal purposes (see Ephesians 1). But this does not mean that God is some kind of Robot-Automaton who cannot interact with His creatures and respond to them.

God promised to judge the Ninevites but then withheld judgment after the entire city repented (see the Book of Jonah). Many people fail to realize that God has what you might call a built-in repentance clause to His promises of judgment. This clause is found in Jeremiah 18:7-10:

> If at any time I announce that a nation or kingdom is to be uprooted, torn down and destroyed, and if that nation I warned repents of its evil, then I will relent and not inflict on it the disaster I had planned. And if at another time I announce that a nation or kingdom is to be built up and planted, and if it does evil in my sight and does not obey me, then I will reconsider the good I had intended to do for it.

What we see here is that God changes His policy toward man when He beholds a change in the actions of man. God is a God of mercy. And when He sees repentance, He responds with mercy and grace. We should all be thankful that God is this way. If God gave us what we actually deserved, we'd all end up in hell.

Does God always heal when Christians ask for it?

No. Sometimes God may have something He wants to teach a believer by allowing him or her to go through a time of sickness. God allowed Epaphroditus (Philippians 2:25-27), Trophimus (2 Timothy 4:20), Timothy (1 Timothy 5:23), Job (Job 1–2), and Paul (2 Corinthians 12:9) to suffer through periods of sickness. He does the same with us.

While the healing of our bodies in our mortal state is not guaranteed in the atonement, ultimate healing (in terms of our resurrection bodies) *is* guaranteed in the atonement. Our resurrection bodies will never get sick, grow old, or die (see 1 Corinthians 15:50f.). That's something to look forward to.

Today when Christians get sick, they should certainly pray for healing (see James 5:15). As well (contrary to certain televangelists' messages), we should not be hesitant about going to the doctor. God can work a healing directly, or He can work a healing through the instrumentality of a doctor. God never portrays doctors in a negative light. Jesus Himself said, "It is not the healthy who need a doctor, but the sick" (Matthew 9:12). But if we remain sick, we must continue to trust in God and rely on His grace, as did the apostle Paul (2 Corinthians 12:9). Our attitude should be that whether we are healthy or sick, we will always rest in God's sufficiency (Philippians 4:13).

Does God hear the prayers of non-Christians?

On the one hand, God is omniscient (Psalm 139:1-5) and hence is aware in every way of the utterances of human beings the world over. Nothing escapes His attention. The real question is, Does God personally *respond* to the prayers of non-Christians?

I think there are cases when He does. For example, God certainly hears the prayer of conversion when an unbeliever finally comes to faith in Christ. I also think that in the process leading up to that person's conversion, God may answer some prayers along the way to show that person that he or she is dealing with the one true God. In other words, God may answer such prayers as a way of confirming that He is real and He is there.

Having said that, it is only Christians—those in the family of God—who can go before God and call Him "Abba" (meaning *Daddy*—Galatians 4:6) and claim the many promises God makes to those in His family (2 Peter 1:4).

Should Christians who are hurting in their relationship with God or struggling with a behavioral problem seek help from pastoral counseling, or is it better to join a recovery group?

From my perspective, the pastor of the local church should be the primary counselor for the Christian. This is not to say that a biblically oriented recovery group is never warranted. Sometimes it may be. But why not make the pastor—who interprets life's problems through the lens of Scripture—the first step in the recovery process? Through a solid course of biblical (nonhumanistic) counseling from the pastor, the counselee may obtain all he or she needs to deal with his or her problem.

Such biblical counseling should include:

An emphasis on the importance of becoming biblically literate. Biblical doctrine enables us to develop a realistic worldview, without which we are doomed to ineffectual living (Romans 12:3; 2 Timothy 4:3,4). Moreover, doctrine can protect us from false beliefs that can lead to destructive behavior (1 Timothy 4:1-6; 2 Timothy 2:17-19; Titus 1:11).

An emphasis on what the Bible says about the nature of man. This includes his soul (1 Peter 2:11), his spirit (Romans 8:16), his heart (Hebrews 4:12), his conscience (1 Peter 2:19), his mind (Romans 12:2), as well as his sin nature and its effects (2 Corinthians 4:4; Ephesians 4:18; Romans 1:18–3:20). An accurate understanding of man's nature is a prerequisite for prescribing the correct treatment for a particular behavioral problem.

A thorough understanding of man's sin nature. This is especially important. Too often, "recovery" experts speak of getting rid of "character defects" in the patient. However, the whole "old" self is defective or depraved (2 Corinthians 4:4; Ephesians 4:18; Romans 1:18–3:20) and must go. As one critic put it, we do not need a tune-up in our lives. We need a brand new engine.

An emphasis on the threefold enemy of the Christian. This enemy includes: (1) the world (including the things of the world, which are expressions of "the cravings of sinful man, the lust of his eyes and the boasting of what he has and does," 1 John 2:16); (2) the flesh (the sinful nature itself, which is bent on sexual immorality, impurity, discord, jealousy, fits of rage, selfish ambition, dissensions, factions and envy, and drunkenness, Galatians 5:20, 21); and (3) the devil (who seeks to tempt us [1 Corinthians 7:5], deceive us [2 Corinthians 11:14], afflict us [2 Corinthians 12:7], and hinder us [1 Thessalonians 2:18]). All three of these "enemies" have some bearing on human behavior.

An emphasis on dependence upon the Holy Spirit. Scripture tells us that self-control is the fruit of the Holy Spirit (Galatians 5:22). And as we "walk" in the spirit—as we habitually depend upon the Spirit (verse 25)—such fruit will inevitably grow in our lives.

An emphasis on the sufficiency of God's grace. In the midst of trying circumstances (2 Corinthians 12:9, 10), as Paul discovered, God's grace enables us to cope with difficulties that can be overwhelming when approached through human strength alone.

An emphasis on faith. Scripture says that without faith it is impossible to please God (Hebrews 11:6). It is also true that without faith in God it is impossible to effectively deal with behavioral problems and live victorious Christian lives (cf. 1 Thessalonians 5:8).

A counseling regimen based on these and other practical truths may completely solve the counselee's problem. But if, during the course of biblical counseling, it is determined that a biblically oriented (nonhumanistic) recovery group would be helpful, then it becomes an option at that point.

I'm convinced that small groups can be beneficial—if the purpose of the small group is to console, compassionately listen, empathize, and share experiences with one another. These are the hallmarks of true friendship, and such activity can contribute greatly to the healing of an individual who has been ravaged in some way in our impersonal and often callous world.

During the time the counselee is attending the group, however, I believe he or she should continue to meet with the pastor so progress can be monitored. This way, the pastor can still play a significant role in the recovery process and continue to offer instructive counsel and prayer support. And once the person has recovered, he or she can then serve as a shining example to others of the truth of Paul's inspiring affirmation: "I can do all things through Him who strengthens me" (Philippians 4:13 NASB).

18

~

The Sin Problem

What is "original sin"?

When Adam and Eve sinned, it didn't just affect them in an isolated way. It affected the entire human race. In fact, ever since then, every human being born into the world has been born in a state of sin.

The apostle Paul said that "sin entered the world through one man, and death through sin, and in this way death came to all men, because all sinned" (Romans 5:12). Indeed, "through the disobedience of the one man the many were made sinners" (Romans 5:19; see also 1 Corinthians 15:21,22).

In Psalm 51:5 David said, "Surely I was sinful at birth, sinful from the time my mother conceived me." According to this verse human beings are born into the world in a state of sin. The sin nature is passed on *from conception*. This is why Ephesians 2:3 says we are "by nature objects of wrath." Every one of us is born into this world with a sin nature.

Was death the result of sin?

Yes, I believe so. In Scripture there is a direct connection between sin and death (Romans 5:12). One causes the other. Death came into the universe as a result of sin (Genesis 2:17).

This means that death is not natural. It is an unnatural intruder. God intended human beings *to live*. Death is therefore something foreign and hostile to human life. Death has arisen because of our rebellion against God; it is a form of God's judgment.

But there is grace even in death. For death, as a judgment against sin, serves to prevent us from living forever in a state of sin. When Adam and Eve sinned in the Garden of Eden (Genesis 2:17; 3:6), God assigned an angel to guard the Tree of Life. This was to protect against Adam and Eve eating from the Tree of Life while they were yet in a body of sin. How horrible it would be to live eternally in such a state.

By death, then, God saw to it that man's existence in a state of sin had definite limits. And by sending a Savior into the world—the Lord Jesus Christ—God made provision for taking care of the sin problem (John 3:17). Those who believe in Him will live eternally at His side, the sin problem having been banished forever.

Does God punish children for their parents' sins (Numbers 14:18)?

No, I don't think so. The primary verse of dispute is Numbers 14:18, where we read, "The LORD is slow to anger, abounding in love and forgiving sin and rebellion. Yet he does not leave the guilty unpunished; he punishes the children for the sin of the fathers to the third and fourth generation."

I believe it is the consistent teaching of Scripture that God punishes people for *their own* sins. In Deuteronomy 24:16 we read, "Fathers shall not be put to death for their children, nor children put to death for their fathers; each is to die for his own sin." Moreover, in Ezekiel 18:14-20 we read that children will not die for the sins of their fathers.

So, how are we to interpret Numbers 14:18? I think this verse is referring to the fact that parents pass on to their children sinful patterns of behavior. A parental environment of alcoholism may produce a child who ends up drinking.

A parental environment of yelling may produce a child who verbally abuses others.

There are all kinds of examples of this type of thing in Scripture. Ahaziah "did evil in the eyes of the LORD, because he walked in the ways of his father and mother" (1 Kings 22:52). His mother "encouraged him in doing wrong" (2 Chronicles 22:3). Similarly, in Jeremiah 9:14 we read of those who "followed the Baals, as their fathers taught them." So, again, Numbers 14:18 is basically dealing with sinful patterns of behavior being passed on from one generation to the next.

Is it possible for the Christian to attain sinless perfection in this life?

No. A number of scriptural facts rule this out as a possibility. To begin, 1 John 1:8 tells us, "If we claim to be without sin, we deceive ourselves and the truth is not in us." Since this epistle was written to Christians (1 John 2:12-14,19; 3:1; 5:13), it seems clear that Christians in mortal life should never make the claim to have attained perfection.

Second, this view doesn't take adequate account of the fact that each of us is born into the world with a "sinful nature" that stays with us until we die (Ephesians 2:3). The presence of the sin nature would seem to make any form of perfectionism impossible.

Third, the great saints of the Bible seemed to all recognize their own intrinsic sinfulness (Isaiah 6:5; Daniel 9:4-19; Ephesians 3:8). If anyone could have attained perfection, certainly Isaiah, Daniel, and the apostle Paul would have been contenders. But none of them succeeded. Why? Because they still had the sin nature in them that erupted in their lives from time to time.

So, for us to claim to be able to attain sinless perfection is, in the words of one theologian, a perfect error.

How can we respond to those who say that Jesus taught that man's basic problem is ignorance of his divinity?

The biblical Jesus taught that human beings have a grave sin problem that is altogether beyond their means to solve. He taught that human beings are by nature evil (Matthew 12:34; Luke 11:13) and that man is capable of great wickedness (Mark 7:20-23; Luke 11:42-52). Moreover, Jesus said that man is utterly lost and that he is a sinner (Luke 15:10), that he is in need of repentance before a holy God (Mark 1:15), and that he needs to be born again (John 3:3,5,7).

Jesus often spoke of man's sin with metaphors that illustrate the havoc sin can wreak in one's life. He described human sin as a blindness (Matthew 15:14; 23:16-26); a sickness (Matthew 9:12); being enslaved in bondage (John 8:34); and living in darkness (John 3:19-21; 8:12; 12:35-46). Moreover, Jesus taught that this is a universal condition and that all people are guilty before God.

Jesus also taught that it is not only external acts that render a person guilty of sin, but inner thoughts as well (Matthew 5:28). He taught that from within the human heart come "evil thoughts, sexual immorality, theft, murder, adultery, greed, malice, deceit, envy, slander, arrogance and folly. 'All these evils,' Jesus said, 'come from inside and make a man "unclean"'" (Mark 7:21-23). Moreover, Jesus affirmed that God is fully aware of every person's sins—both external acts and inner thoughts; nothing escapes His notice (Matthew 10:26; 22:18; Luke 6:8; John 4:17-19). Man is quite obviously *not* divine!

What is the "sin unto death" mentioned in 1 John 5:16?

The "sin unto death" in 1 John 5:16,17 has been the cause of much concern among many believers. Various interpretations have been proposed down through the centuries. Some believe it refers to the spiritual death of unbelievers. Others believe that it refers to the physical death of believers as a result of committing either (1) a particular identifiable sin that is seen as the sin unto death; or (2) a sin (*any* sin) that is persistently committed in an unrepentant attitude.

From my understanding of John's writings (primarily his Gospel and three epistles), the sin unto death might be viewed as a permanent separation of the believer into the *kosmos* (the fallen world system) which subsequently ends up killing him. There is a very close relationship in John's writings between sin, death, and the kosmos. A believer's relationship to the sin unto death is directly proportional to his relationship to the kosmos, for the kosmos (the evil world) is characterized by sin—and is, in fact, a death system. To become a part of this system and remain entrenched there is subsequently to come within the grips of death.

The way I see it, the sin for which death is a rapid consequence is *permanently retrogressing* into the kosmos death system. Other individual sins—whether related to lust of the flesh, lust of the eyes, or the pride of life—can be committed that will not likely end in death. But in light of the fact that these lesser sins are a part of the kosmos system, it is possible that one such sin (if unrepented of and persisted in) could ultimately lead one to commit the greater sin of *total separation* into the kosmos death system. In such a condition, the kosmos ends up killing the believer. The death system yields its fruit—death.

It is important to note in regard to the sin unto death that this sin *tends* to death, doesn't *guarantee* death, and we're talking about *physical* death only. Death is, so to speak, its natural consequence, if it continues.

We can summarize things this way: (1) Sin is an integral part of the kosmos, which is a death system; (2) Believers have a sin nature, and they are not immune to committing sins which are rooted in the kosmos; (3) Such sins committed by believers will never result in their spiritual death; (4) Most sins committed by believers will not result in physical death; but (5) One sin that can lead to the physical death of the believer is that of separating himself headlong into the kosmos and remaining there in a *permanent state of retrogression*. In such a state, death for the believer may be imminent if there is no repentance. But he is still saved and will enjoy eternal life with Christ in heaven.

PART 6

~

THE GOOD NEWS OF SALVATION

The Gospel of Salvation

Eternal Security

God's Part, Man's Part

The Role of Baptism

Our Role as Witnesses

The Church: The Community of the Redeemed

19

~

The Gospel of Salvation

Are the heathen really lost?

Yes. If the heathen are not really lost, then many of the teachings of Christ become absurd. For example, John 3:16—"For God so loved the world that he gave his one and only Son, that whoever believes in him shall not perish but have eternal life"—becomes meaningless.

If the heathen are not lost, Christ's postresurrection and preascension commands to His disciples are a mockery. In Luke 24:47 Christ commanded "that repentance and remission of sins should be preached in his name among all nations" (KJV). Similarly, in Matthew 28:19 He said, "Therefore go and make disciples of all nations, baptizing them in the name of the Father and of the Son and of the Holy Spirit." These verses might well be stricken from the Scriptures if human beings without Christ are not lost.

If the heathen are not really lost, then the Lord's words were meaningless when He said to His disciples, "As the Father has sent me, I am sending you" (John 20:21). Why did the Father send Him? Jesus Himself explained that "the Son of Man came to seek and to save what was lost" (Luke 19:10).

If the heathen do not need Christ and His salvation, then neither do we. Conversely, if we need Him, *so do they*. The Scriptures become a bundle of contradictions, the Savior becomes a false teacher, and the Christian message becomes "much ado about nothing" if the heathen are not lost.

Scripture makes it very plain: "Salvation is found in no one else, for there is no other name under heaven given to men by which we must be saved" (Acts 4:12). The Bible says, "There is one God and one mediator between God and men, the man Christ Jesus" (1 Timothy 2:5).

Other religions do not lead to God. The one sin for which God judged the people of Israel more severely than any other was that of participating in heathen religions. Again and again the Bible implies and states that God hates, despises, and utterly rejects anything associated with heathen religions and practices. Those who follow such idolatry are not regarded as groping their way to God but rather as having turned their backs on Him, following the ways of darkness.

Now, I must point out the scriptural teaching that God has given a certain amount of "light" to every single person in the world. Everyone has some sense of God's law in his or her heart. As John Blanchard put it so well, everyone

> has some conception of the difference between right and wrong; he approves of honesty; he responds to love and kindness; he resents it if someone steals his goods or tries to injure him. In other words, he has a conscience which passes judgment on his behavior and the behavior of others, something the Bible calls a law written on his heart.[1]

Paul speaks of this law written on human hearts in Romans 2:15.

God has also given witness of Himself in the universe around us. In beholding the world and the universe, it is evident that there is someone who made the world and the universe. Since the creation of the world, God's invisible qualities—His eternal power and divine nature—have been clearly seen and understood from that which He created (Romans 1:20).

We know from other Scripture verses that God is an invisible spirit (John 4:24). The physical eye cannot see Him. But His existence is nevertheless reflected in what He has made—the creation. The *creation*, which is visible, reveals the existence of the *Creator*, who is invisible.

Because all human beings can see the revelation of God in creation, all people—regardless of whether they've heard about Christ or have read the Bible—are held accountable before God. *All are without excuse.* Their rightful condemnation, as objects of God's wrath, is justified because their choice to ignore the revelation of God in creation is indefensible (see Psalm 19:1-6; Romans 1:20).

The Scriptures clearly indicate that those who respond to the limited light around them (such as God's witness of Himself in the universe) will receive further, more specific "light." This is illustrated in the life of Cornelius. This Gentile was obedient to the limited amount of "light" he had received—that is, he had been obedient to Old Testament revelation (Acts 10:2). But he didn't have enough "light" to believe in Jesus Christ as the Savior. So God sent Peter to Cornelius's house to explain the gospel, after which time Cornelius believed in Jesus and was saved (Acts 10:44-48).

In view of the above, we must not allow God's name to be impugned by those who imply that God is unfair if He judges those who have never heard the gospel. As we have seen, God has given a witness of Himself to *all* humanity. Moreover, God desires all to be saved (1 Timothy 2:4) and doesn't want anyone to perish (2 Peter 3:9). He certainly takes no pleasure in the death of the unsaved (Ezekiel 18:23).

Let us remember that God is a *fair* Judge. "It is unthinkable that God would do wrong, that the Almighty would pervert justice" (Job 34:12). "Will not the Judge of all the earth do right?" (Genesis 18:25).

Does the Bible teach universalism—the view that all humanity will eventually be saved?

Universalism states that sooner or later all people will be saved. This position holds that the concepts of hell and punishment are inconsistent with a loving God.

The older form of universalism, originating in the second century, taught that salvation would come after a temporary period of punishment. The more recent form of universalism declares that all human beings are now saved, though all do not realize it. Therefore the job of the preacher and the missionary is to tell people they are already saved. Certain passages—John 12:32, Philippians 2:11, and 1 Timothy 2:4—are typically twisted out of context in support of universalism. Such passages, interpreted properly, do not support universalism.

John 12:32 says that Christ's work on the cross makes possible the salvation of both Jews and Gentiles. Notice, however, that the Lord—in the same passage—warned of judgment of those who reject Christ (verse 48).

Philippians 2:10,11 assures us that someday all people will acknowledge that Jesus is Lord, but not necessarily as Savior. (Even those in hell will have to acknowledge Christ's Lordship.)

First Timothy 2:4 expresses God's desire that all be saved, but does not promise that all *will* be. This divine desire is only realized in those who exercise faith in Christ (Acts 16:31).

The Scriptures consistently categorize people into one of two classes (saved/unsaved, also called believers/unbelievers), and portray the final destiny of every person as being one of two realities (heaven or hell).

In Matthew 13:49 Jesus said, "This is how it will be at the end of the age. The angels will come and separate the wicked from the righteous." Two classes are mentioned—

unbelievers and believers, spoken of as "the wicked" and "the righteous."

In Matthew 25:32 Jesus said that following His second coming, "All the nations will be gathered before him, and he will separate the people one from another as a shepherd separates the sheep from the goats." Here believers and unbelievers are differentiated by the terms "sheep" and "goats." The sheep will enter into God's kingdom (verse 34) and inherit eternal life (verse 46). The goats go into eternal punishment (verse 46).

Clearly, then, the Scriptures speak of two categories of people (the saved and the unsaved) and two possible destinies (heaven for the saved, hell for the unsaved). And each respective person ends up in one of these places based upon whether or not he or she placed saving faith in Christ during his or her time on earth (Acts 16:31).

What is the gospel?

Perhaps the best single definition of the gospel in Scripture is found in 1 Corinthians 15:3, 4: "For what I received I passed on to you as of first importance: that Christ died for our sins according to the Scriptures, that he was buried, that he was raised on the third day according to the Scriptures." The "gospel," according to this passage, has four components: (1) man is a sinner; (2) Christ is the Savior; (3) Christ died as man's substitute; and (4) Christ rose from the dead. This is the gospel Paul and the other apostles preached; it is the gospel we too must preach.

What are some faulty concepts people have of the gospel?

There are a number of misconceptions that people have had about the gospel. Following are three examples:

1. Some have taught that one must plead for mercy before one can be saved. However, this idea is never found in Scripture. Salvation comes by faith in Christ (John 3:16; Acts 16:31). God provides pardon for anyone who believes; no one has to plead for it.

2. Some have taught that we must follow Christ's example and seek to live as He lived in order to be a Christian. *The Imitation of Christ* by Thomas à Kempis has been understood by many to teach that we become Christians by living as Christ did and obeying His teachings, seeking to behave as He behaved. From a scriptural perspective, we simply do not have it in us to live as Christ lived. We are fallen human beings (Romans 3:23). Only the Holy Spirit working in us can imitate Christ in our lives (Galatians 5:16-23).

3. Some have inadvertently communicated that prayer is a necessary component in becoming saved. In other words, one must pray the "prayer of repentance." The scriptural perspective is that even though prayer may be a vehicle for the expression of one's faith, it is the faith that brings about salvation, not the prayer through which that faith is communicated. In fact, one can bypass prayer altogether by simply exercising faith in one's heart, and one becomes saved at that moment.

We must always remember that salvation is a free gift that we receive by faith in Christ (Ephesians 2:8, 9). This is the glorious message of the gospel.

Does Psalm 19:1 tell us the gospel of Jesus Christ can be found in the stars?

I don't think so. That's not to deny that there's a "witness" in the stars, but you'll never find the gospel there. Psalm 19:1 tells us, "The heavens declare the glory of God; the skies proclaim the work of his hands." People all over the world can understand something of God's power and glory by observing the stellar universe (Romans 1:20). But they can't read the gospel message from the stars.

According to the New Testament, the gospel is something that is objectively communicated. It is not subjectively observed in images one constructs while looking at the stars. As noted earlier in the chapter, the content of this gospel is provided by the apostle Paul in 1 Corinthians 15:1-4, and involves four primary components: (1) man is a sinner; (2) Christ is the Savior; (3) Christ died as man's substitute; and (4) Christ rose from the dead.

The word *gospel* occurs more than 100 times in the New Testament, but not once is it ever associated with the stars. Hence, though the "gospel in the stars" theory may be intriguing, it has virtually no biblical basis.

There are two further points that bear mentioning. First, there is no uniform zodiac constellation. Some claim there are 24 zodiac signs, while others count eight, ten, or 14. This makes it impossible to interpret the stars in a uniform way.

Moreover, there is no uniform message behind the stars. The star-formed zodiac signs can be assigned whatever meaning the interpreter subjectively decides upon; the purported messages behind the signs are completely arbitrary.

What is the theological doctrine known as "justification"?

Humankind's dilemma of "falling short" pointed to the need for a solution—and that solution is found in justification (Romans 3:24). The word *justification* is a legal term and involves being "declared righteous" or "acquitted." Negatively, the word means that one is once-and-for-all pronounced *not guilty* before God. Positively, the word means that man is once-and-for-all pronounced *righteous*. The very righteousness of Christ is imputed to the believer's life. From the moment that we place faith in Christ, God sees us through the lens of Christ's righteousness.

Though the Jews had previously tried to earn a right standing with God by works, Paul indicated that God's declaration of righteousness (justification) is given "freely by his grace" (Romans 3:24). The word grace literally means "unmerited favor." It is because of God's unmerited favor that human beings can freely be "declared righteous" before God. And this declaration occurs the moment a person exercises faith in Christ.

But this doesn't mean God's declaration of righteousness has no objective basis, because it does: Paul said that redemption "came by Christ Jesus." The word *redemption* literally means "ransom payment." This is a word adapted from the slave market. We were formerly enslaved to sin and Satan, but Jesus ransomed us by His death on the cross. His shed blood was the ransom payment (Romans 3:25).

What is the difference between the Roman Catholic view of justification and the Protestant view?

Justification in the Roman Catholic view involves a transformation whereby the individual actually *becomes* righteous. It is viewed as a process by which God gradually perfects us. This process is furthered by good works and participation in the sacraments.[2]

By contrast, Protestants view justification as a singular and instantaneous event in which God declares the believing sinner to be righteous. Justification viewed in this way is a judicial term in which God makes a legal declaration. It is not based on performance or good works. It involves God's pardoning of sinners and restoring them to a state of righteousness. This declaration of righteousness takes place the moment a person trusts in Christ for salvation (Luke 7:48-50; Acts 10:43; Romans 3:25, 28, 30; 8:33, 34; Galatians 4:21–5:12; 1 John 1:7–2:2).

It must also be noted that evangelicals believe in justification *by faith in Christ alone*. Good works do not contribute to justification at all but are rather viewed as the result of justification. Salvation comes about through faith (Romans 4; Galatians 3:6-14). Good works, however, are a by-product of salvation (Matthew 7:15-23). Good works should result from the changed purpose for living that salvation brings.

Where does the word Christian come from?

The word *Christian* is used only three times in the New Testament—the most important of which is Acts 11:26 (cf. Acts 26:28 and 1 Peter 4:16). In Acts 11:26, we are told simply and straightforwardly, "The disciples were called Christians first at Antioch." This would have been around A.D. 42, about a decade after Christ died on the cross and was resurrected from the dead.

Up until this time the followers of Jesus had been known among themselves by such terms as "brethren" (Acts 15:1, 23 NASB), "disciples" (Acts 9:26), "believers" (Acts 5:14 NASB), and "saints" (Romans 8:27). But now, in Antioch, they are called Christians.

What does the term mean? The answer is found in the "ian" ending—for among the ancients this ending meant "belonging to the party of." "Herodians" belonged to the party of Herod. "Caesarians" belonged to the party of Caesar. "Christians" belonged to Christ. And Christians were loyal to Christ, just as the Herodians were loyal to Herod and Caesarians were loyal to Caesar.

The significance of the name *Christian* was that these followers of Jesus were recognized as a distinct group. They were seen as distinct from Judaism and as distinct from all other religions of the ancient world. We might loosely translate the term Christian, "those who belong to Christ," "Christ-ones," or perhaps "Christ-people." *They are ones who follow the Christ.*

Why are Christians called "saints"?

Many people have wrongly concluded that only certain unusually holy and pure people become "saints." But Scripture indicates that all who believe in Jesus Christ are properly categorized as saints. The word literally means, "one who is set apart" (see Romans 1:7; Philippians 1:1).

A saint is not one who has, in his or her own strength and power, attained a certain level of purity. Rather, a saint is one who has believed in Jesus Christ and has accordingly been washed from the stain of sin. Because of Jesus we are clean. We are saints not because of what we can do but because of what Jesus has already done for us. He died on the cross and thereby did away with the sin problem for all who believe in Him.

Do the Scriptures teach that the gospel can be preached to the dead, thereby implying that there is a second chance to become saved following death?

No. But there are two verses that are often misinterpreted in regard to this issue—1 Peter 3:18,19 and 1 Peter 4:6. Let's take a brief look at each.

1 Peter 3:18,19. This passage says, "For Christ ... was put to death in the body but made alive by the Spirit, through whom also he went and preached to the spirits in prison."

Difficult passages like this must be interpreted according to the clearer passages of Scripture. The clear passages of Scripture tell us that immediately following the moment of death comes the judgment (Hebrews 9:27). There is no possibility of redemption beyond death's door (Luke 16:19-31). *Now* is the day of salvation (2 Corinthians 6:2). Hence, whatever 1 Peter 3:18,19 means, it doesn't refer to the possibility of responding to the gospel following the moment of death.

Many evangelical scholars believe that the "spirits in prison" referred to in this passage are fallen angels who grievously sinned against God. The idea here is that these spirits are the fallen angels of Genesis 6:1-6 who were disobedient to God during the days of Noah. This same group of evil angels is mentioned in 2 Peter 2:4,5 and Jude 6. According to this interpretation, these evil angels disobeyed God, left their first estate (they forsook their proper angelic realm), and somehow entered into sexual relations with human women.

The Greek word for "preach" (*kerusso*) in 1 Peter 3:19 is not the word used for preaching the gospel but rather points to a proclamation—as in a proclamation of victory. This passage may imply that the powers of darkness thought they had destroyed Jesus at the crucifixion, but that in raising Him from the dead God turned the tables on them—and Jesus Himself proclaimed their doom. If this is the correct interpretation, it is clear that the verse has nothing whatsoever to do with human spirits hearing and responding to the gospel in the afterlife.

Another possible interpretation is that between His death and resurrection, Jesus went to the place of the dead and "preached" to the wicked contemporaries of Noah. The "preaching," however, was not a gospel message but was rather a proclamation of victory.

Still others believe this passage has reference to Christ preaching *through the person of Noah* to those who, because they rejected his message, are *now* spirits in prison. One must keep in mind that 1 Peter 1:11 tells us that the "Spirit of Christ" spoke through the Old Testament prophets. And Noah is later described as a "preacher of righteousness" (2 Peter 2:5). Hence, it may be that the Spirit of Christ preached through Noah to the ungodly humans who, at the time of Peter's writing, were "spirits in prison" awaiting final judgment.[3]

Regardless of which of the above interpretations is correct, evangelical scholars unanimously agree that this passage does not teach that people can hear and respond to the gospel in the next life. Passages like 2 Corinthians 6:2 and Hebrews 9:27 make this emphatically clear.

1 Peter 4:6. This verse says, "For this is the reason the gospel was preached even to those who are now dead, so that they might be judged according to men in regard to the body, but live according to God in regard to the spirit."

This is another difficult verse that must be interpreted in light of what clear verses of Scripture teach. Though evangelical scholars have offered several interpretations of this verse, perhaps the best view is that the verse refers to those who are *now* dead but who heard the gospel *while they were yet alive*. This especially makes sense in view of the tenses used: the gospel was preached (in the past) to those who are dead (presently). "The preaching was a past event.... It is necessary to make it clear that the preaching was done not after these people had died, but while they were still alive."[4]

In interpreting these words from 1 Peter, it is good to keep in mind the words of Jesus in Luke 16:19-31. Once the rich man had died and ended up in a place of great suffering, he had no further opportunity for redemption. Nothing could be done at that point to ease his situation at all (Luke 16:24). This clearly illustrates the urgency in the words found in 2 Corinthians 6:2, "*Now* is the day of salvation." There are no opportunities beyond death's door. One must choose *for* or *against* the Christ of the Bible in this life.[5]

20

~

Eternal Security

Is it true that faith in Christ alone saves a person?

Yes. Recall that in Acts 16:31 the jailer asked Paul and Silas how to be saved. They responded, "Believe in the Lord Jesus, and you will be saved." The jailer believed and immediately became saved.

Close to 200 times in the New Testament salvation is said to be by faith alone—with no works in sight. Consider the following:

- ✓ John 3:15 tells us that "everyone who believes in him may have eternal life."

- ✓ John 5:24 says, "I tell you the truth, whoever hears my word and believes him who sent me has eternal life and will not be condemned; he has crossed over from death to life."

- ✓ In John 11:25 Jesus says, "I am the resurrection and the life. He who believes in me will live, even though he dies."

- ✓ John 12:46 says, "I have come into the world as a light, so that no one who believes in me should stay in darkness."

- ✓ John 20:31 says, "But these are written that you may believe that Jesus is the Christ, the Son of God, and that by believing you may have life in his name."

If salvation were not by faith alone, then Jesus' message in the Gospel of John—manifest in the above quotations—would be deceptive, stating that there is one condition for salvation when there are allegedly two—faith *and* works.

I must emphasize that we are saved *by* faith but *for* works. Works are not the condition of our salvation, but a consequence of it. We are saved not by works, but by the kind of faith that produces works.

What does James 2:17,26 mean when it says that faith without works is dead?

Martin Luther said it best: James 2 is not teaching that a person is saved by works. Rather a person is "justified" (declared righteous before God) by faith alone, but *not by a faith that is alone.* In other words, genuine faith will always *result* in good works in the saved person's life.

James is writing to Jewish Christians ("to the twelve tribes"—James 1:1) who were in danger of giving nothing but lip service to Jesus. His intent, therefore, is to distinguish true faith from false faith. He shows that true faith results in works, which become visible evidences of faith's invisible presence. In other words, good works are the "vital signs" indicating that faith is alive.

Apparently some of these Jewish Christians had made a false claim of faith. "It is the spurious boast of faith that James condemned. Merely claiming to have faith is not enough. Genuine faith is evidenced by works."[1] Indeed, "Workless faith is worthless faith; it is unproductive, sterile, barren, dead! Great claims may be made about a corpse that is supposed to have come to life, but if it does not move, if there are no vital signs, no heartbeat, no perceptible pulse, it is still dead. The false claims are silenced by the evidence."[2]

The fact is, apart from the spirit, the body is dead; it's a lifeless corpse. By analogy, apart from the evidence of good works, faith is dead. It is lifeless and nonproductive. That is what James is teaching in this passage.

What about James 2:21? Does this verse teach that Abraham was justified before God by works and not by faith?

No. In this verse James is not talking about justification *before God* but rather justification *before man*. This is clear from the fact that James stressed that we should "show" (James 2:18) our faith. That is, our faith must be something that can be seen by others in "works" (verses 18–20).

Note that James acknowledged that Abraham was justified before God by faith, not works, when he said, "Abraham believed God, and it was accounted to him for righteousness" (James 2:23 NKJV). When he said that Abraham was "justified by works," he was speaking of what Abraham did that could be seen by men, namely, he offered his son Isaac on the altar (verses 21, 22).

Contrary to James, who talked about justification *before men*, the apostle Paul spoke about justification *before God*. Paul declared, "But to him who does not work but believes on Him who justifies the ungodly, his faith is accounted for righteousness" (Romans 4:5 NKJV). It is "not by works of righteousness which we have done, but according to His mercy He saved us" (Titus 3:5 NKJV). For "by grace you have been saved through faith, and that not of yourselves; it is the gift of God, not of works, lest anyone should boast" (Ephesians 2:8, 9 NKJV).

How do we relate Paul's teaching to that of James? While Paul is stressing the *root* of justification (faith in God), James is stressing the *fruit* of justification (works before men). But each man acknowledges both doctrines. Paul, for example, taught that we are saved by grace through faith, but then he quickly adds, "We are His workmanship, created in Christ

Jesus for good works, which God prepared beforehand that we should walk in them" (verse 10 NKJV).

What is the "Lordship salvation" issue all about?

The issue involved in Lordship salvation is the nature of salvation and saving faith: What *is* saving faith? What does it mean to receive Jesus as Lord and Savior?

Lordship salvation advocates say that in order to be saved, one must not only believe and acknowledge that Christ is Savior, but also be willing to submit to His Lordship. In other words, there must be—at the moment one trusts in Christ for salvation—a willingness to commit one's life absolutely to the Lord, even though the actual practice of a committed life may not follow immediately or completely.

Non-Lordship proponents argue that such a presalvation commitment to Christ's Lordship compromises salvation by grace ("unmerited favor"). They argue that accepting Jesus as Lord does not refer to a subjective commitment to Christ's Lordship in one's life, but rather involves a repentance (a changing of one's mind) about one's ideas of who Christ is (Messiah-God) and exercising faith in Him. Repentance from sin is what *follows* in the Christian's daily walk with the Lord. This is my position.

Martin Luther gives us a good insight on this issue. He said that "faith alone justifies, but not the faith that is alone." He said that "works are not taken into consideration when the question respects justification. But true faith will no more fail to produce them than the sun can cease to give light."

What does the Bible say about our eternal security in salvation?

I believe that once a person exercises saving faith in Jesus Christ, he or she is forever in the family of God. God never kicks anyone out of His forever family. A number of Scripture passages support this view. For example, in 1 Corinthians 12:13 we are told that at the moment of salvation the Holy Spirit places us in the body of Christ. Once we're infused into the body of Christ, we're never excised from the body. In fact, Ephesians 1:13 and 4:30 indicate that at the moment of believing in Jesus Christ for salvation, we are permanently "sealed" by the Holy Spirit. At that point, we are God's everlasting property. That seal guarantees that we'll make it to heaven.

Moreover, we read in John 10:28-30 that it is the Father's purpose to keep us secure despite anything that might happen once we've trusted in Christ. Nothing can snatch us out of His hands. God's plans cannot be thwarted (Isaiah 14:24). Further, Romans 8:29-39 portrays an unbroken chain that spans from the predestination of believers to their glorification in heaven. This indicates the certainty of all believers reaching heaven.

Another fact we need to keep in mind is that Christ regularly prays for each Christian (Hebrews 7:25). With Jesus interceding for us, we're secure. (His prayers are always answered!)

Of course, the fact that a believer is secure in his salvation doesn't mean he is free to sin. If the Christian sins and remains in that sin, Scripture says that God will discipline him or her just as a father disciplines his children (see Hebrews 12:7-11).

Does Hebrews 6:4-6 teach that Christians can lose their salvation?

No. In Hebrews 6:4-6 we read:

> It is impossible for those who have once been enlightened, who have tasted the heavenly gift, who have shared in the Holy Spirit, who have tasted the goodness of the word of God and the powers of the

> coming age, if they fall away, to be brought back to repentance, because to their loss they are crucifying the Son of God all over again and subjecting him to public disgrace.

Those who subscribe to Arminian theology believe this passage indicates that a Christian can indeed lose his or her salvation. If this interpretation is correct, one would also have to conclude that it is impossible to be saved a second time.

Others interpret this passage as referring to people who have a "said faith" as opposed to a "real faith" in Jesus Christ. They are professed believers, but not genuine believers. It is suggested that the "falling away" is from the knowledge of the truth, not from an actual personal possession of it.

Still others interpret this passage as a warning to Christians to move on to spiritual maturity. I subscribe to this third view. Note that the context of Hebrews 6:4-6 is set for us in verses 1-3 (emphasis added):

> Therefore let us leave the elementary teachings about Christ and *go on to maturity*, not laying again the foundation of repentance from acts that lead to death, and of faith in God, instruction about baptisms, the laying on of hands, the resurrection of the dead, and eternal judgment. And God permitting, we will do so.

The context clearly deals with going on to maturity. This was an important issue for the Jews of the first century who had converted to Christ and become Christians. The Jews living in and around the Palestine area were under the authority of the High Priest. The High Priest had sufficient influence to cause a Jew to lose his job, have his kids kicked out of synagogue school, and much more. Many scholars believe that when some Jews became Christians in the first century, the High Priest put some heavy-duty pressure (*persecution*) on them.

This caused some of the Jewish Christians to become a bit gun-shy in their Christian lives. They weren't as open about their Christian faith. Perhaps they thought that if they kept quiet about their faith and withdrew from external involvement in Christian affairs (like church attendance), the High Priest would lighten up on them.

The author of the book of Hebrews saw this as a retreat from spiritual maturity in Christ. He thus encouraged them to move on to maturity in Christ.

Though it is impossible for a Christian to actually "fall away" from salvation, the author of the book uses this phrase to put his warning about moving onto spiritual maturity in strong terms. Theologian Charles Ryrie explains it this way: "It is similar to saying something like this to a class of students: 'It is impossible for a student, once enrolled in this course, if he turns the clock back [which cannot be done], to start the course over. Therefore, let all students go on to deeper knowledge.'"[3]

The motivation of Hebrews 6:4-6, then, is not "Shape up or you lose your salvation." Rather it is, "In view of the fact that you're already in the school of Christ and have made a commitment, let's move on to maturity." This was a message those first-century Jewish converts really needed to hear.

Can a Christian have his or her name blotted out of the Book of Life (Revelation 3:5)?

No, I don't think so. Revelation 3:5 says, "He who overcomes will, like them, be dressed in white. I will never blot out his name from the book of life, but will acknowledge his name before my Father and his angels."

To begin, notice that the same John who wrote the Book of Revelation wrote elsewhere about the absolute security of each individual believer (see John 5:24; 6:35-37, 39; 10:28, 29).

Hence, however Revelation 3:5 is interpreted, it shouldn't be interpreted to mean a believer can lose his or her salvation.

Theologian John F. Walvoord points out that "while this passage may imply that a name could be erased from the book of life, actually it only gives a positive affirmation that their names *will not* be erased."[4] This may thus be considered not a threat but indeed an assurance that saved peoples' names will always *be* in the Book of Life. This seems to be the gist of what other verses communicate about the Book of Life. For example, in Luke 10:20 Jesus said to the disciples, "Do not rejoice that the spirits submit to you, but rejoice that your names are written in heaven" (Luke 10:20). In Hebrews 12:23 we read of "the church of the firstborn, whose names are written in heaven."

~

God's Part, Man's Part

Is God's election of people to salvation based on His foreknowledge or on His divine sovereignty?

This is a complicated and much-debated issue. Let's take a brief look at both views.

View #1. The first view is that God's election is based on His foreknowledge. This view says that God used His foreknowledge to look down the corridors of time to see who would respond favorably to His gospel message, and on that basis He elected certain persons to salvation. The argumentation for this view is as follows:

✓ Scripture teaches that God's salvation has appeared to all men, not merely the elect (Titus 2:11).

✓ The Bible teaches that Christ died for all (1 Timothy 2:6; 4:10; Hebrews 2:9; 1 John 2:2).

✓ There are numerous exhortations in Scripture to turn to God (Isaiah 31:6; Joel 2:13f.; Acts 3:19), to repent (Matthew 3:2; Luke 13:3,5; Acts 2:38; 17:30), and to believe (John 6:29; Acts 16:31; 1 John 3:23).

✓ Scripture seems to indicate that election is based on God's foreknowledge of who would respond positively to such exhortations (Romans 8:28-30; 1 Peter 1:1f.).

There are some substantial arguments against this view, however. To begin, there are statements indicating that the Father *gave* certain ones to Christ (John 6:37; 17:2, 6, 9). Christ said, "No one can come to Me, unless the Father who sent Me draws him" (John 6:44 NASB). Moreover, in Romans 9:10-16 God is said to have chosen Jacob rather than Esau, even before they were born and before they had done either good or bad.

We read in Acts 13:48 that "as many as had been appointed to eternal life believed" (NASB). Ephesians 1:5-8 and 2:8-10 represent salvation as originating in the choice of God and as being all of grace (see also Acts 5:31; 11:18; Romans 12:3; 2 Timothy 2:25). Finally, many claim that if election is not unconditional and absolute, then God's whole plan is uncertain and liable to miscarriage.

View #2. The second view (my view) is that God's election is based on His sovereign choice. The arguments for this view include the following:

✓ Biblical statements support election by choice (Acts 13:48).

✓ The whole process of salvation is a gift of God (Romans 12:3; Ephesians 2:8-10).

✓ Certain verses speak of human beings having been given to Christ (John 6:37; 17:2), and of the Father drawing men to Christ (John 6:44).

✓ There are examples in Scripture of the sovereign calling of God upon individuals, like Paul (Galatians 1:15) and Jeremiah (Jeremiah 1:5), even before they were born.

✓ Election is necessary in light of man's total depravity (Job 14:1; Jeremiah 13:11; Romans 3:10-20).

✓ Election is necessary because of man's inability to initiate a relationship with God on his own (due to his sin nature). (Ephesians 2:1).

✓ Election is compatible with God's sovereignty (Jeremiah 10:23; Proverbs 19:21).

✓ Election is portrayed as being from all eternity (2 Timothy 1:9).

✓ It is on the basis of election by choice that the appeal to a godly life is made (Colossians 3:12; 2 Thessalonians 2:13; 1 Peter 2:9).

Two primary arguments have been suggested against this view:

(1) First, it is argued that if election is limited by God, then surely the atonement must be limited as well. However, this conclusion is clearly refuted by John 1:29, 3:16, 1 Timothy 2:6, Hebrews 2:9, and 1 John 2:2.

(2) It is argued that election by choice makes God responsible for "reprobation." However, those not included in election suffer only their due reward. God does not "elect" a person to hell. Those not elected to salvation are left to their own self-destructive ways.

Whichever view one concludes is the correct one, the following facts should be kept in mind:

✓ God's election is loving (Ephesians 1:4-11).

✓ Election glorifies God (Ephesians 1:12-14).

✓ The product of election is a people who do good works (Ephesians 2:10; cf. Colossians 3:12).

I've heard people describe Reformed theology with the acronym TULIP. What does this mean?

This acronym represents the five pillars of Reformed theology:

Total depravity. This doctrine does not mean that human beings are completely devoid of any good impulses, but rather says that every human being is engulfed in sin to such a severe degree that there is nothing he or she can do to earn merit of any kind before God.

Unconditional election. This doctrine says that God's choice of certain persons to salvation is not dependent upon any foreseen virtue or faith on their part but rather is based on His sovereignty.

Limited atonement. This doctrine says that Christ's atoning death was only for the elect.

Irresistible grace. This doctrine involves the idea that those whom God has chosen for eternal life will, as a result of God's grace, come to faith and thus to salvation. This view is also called efficacious grace.

Perseverance of the saints. This is the teaching that those who are genuine believers will endure in the faith to the end.

What do Arminians believe?

Arminianism is a theological movement that stemmed from the teachings of Dutch theologian Jacobus Arminius (1560–1609). We can summarize the beliefs of Arminianism under the following five pillars:

1. God elected people to salvation who He foreknew would of their own free will believe in Christ and persevere in the faith.

2. In His atonement at the cross, Jesus provided redemption for all humankind, making all humankind savable. But Christ's atonement becomes effective only for those who believe in Jesus.

3. Human beings cannot save themselves. The Holy Spirit must effect the new birth.

4. Prevenient grace from the Holy Spirit enables the believer to respond to the gospel and cooperate with God in salvation.

5. Believers have been empowered by God to live a victorious life, but they are capable of turning from grace and losing their salvation.

Arminians obviously believe quite differently from Calvinists. For example, Calvinists believe that God elected people according to His sovereign will and not based on His foreknowledge of how humans would respond to the gospel. Calvinists believe that Christ died only for the elect. Calvinists also believe that genuine believers will endure in the faith to the end.

What is the doctrine known as "limited atonement"?

Limited atonement (a doctrine I disagree with) is the view that Christ's atoning death was only for the elect. Another way to say this is that Christ made no atoning provision for those who are not of the elect. Following are some of the key verses the advocates of limited atonement cite in favor of their position. I've italicized the relevant portions of each verse:

✓ Matthew 1:21: "She will give birth to a son, and you are to give him the name Jesus, because he will save *his people* from their sins."

✓ Matthew 20:28: "The Son of Man did not come to be served, but to serve, and to give his life as a ransom *for many*."

✓ Matthew 26:28: "This is my blood of the covenant, which is poured out *for many* for the forgiveness of sins."

✓ John 10:15: "I lay down my life for *the sheep*."

✓ Acts 20:28: "Keep watch over yourselves and all the flock of which the Holy Spirit has made you overseers. Be shepherds of the *church of God*, which he bought with his own blood."

✓ Ephesians 5:25: "Husbands, love your wives, just as Christ loved *the church* and gave himself up for her."

✓ Hebrews 9:28: "So Christ was sacrificed once to take away the sins of *many people*; and he will appear a second time, not to bear sin, but to bring salvation *to those* who are waiting for him."

✓ John 15:13: "Greater love has no one than this, that he lay down his life for his *friends*."

Upon first reading, verses such as these seem to support the idea that Christ died on the cross not for all people but for a particular group of people—the "many," the "church of God," His "sheep," His "friends." Many Reformed theologians believe the doctrine of *un*limited atonement (the doctrine that Christ died for the sins of *all* people) is utterly disproven by such verses.

Proponents of limited atonement set forth a number of arguments which they believe conclusively proves the truth of the doctrine. Following are eight of the more notable arguments:

(1) The Bible says Christ died for a specific group of people. Those for whom He suffered and died are variously called His "sheep" (John 10:11,15), His "church" (Acts 20:28; Ephesians 5:25-27), His "people" (Matthew 1:21), and the "elect" (Romans 8:32-35 NASB).

(2) Since the elect were chosen before the foundation of the world (Ephesians 1), Christ could not honestly be said to have died *for all* human beings. It would have been a waste and a lack of foresight on the part of God to have Christ die for those whom He had not chosen to salvation.

(3) Some advocates of limited atonement say Christ is defeated if He died for all men and all men aren't saved.

(4) Some advocates of limited atonement say that if Christ died for all people, then God would be unfair in sending people to hell for their own sins. It is argued that no law or court allows payment to be exacted twice for the same crime, and God will not do that either. Christ paid for the sins of the elect; the lost pay for *their own* sins.

(5) Since Christ didn't pray for everyone in His High Priestly prayer in John 17, but prayed only for *His own*, Christ must not have died for everyone. It is argued that since the intercession is limited in extent, the atonement must be, too.

(6) Some advocates of limited atonement have charged that unlimited atonement tends toward universalism. Hence, unlimited atonement cannot be the correct view.

(7) In the Middle Ages such scholars as Prosper of Aquitaine, Thomas Bradwardine, and John Staupitz taught limited atonement. It is claimed that even though John Calvin did not explicitly teach the doctrine, it seems implicit in some of his writings. Calvin's successors then made limited atonement explicit and included it in Reformed confessions of faith such as the Canons of Dort and the Westminster Confession of Faith.

(8) Though terms such as "all," "world," and "whosoever" are used in Scripture in reference to those for whom Christ died (for example, John 3:16), these words are to be understood in terms of the elect. In other words, "all" refers to "all *of the elect*" or "all *classes of men*" (Jew and Gentile). Similarly, the word "world" is said to refer to the "world *of the elect*" or to people without distinction (Jews and Gentiles). The word "whosoever" is interpreted to mean "whosoever of the elect."

Based on arguments such as these, Reformed scholars believe that Christ died *only for the elect*. However, I believe the above logic is flawed (see below).

What are the scriptural arguments that prove the doctrine of unlimited atonement?

I believe the doctrine of unlimited atonement is the scriptural view, and there are numerous verses that support it. Following is a sampling (with relevant portions italicized):

In Luke 19:10 we read, "For the Son of Man came to seek and to save *what was lost*." The "lost" in this verse refers to the *collective whole* of lost humanity, not just to the lost elect. This is the most natural understanding of this verse.

In John 1:29 we read, "The next day John saw Jesus coming toward him and said, 'Look, the Lamb of God, who takes away the sin *of the world!*'" What is the "world" here? The world represents humanity in its fallen state, alienated from its Maker. Reformer John Calvin says of this verse, "When he says the sin *of the world*, he extends this favor indiscriminately to the whole human race."[1] Though Calvin is often cited in favor of limited atonement, here is a clear statement in which unlimited atonement is his view.

In John 3:16 we read, "For God so loved *the world* that he gave his one and only Son, that *whoever* believes in him shall not perish but have eternal life." It is critical to observe that John 3:16 cannot be divorced from the context that is set in verses 14 and 15, wherein Christ alludes to Numbers 21. In this passage Moses is seen setting up the brazen serpent in the camp of Israel, so that if "any man" looked to it, he experienced physical deliverance. In verse 15 Christ applies the story spiritually when He says that "everyone who" believes on the uplifted Son of Man shall experience spiritual deliverance.

In John 4:42 we read, "They said to the woman, 'We no longer believe just because of what you said; now we have heard for ourselves, and we know that this man really is the Savior *of the world*.'" It is quite certain that when the Samaritans called Jesus "the Savior of the world," they were not thinking of the world of the elect.

First Timothy 4:10 says, "We have put our hope in the living God, who is the Savior *of all men,* and especially of those who believe." There is a clear distinction in this verse between "all men" and "those who believe." Apparently the Savior has done something for *all* human beings, though it is less in degree than what He has done for those who believe.[2] In other words, Christ has made a provision of salvation for all men, though it only becomes effective for those who exercise faith in Christ.

Hebrews 2:9 says, "But we see Jesus, who was made a little lower than the angels, now crowned with glory and honor because he suffered death, so that by the grace of God he might taste death *for everyone.*" The Greek word *everyone* (*pantos*) is better translated "each." Why use the word *pantos* (each) rather than *panton* (all)? The singular brings out more emphatically the applicability of Christ's death to each individual human being. Christ tasted death for every single person.

Romans 5:6 says, "At just the right time, when we were still powerless, Christ died *for the ungodly.*" It doesn't make much sense to read this as saying that Christ died for the ungodly among the elect. Rather the verse, read plainly, indicates that Christ died for *all* the ungodly of the earth.

Romans 5:18 tells us, "Consequently, just as the result of one trespass was condemnation *for all men,* so also the result of one act of righteousness was justification that brings life *for all men*" (italics added). Commenting on this verse, Calvin said, "Though Christ suffered for the sins of the whole world, and is offered through God's benignity indiscriminately to all, yet all do not receive Him."[3] This sounds very much like Calvin was teaching unlimited atonement.

First John 2:2 says, "He is the atoning sacrifice for our sins, and not only for ours but also for the sins *of the whole world.*" A natural reading of this verse, without imposing

theological presuppositions on it, supports unlimited atonement. In fact, a plain reading of this verse would seem to
deal a knockout punch to the limited atonement position. It
simply would not make sense to interpret this verse as
saying, "He is the atoning sacrifice for our [*the elect*] sins,
and not only for ours [*the elect*] but also for the sins of the
whole world [*of the elect*]."

Isaiah 53:6 says, "*We all*, like sheep, have gone astray,
each of us has turned to his own way; and the LORD has laid
on him the iniquity *of us all*" (italics added). This verse
doesn't make sense unless it is read to say that the same
"all" that went astray is the "all" for whom the Lord died.

In 2 Peter 2:1, we are told that Christ even paid the price
of redemption for false teachers who deny Him: "But there
were also false prophets among the people, just as there will
be false teachers among you. They will secretly introduce
destructive heresies, even denying the sovereign Lord who
bought them—bringing swift destruction on themselves."
This passage seems to point out quite clearly that people for
whom Christ died may be lost; there is a distinction
between those for whom Christ died and those who are
finally saved.

John 3:17 says, "For God did not send his Son into *the
world* to condemn *the world*, but to save *the world* through
him" (italics added). Commenting on this verse, Calvin said
that "God is unwilling that we should be overwhelmed
with everlasting destruction, because He has appointed His
Son to be the salvation *of the world*."[4] Calvin also stated,
"The word *world* is again repeated, that no man may think
himself wholly excluded, if he only keeps the road of
faith."[5] Clearly God has made the *provision* of salvation
available to all human beings.

In keeping with the above verses, there are also many
verses which indicate that the gospel is to be universally
proclaimed to *all* human beings. Such a universal procla-

mation would make sense only if the doctrine of unlimited atonement were true. Consider the following:

✓ Matthew 24:14 says, "And this gospel of the kingdom will be preached *in the whole world* as a testimony *to all nations*, and then the end will come" (italics added).

✓ Matthew 28:19 says, "Therefore go and make disciples *of all nations*, baptizing them in the name of the Father and of the Son and of the Holy Spirit" (italics added).

✓ In Acts 1:8 Jesus said, "But you will receive power when the Holy Spirit comes on you; and you will be my witnesses in Jerusalem, and in all Judea and Samaria, and *to the ends of the earth*" (italics added).

In view of such passages, it is legitimate to ask, if Christ died only for the elect, how can an offer of salvation be made to all persons without some sort of insincerity, artificiality, or dishonesty being involved in the process? Is it not improper to offer salvation to everyone if in fact Christ did not die to save everyone? The fact is, those who hold to limited atonement cannot say to any sinner with true conviction, "Christ died *for you.*"

How, then, do we put the "limited" and "unlimited" verses together so that, taken as a whole, all the verses are interpreted in a harmonious way without contradicting each other? I believe that seemingly restrictive references can be logically fit into an unlimited scenario much more easily than universal references can be made to fit into a limited atonement scenario.

The two sets of passages—one seemingly in support of limited atonement, the other in support of unlimited atonement—are not irreconcilable. While it is true that the benefits of Christ's death are referred to as belonging to God's "sheep," His "people," and the like, it would have to be shown that Christ died *only* for them in order for limited atonement to be true. No one denies that Christ died for God's "sheep" and His "people." It is only denied that Christ died *exclusively* for them.[6] Certainly if Christ died for the whole of humanity, there is no logical problem in saying that He died for a specific *part* of the whole.[7]

～

The Role of Baptism

Is the correct mode of baptism immersion or sprinkling?

Christians are divided on this issue. Those who argue for sprinkling point out that a secondary meaning of the Greek word *baptizo* is "to bring under the influence of." This fits sprinkling better than immersion. Moreover, it is argued, baptism by sprinkling better pictures the coming of the Holy Spirit upon a person.

It is also suggested that immersion would have been impossible in some of the baptisms portrayed in Scripture. It is believed that in Acts 2:41, for example, it would have been impossible to immerse all 3,000 people who were baptized. The same is said to be true in regard to Acts 8:38, 10:47, and 16:33.

Those who hold to the immersion view (like I do) respond to the above by pointing out that the primary meaning of the Greek word *baptizo* is "to immerse." And the prepositions normally used in conjunction with *baptizo* (such as "into" and "out of" the water) clearly picture immersion and not sprinkling. The Greek language has perfectly acceptable words for "sprinkling" and "pouring," but these words are *never* used in the context of baptism in the New Testament.

It is noteworthy that the ancient Jews practiced baptism by immersion. Hence, it is likely that the Jewish converts to

Christianity (including the disciples, who came out of Judaism) would have followed this precedent.

Certainly baptism by immersion best pictures the significance of death to the old life and resurrection to the new life in Christ (Romans 6:1-4). And, despite what sprinkling advocates say, in *every instance* of water baptism recorded in the New Testament, immersion was practiced. Arguments that there was not enough water to accomplish immersion are weak and unconvincing. Archeologists have uncovered ancient pools all over the Jerusalem area.

I should point out that though immersion is the biblical norm of baptism, it is not an inflexible norm. God accepts the believer on the basis of his or her faith in Christ and the desire to obey Him, not on the basis of how much water covers the body at the moment of baptism.

Does Acts 2:38 teach that a person must be baptized in order to be saved?

No. Admittedly, this is not an easy verse to interpret. But a basic principle of Bible interpretation is that difficult passages are to be interpreted in light of the easy, clear verses. One should never build a theology on difficult passages.

Now, the great majority of passages dealing with salvation in the New Testament affirm that salvation is by faith alone. A good example is John 3:16-17: "For God so loved the world that he gave his one and only Son, that whoever believes in him shall not perish but have eternal life. For God did not send his Son into the world to condemn the world, but to save the world through him." In view of such clear passages, how is Acts 2:38 to be interpreted?

A single word in the verse gives us the answer. The verse reads, "Peter replied, 'Repent and be baptized, every one of you, in the name of Jesus Christ *for* the forgiveness of your sins. And you will receive the gift of the Holy Spirit'" (emphasis added).

Students of the Greek language have often pointed out that the Greek word "for" (*eis*) is a preposition that can indicate *causality* ("in order to attain") or a *result* ("because of"). An example of using "for" in a *resultant* sense is the sentence, "I'm taking an aspirin *for* my headache." Obviously this means I'm taking an aspirin *as a result of* my headache. I'm not taking an aspirin *in order to attain* a headache.

An example of using "for" in a *causal* sense is the sentence, "I'm going to the office *for* my paycheck." Obviously this means I'm going to the office *in order to attain* my paycheck.

Now, in Acts 2:38 the word "for" is used in a resultant sense. The verse might be paraphrased, "Repent, and be baptized every one of you in the name of Jesus Christ *because of* (or *as a result of*) the remission of sins." The verse is not saying, "Repent, and be baptized every one of you in the name of Jesus Christ *in order to attain* the remission of sins."

Hence, this verse, properly interpreted, indicates that water baptism *follows* the salvation experience.

Does Mark 16:16 teach that a person must be baptized in order to be saved?

This is another difficult passage. But, as noted above, a basic principle of Bible interpretation is that difficult passages are to be interpreted in light of the easy, clear verses.

Now, notice the latter part of the verse: "Whoever believes and is baptized will be saved, but *whoever does not believe will be condemned*" (Mark 16:16). It is *unbelief* that brings damnation, not a lack of being baptized. When one rejects the gospel, refusing to believe it, that person is damned.

In regard to the question of whether baptism is necessary for salvation, consider the words of the apostle Paul: "For Christ did not send me to baptize, but to preach the gospel—not with words of human wisdom, lest the cross of Christ be emptied of its power" (1 Corinthians 1:17). Paul here draws a clear distinction between baptism and the gospel. And since it is the gospel that saves (1 Corinthians 15:1, 2), baptism is clearly not necessary to attain salvation.

That's not to say that baptism is unimportant. I believe that baptism should be the first act of obedience to God following a person's conversion to Christ. But even though we should obey God and get baptized, we mustn't forget that our faith in Christ, not baptism, is what saves us (Acts 16:31; John 3:16). Baptism is basically a public profession of faith. It says to the whole world, "I'm a believer in Christ and have identified my life with Him."

Does John 3:1-5 teach that a person must be baptized in order to be saved?

Some have concluded that the reference to being "born of water" (John 3:5) means one must be baptized in order to be saved. But this is not what Jesus was intending to teach.

Consulting the context of John 3 clears up Jesus' intended meaning. Let us begin by emphasizing that being "born again" (literally, "born from above") simply refers to the act of God by which He gives eternal life to the one who believes in Christ (John 3:3; Titus 3:5). Being "born again" thus places one into God's eternal family (1 Peter 1:23) and gives the believer a new capacity and desire to please the Father (2 Corinthians 5:17).

Now, critical to a proper understanding of John 3:1-5 is verse 6: "That which is born of the flesh is flesh, and that which is born of the Spirit is spirit" (NASB). Flesh can only reproduce itself as flesh—and flesh cannot pass muster with God (cf. Romans 8:8). The law of reproduction is "after its kind" (see Genesis 1). So, likewise, the Spirit produces spirit.

In Nicodemus's case, we find a Pharisee who would have been trusting in his physical descent from Abraham for entrance into the Messiah's kingdom. The Jews believed that because they were physically related to Abraham, they were in a specially privileged position before God. Christ, however, denied such a possibility. Parents can transmit to their children only the nature which they themselves possess. Since each parent's nature, because of Adam's sin, is sinful, each parent transmits a sinful nature to the child. And what is sinful cannot enter the kingdom of God (verse 5). The only way one can enter God's kingdom is to experience a spiritual rebirth, and this is precisely what Jesus is emphasizing to Nicodemus.

The problem is, Nicodemus did not initially comprehend Jesus' meaning. Nicodemus wrongly concluded that Jesus was speaking of something related to physical birth, but could not understand how a person could go through physical birth a second time (John 3:4). So, Jesus picked up on Nicodemus' line of thought and sought to move the argument from physical birth to spiritual birth.

Notice how Jesus went about His explanation to Nicodemus. He first speaks about being "born of water and the Spirit" in John 3:5 (NASB), and then explains what He means by this in verse 6. It would seem that "born of water" in verse 5 is parallel to "born of the flesh" in verse 6, just as "born of . . . the Spirit" in verse 5 is parallel to "born of the Spirit" in verse 6. Jesus' message, then, is that just as one has had a physical birth to live on earth, so one must also have a spiritual birth in order to enter the kingdom of God. One must be "born from above." The verse thus has nothing whatsoever to do with water baptism.

Are we to be baptized only "in the name of Jesus" (Acts 2:38), and not in the name of the Father, the Son, and the Holy Spirit?

No. This idea is based on a misinterpretation of Acts 2:38: "Repent and be baptized, every one of you, *in the name of Jesus Christ* for the forgiveness of your sins. And you will receive the gift of the Holy Spirit" (emphasis added).

As a backdrop, it is important to understand that the phrase *in the name of* in biblical times carried the meaning "by the authority of." Seen in this light, the phrase in Acts 2:38 cannot be interpreted to be some kind of a magic baptismal formula. The verse simply indicates that people are to be baptized *according to the authority of* Jesus Christ. The verse does not mean that the words "in the name of Jesus" must be liturgically pronounced over each person being baptized.

If we were consistent in using the strict "baptism only in the name of Jesus" logic, we'd have to pronounce the words "in the name of Jesus" over everything we did. For, indeed, Colossians 3:17 instructs us, "Whatever you do in word or deed, do all *in the name of the Lord Jesus,* giving thanks through Him to God the Father" (NASB, emphasis added). Clearly the words "in the name of Jesus" are not intended as a formula.

I believe that a baptism "in the name of Jesus" makes good sense in the context of Acts 2, because the Jews ("men of Judea" [verse 14], "men of Israel" [verse 22]), to whom Peter was preaching, had rejected Christ as the Messiah. It is logical that Peter would call on them to repent of their rejection of Jesus the Messiah and become publicly identified with Him via baptism.

Does the reference to "baptism for the dead" in 1 Corinthians 15:29 mean that we can be baptized on behalf of our dead loved ones?

No. Scripture is abundantly clear that this life (on earth) is the only time we have to choose either *for* or *against* Christ. Once we die, all opportunities vanish. Hebrews 9:27 tells us, "It is appointed unto men once to die, but after this the judgment" (KJV).

Notice that throughout 1 Corinthians, the apostle Paul refers to the Corinthian believers and himself using first-person pronouns ("we," "I"). But when he comes to 1 Corinthians 15:29—the verse dealing with baptism for the dead—Paul switches to the third person ("they"). A plain reading of the text would seem to indicate that Paul is referring to people outside the Christian camp in Corinth. And he seems to be disassociating himself from the group practicing baptism for the dead. Some believe Paul is referring to a cultic practice in Corinth, a city permeated with false beliefs (cf. 1 Corinthians 5, 12).

Whatever "baptism for the dead" is, Paul certainly did not encourage his hearers in any way to practice it. He merely used the case as an illustration. There is no mention of baptism for the dead in the Bible up until Paul—and no mention afterward. Christ does not mention it, nor do any of the other apostles.

The fact that there are no further opportunities for salvation following death is illustrated in Luke 16:19-31, which deals with the fate of the rich man and Lazarus. Once the rich man had died and ended up in a place of great suffering, he had no further opportunity for redemption. Nothing could be done at that point to ease his situation at all (verse 24). No "baptism for the dead" would have had any effect on his—or anyone else's—situation.

This emphasizes the importance of the words in 2 Corinthians 6:2, "Now is the day of salvation" (NASB). There are no opportunities beyond death's door. One must choose *for* or *against* the Christ of the Bible in this life.

Is infant baptism a biblical practice?

It is often argued that infant baptism is analogous to circumcision in the Old Testament, which was done to infant boys. Moreover, it is argued that household baptisms in the New Testament must have included infants (Acts 16:33).

I don't agree with this view. It seems to me that the biblical pattern is that a person always get baptized *following* his or her conversion experience (see Acts 16:29-34 for one of many examples). Moreover, household baptisms such as the one described in Acts 16:33 do not specify the presence of any infants. Having said that, it is certainly permissible and right for young children who have trusted in Christ to get baptized.

~

Our Role as Witnesses

Is there a sense in which all of us are missionaries?

Yes. A Christian leader once said, "Every heart with Christ is a missionary; every heart without Christ is a mission field." Christians can be missionaries wherever they are—whether it be abroad or in our home country. We can be missionaries in our schools, shopping centers, libraries, theaters, the workplace, and anywhere we happen to be.

Some people claim that Jesus is "one of many ways to God." As witnesses of Christ, how can we respond to this idea?

This line of thinking tries to argue that all the leaders of the world religions were pointing to the same God. This is not true, however. The reason we can say this is that the leaders of the different world religions had different (and *contradictory*) ideas about God. For example:

✓ Jesus taught that there is only one God and that He is triune in nature (Matthew 28:19).

✓ Muhammad taught that there is only one God, but that God cannot have a son.

✓ Krishna in the Bhagavad Gita (a Hindu scripture) indicated he believed in a combination of polytheism (there are many gods) and pantheism (all is God).

✓ Confucius believed in many gods.

✓ Zoroaster taught that there is both a good god and a bad god.

✓ Buddha taught that the concept of God was essentially irrelevant.[1]

Obviously, these religious leaders were not pointing to the same God. If one was right, all the others were wrong. If Jesus was right (and *He is*), then all the others are wrong.

Jesus claimed that what He said took precedence over all others. He said He is humanity's *only* means of coming into a relationship with God (John 14:6). This was confirmed by those who followed Him (Acts 4:12; 1 Timothy 2:5). And Jesus warned His followers about those who would try to set forth a different "Christ" (Matthew 24:4,5).

It's important to understand that Jesus is totally unique. He proved the veracity of all He said by resurrecting from the dead (Acts 17:31). None of the other leaders of the different world religions did that. Jesus' resurrection proved that He was who He claimed to be—the divine Messiah (Romans 1:4).

How can we go about witnessing to Jews?

I like to witness to Jews using the method suggested by Stuart Dauermann.[2] As one reads through the Bible, we find progressively detailed prophecies about the identity of the Messiah. Obviously, as the prophecies become increasingly detailed, the field of qualified "candidates" becomes increasingly narrow.

In showing a Jewish person that Jesus is the Messiah, one effective approach is to begin with broad prophecies and then narrow the field to include increasingly specific and detailed prophecies. You might use circles to graphically illustrate your points as you share these prophecies.

As suggested by Dauermann, seven increasingly detailed "circles of certainty" include:

1. The Messiah's humanity (Genesis 3:15).

2. The Messiah's Jewishness (Genesis 12:1-3; 28:10-15).

3. The Messiah's tribe (Genesis 49:10).

4. The Messiah's family (2 Samuel 7:16; Jeremiah 23:5,6).

5. The Messiah's birthplace (Micah 5:2).

6. The Messiah's life, rejection, and death (Isaiah 52:13; 53).

7. The chronology of Messiah's appearing (Daniel 9:24-26).

Let us look at these in a little more detail.

Circle 1: The Messiah's humanity. Scripture says that the Messiah had to become a human being. This circle is obviously a very large circle. The Messiah's humanity is predicted in Genesis 3:15 and fulfilled in Galatians 4:4,5. (You'll want to open your Bible and read these verses aloud while witnessing.)

Circle 2: The Messiah's Jewishness. Scripture says the Messiah had to be Jewish—that is, He had to be a descendant of Abraham, Isaac, and Jacob. This narrows the circle considerably. Of all human beings who have ever lived, only *Jewish* human beings would qualify. Read aloud from Genesis 12:1-3, where God makes a covenant with Abraham (the "father" of the Jews). You might also read aloud from Genesis 28:10-15, which shows that the promised seed was to come through the line of Abraham, Isaac, and Jacob.

Circle 3: The Messiah's tribal identity. The circle gets even narrower when it is demonstrated that the Messiah had to come from the tribe of Judah. This is demonstrated in Genesis 49:10. Here Jacob is on his deathbed. Before he dies, he affirms that the scepter (of the ruling Messiah) would be from the tribe of Judah.

Circle 4: The Messiah's family. Scripture tells us that the Messiah had to be from David's family. This narrows the circle still further. The Messiah's descent from David's family is affirmed in 2 Samuel 7:16 and reaffirmed in Jeremiah 23:5, 6.

Circle 5: The Messiah's birthplace. Scripture clearly prophesies that the Messiah was to be born in Bethlehem. This narrows the circle of possible candidates for the Messiah tremendously. Read aloud from Micah 5:2.

Circle 6: The Messiah's manner of life, rejection, and death. Point the Jewish person to Isaiah 53:1-9. Note from these verses that: (1) The Messiah was to be despised and rejected by His fellow Jews. (2) He would be put to death following a judicial proceeding. (3) He would be guiltless. Obviously these facts about the Messiah narrow the circle still further.

Circle 7: The Messiah's chronology. Point the Jewish person to Daniel 9:24-26. Regarding this passage, note the following facts: (1) The city of Jerusalem would be rebuilt, as would the Temple. (2) The Messiah would come. (3) The Messiah would then be "cut off" (die), but not for Himself. (4) The city and the Temple would then be destroyed. Note especially that the Messiah had to come and die *prior* to the destruction of the second temple, which occurred in A.D. 70.

Clearly, this narrows the circle of potential candidates incredibly. Is there anyone who has fulfilled all these conditions? Is there anyone who was a human being, a Jew, from the tribe of Judah and the family of David, born in Bethlehem, was despised and rejected by the Jewish people, died as a result of a judicial proceeding, was guiltless, and came and died before the destruction of the second temple in A.D. 70?

Yes! His name was Jesus!

How can we arouse the liberal Christian's interest in true Christianity?

Emphasize that Christianity ultimately is a relationship, not a religion. Christianity is not just a set of doctrines or creeds—a "dead orthodoxy." Rather it involves a personal relationship with the living Lord of the universe. This is the most important truth you will want to leave the liberal to ponder because this is the ingredient of true Christianity that the liberal "Christian" is most painfully lacking.

Liberal Christians admit that one of their goals has been to make Christianity relevant to the masses of humanity by stripping the Bible of miracles. (They think modern people cannot accept such unscientific concepts.) The paradox, however, is that for everyone to whom Christianity is "made relevant," there are thousands for whom it is made *ir*relevant. For, indeed, the liberal version of Christianity lacks an authentic and supernatural spirituality to help people and give them hope in the midst of life's problems. You can capitalize on this deficiency by talking about how a personal relationship with Jesus provides all the strength you need to deal with life's harsh realities.

In addressing the spiritual bankruptcy of liberalism, you can also use the liberal's recognition of God's love as a launching pad to emphasize that God loved humankind so much that He sent Jesus into the world to die on the cross to rescue humankind from hell. Be sure to note that Jesus— love incarnate—spoke of God's wrath and the reality of hell in a more forceful way than any of His disciples ever did (see, for example, Matthew 25:46). Hence, God's love is not incompatible with the reality of hell. Jesus affirmed that His mission of love was to provide atonement for human sin (for which there is plenty of empirical evidence in our world) by His sacrificial death on the cross (Mark 10:45; John 12:23-27).

Inform the liberal that if he or she really wants to experience the love of God, the place to begin is a living relationship with Jesus Christ. Then tell him or her about your relationship with Jesus. There's no better way to close a discussion with a liberal Christian than by giving your testimony, focusing on how your personal relationship with Jesus has changed your life forever.

How can we witness to Muslims?

Witnessing to a Muslim can be a challenging experience. Though there are whole books written on this topic, the place to begin would be the following:

1. Don't start off your conversation by slamming the prophet Muhammad. That will close the Muslim's mind. You don't want to do that. Your conversation will essentially be over if you start out by saying bad things about someone the Muslim has revered his or her entire life.

2. Appeal to the Quran (the Muslim's holy book), which speaks about Jesus in a very positive way. In fact, the Quran speaks of Jesus' virgin birth, His ability to heal people and raise them from the dead, His being the Messiah, His being an "all-righteous" one, and His eventual return to judge the earth (Quran 3:45,49; 4:158; 82:22). Use these statements from the Quran as a launching pad to talk about the biblical view of Jesus—that He is God in human flesh who came to redeem humankind by dying on the cross.

3. Since Muslims believe in a works-oriented salvation,[3] share with them what the Bible says about this. Romans 3:20 tells us, "Therefore no one will be declared righteous in his sight by observing the law; rather, through the law we become conscious of sin." Galatians 3:24 says, "So the law was put in charge to lead us to Christ that we might be jus-

tified by faith." Emphasize the grace of God: "For it is by grace you have been saved, through faith—and this not from yourselves, it is the gift of God—not by works, so that no one can boast" (Ephesians 2:8, 9).

4. Give him or her a copy of the New Testament and ask your friend to read the Gospel of John. Tell him or her that you'd be interested in meeting again to talk about what John's Gospel says about Jesus. Be sure to bathe all your subsequent witnessing encounters in prayer.

WITNESSING TO CHILDREN

Is there an "age of accountability"—that is, an age at which children become responsible before God?

Yes—though the "age" is not the same for every child. Obviously, some children mature faster than others. A verse that relates to this issue is James 4:17, where we read: "Anyone, then, who knows the good he ought to do and doesn't do it, sins." It would seem from this verse that when a child truly comes into a full awareness and moral understanding of "oughts" and "shoulds," he or she *at that point* has reached the age of accountability.

Is it possible to evangelize little children, or should we wait until they are older?

I think evangelist Billy Graham is right when he says that "conversion is so simple that the smallest child can be converted."[4] The great Charles Spurgeon likewise said, "Children need to be saved and *may* be saved."[5]

The apostle Paul, speaking to young Timothy, said, "*From infancy* you have known the holy Scriptures, which are able to make you wise for salvation through faith in Christ Jesus" (2 Timothy 3:15, emphasis added). Obviously, if Timothy had been taught the Scriptures from infancy, it's never too early to begin sharing gospel truths with our children.

Timothy's mother started his training in the Scriptures at a very early age and *continued* this training throughout his childhood. I say this because of the present tense verb in this verse (*"you have known* the holy Scriptures"). The present tense indicates continuous, ongoing action. Timothy's mother didn't just sporadically talk to him about the Scriptures; she *regularly* spoke to him about the Scriptures.

There are many people I can think of who have followed Timothy's lead in becoming Christians at a very young age. Corrie ten Boom became saved at age five, revivalist Jonathan Edwards at age seven, Billy Graham at age six, and his wife Ruth at age four.[6]

The condition of salvation is simple faith in Christ (Acts 16:31). It is a fact that the most trusting people in the world are children. Children have not acquired the obstructions to faith that often come with education. No wonder, then, that the Scriptures instruct us to become like children in order to enter into the kingdom of God (Matthew 18:3). As adults, we must develop the same kind of trust that little children naturally have.

How can we lead our children to Christ?

There is no set formula for evangelizing your child. But the following six pointers may be helpful to you.

1. *Read Bible stories to your child that illustrate being lost and getting saved.* Children love to hear stories. Two of my favorite Bible stories that illustrate this truth are the parable of the lost sheep (Luke 15:4-7) and the parable of the lost coin (Luke 15:8-10).

2. *Use stories to explain humanity's sin problem.* I like to illustrate the sin problem by talking about a bow and arrow. If you aim at a target with the bow and arrow, sometimes you "miss the target." This is one of the meanings of the

word "sin" in the New Testament. In our lives, we "miss the target" when we don't live as God wants us to.

3. Explain what Jesus accomplished at the cross. God loves us very much. But because each of us has "missed the target" in our lives, there is a wall or barrier between us and God. Our relationship with God has been broken. Jesus, by dying on the cross, took the punishment for our sins so we wouldn't have to. Jesus has thereby made it possible for us to have our relationship with God restored.

I like to talk about the "certificate of debt" mentioned in Colossians 2:14 (NASB) as a means of illustrating this. (You might call it a "bad behavior list" when speaking to your child.) Back in ancient days, whenever someone was found guilty of a crime, the offender was put in jail and a bad behavior list was posted on the jail door. This paper listed all the crimes the offender was found guilty of. Upon release, after serving the prescribed time in jail, the offender was given the bad behavior list, and on it was stamped, "Paid in full."

Christ took the bad behavior list of each of our lives and nailed it to the cross. He paid for all our sins at the cross. Jesus' sacrifice "paid in full" the price for our sins. Because of Him, the "bad behavior list" of our whole life has been tossed into the trash can. Our relationship with God is restored.

4. Explain that salvation is a free gift that is received through faith in Jesus. Read Ephesians 2:8, 9 to your child. This verse says salvation is a gift from God. A gift cannot be earned. It's free.

You might illustrate this truth with your child's birthday. Most kids on their birthday receive one or more gifts. But as soon as they receive the gift, they don't go get their allowance so they can pay for it. You can't pay for a gift. *It's free.* All you have to do is receive it.

Similarly, you can't buy the gift of salvation. God gives it to us free. All we have to do is receive it.

We "receive" this wonderful gift by placing our faith in Jesus. Placing faith in Jesus is not a complicated thing. It involves taking Jesus at His word. Faith involves believing that Jesus was who He said He was (God). Faith also involves believing that Jesus can do what He claimed He could do—He can forgive me and come into my life.

5. *Allow your child to ask plenty of questions.* Children are naturally inquisitive. If you let them know they're allowed to ask questions about what you're saying, you can count on them to do so. Don't rush your discussion when sharing the gospel. Allow as much time as it requires.

6. *Lead your child in a simple prayer.* The prayer might go something like this:

> Dear Jesus:
>
> I want to have a relationship with You and get to know You.
>
> I know I can't save myself, because I know I'm a sinner.
>
> Thank You for dying on the cross for me and taking the punishment for my sins.
>
> I believe You died for me, that You rose again, and I accept Your free gift of salvation.
>
> Thank You, Jesus.
>
> Amen.

Ask your child if he really believes what he just said to God in prayer. If he does, he is now saved. He is a Christian. Tell him that the angels in heaven are cheering right now because he became a Christian (Luke 15:10).

24

~

The Church: The Community
of the Redeemed

Does being "saved" make you a part of the universal church?

Yes. The universal church may be defined as the ever-enlarging body of born-again believers who comprise the universal Body of Christ over whom He reigns as Lord. Although the members of the church may differ in age, sex, race, wealth, social status, and ability, they are all joined together as one people (1 Corinthians 12:13). All of them share in one Spirit and worship one Lord (Ephesians 4:3-6). This body is comprised of only believers in Christ. The way you become a member in this universal body is to simply place faith in Jesus Christ. If you're a believer, you're in!

Is it okay for Christians not to attend a local church?

No. Hebrews 10:25 specially instructs us not to forsake "our own assembling together" (NASB). The Christian life as described in Scripture is to be lived within the context of the family of God and not in isolation (cf. Ephesians 3:14,15; Acts 2). Moreover, it is in attending church that we become equipped for the work of ministry (Ephesians 4:12-16). Further, it is within the context of attending church that we can receive the Lord's Supper (cf. 1 Corinthians 11:23-26). The Bible knows nothing of a "lone ranger Christian." Many logs burning together burn very brightly, but when a log falls off to the side, the embers quickly die out (see Ephesians 2:19; 1 Thessalonians 5:10,11; and 1 Peter 3:8).

Was the church existent in Old Testament times?

No. First of all, Matthew 16:18 cites Jesus as saying that "I *will* build" my church (future tense). This indicates that at the moment He spoke these words, the church was not yet existent. This is consistent with the Old Testament, for there is no reference there to the "church." The church is clearly portrayed as distinct from Israel in such passages as 1 Corinthians 10:32, Romans 9:6, and Hebrews 12:18-24.

Scripture indicates that the church was born on the day of Pentecost (see Acts 2; cf. 1:5; 11:15; 1 Corinthians 12:13). We are told in Ephesians 1:19,20 that the church is built on the foundation of Christ's resurrection, meaning that the church couldn't have existed in Old Testament times. The church is also called a "new man" in Ephesians 2:15.

Is Peter the "rock" upon which the church is built (Matthew 16:18)?

No, I don't think so. There are a number of factors in the Greek text that argue against this interpretation. First, whenever Peter is referred to in this passage (Matthew 16), it is in the second person ("you"), but "this rock" is in the third person (verse 18). Moreover, "Peter" (*petros*) is a masculine singular term and "rock" (*petra*) is a feminine singular term. Hence, they do not have the same referent. What is more, the same authority Jesus gave to Peter (Matthew 16:18) is later given to all the apostles (Matthew 18:18). So Peter is not unique.

Ephesians 2:20 affirms that the church is "built on the foundation of the apostles and prophets, with Christ Jesus himself as the cornerstone." Two things are clear from this:

first, that *all* the apostles, not just Peter, are the foundation of the church; second, that the only one who was given a place of uniqueness or prominence was Christ, the cornerstone. Indeed, Peter himself referred to Christ as "the capstone" of the church (1 Peter 2:7) and the rest of believers as "living stones" (verse 5) in the superstructure of the church.

What day do the Scriptures say we should worship on—Saturday or Sunday?

We should worship on Sunday, the "Lord's day." Although the moral principles expressed in the Ten Commandments are reaffirmed in the New Testament, the command to set Saturday apart as a day of rest and worship is the only commandment not repeated. There are very good reasons for this.

✓ New Testament believers are not under the Old Testament law (Romans 6:14; Galatians 3:24,25; Hebrews 7:12).

✓ Jesus resurrected and appeared to some of His followers on the first day of the week (Sunday) (Matthew 28:1).

✓ Jesus continued His appearances on succeeding Sundays (John 20:19,26).

✓ The descent of the Holy Spirit took place on a Sunday (Acts 2:1).

✓ The early church was thus given the pattern of Sunday worship, and this they continued to do regularly (Acts 20:7; 1 Corinthians 16:2).

✓ Sunday worship was further hallowed by our Lord who appeared to John in that last great vision on "the Lord's Day" (Revelation 1:10).

✓ Finally, in Colossians 2:16 we read, "Therefore do
not let anyone judge you by what you eat or drink,
or with regard to a religious festival, a New Moon
celebration or a Sabbath day." This verse indicates
that the distinctive holy days of the Old Testament
are no longer binding on New Testament believers.

It is for these reasons that Christians worship on
Sunday, rather than on the Jewish Sabbath.

What does the New Testament teach on tithing?

I do not believe that Christians today are under the Old
Testament 10-percent tithe system. In fact, we're not oblig-
ated to a percentage tithe at all. There's not a single verse in
the New Testament where God specifies that believers
should give 10 percent of their income to the church.

Before you conclude that I don't think we should finan-
cially support the church, let me rush to say that I believe
the New Testament concept is that of *grace* giving. We are to
freely give as we have been freely given to. And we are to
give as we are able (2 Corinthians 8:12). For some, this will
mean less than 10 percent. But for others whom God has
materially blessed, this will mean much more than 10 percent.

I believe that the starting point for having a right attitude toward giving to the church is that we must first give
ourselves to the Lord. The early church is our example:
"They gave themselves first to the Lord and then to us in
keeping with God's will" (2 Corinthians 8:5). Only when we
have given ourselves to the Lord will we have a proper perspective on money.

We also read in Romans 12:1, "Offer your bodies as
living sacrifices, holy and pleasing to God—this is your
spiritual act of worship." The first sacrifice we make to God
is not financial. Our first sacrifice is that of our own lives. As
we give ourselves unconditionally to the Lord for His ser-

vice, our attitude toward money will be what it should be. God is not interested in your money until He first has your heart.

Some believers who are unreservedly committed to God may only be able to afford giving 2 or 3 percent of their income. But others might be able to afford 25 percent or more. Whatever amount you tithe, just remember that God primarily looks upon your heart.

Is church discipline a biblical mandate?

I believe so. The motive for discipline should be love and the restoration of the offender. According to 1 Corinthians 5, discipline is always for the good of the offender (verses 1-5), the good of the church (verses 6-8), as well as the overall good brought about by the fact that this is a witness to the unsaved world (verses 9-13).

I believe the pastor should make the initial approach in disciplining the offender (cf. 1 Timothy 5:1,2; Matthew 18:15). If this fails, the pastor should make a second attempt accompanied by other spiritual men (Matthew 18:16). Finally, if this fails, the whole church must become involved (Matthew 18:17; cf. 1 Corinthians 5:1-5).

What are the different views of the Lord's Supper?

There are four primary views.

1. The Roman Catholic view is known as transubstantiation. This view says that the elements actually change into the body of Jesus Christ at the prayer of the priest. It is said to impart grace to the recipient. Jesus Christ is viewed as literally present. There is no change in the appearance of the elements, but the elements nevertheless change.

There are a number of problems with this view. First of all, note that Jesus Christ was present with the disciples when He said the elements (bread and wine) were His body and blood (Luke 22:17-19). Obviously He intended that His words be taken figuratively. Further, one must keep in mind the scriptural teaching that drinking blood is forbidden to anyone (Acts 15:29).

2. *The Lutheran view is known as consubstantiation.* This view says that Christ is present *in, with,* and *under* the bread and wine. There is a real presence of Christ but no change in the elements. The mere partaking of the elements after the prayer of consecration communicates Christ to the participant along with the elements.

3. *The Reformed view* is that Christ is spiritually present at the Lord's Supper. It is a means of grace. There is said to be a dynamic presence of Jesus in the elements made effective in the believer as he partakes. The partaking of His presence is not a physical eating and drinking, but an inner communion with His person.

4. *The memorial view* (my view) is that there is no change in the elements. The ordinance is not intended as a means of communicating grace to the participant. The bread and wine are symbols and reminders of Jesus in His death and resurrection (1 Corinthians 11:24, 25). It also reminds us of the basic facts of the gospel (11:26), our anticipation of the Second Coming (11:26), and our oneness as the body of Christ (10:17).

PART 7

~

THE SPIRIT WORLD: ANGELS AND DEMONS

Angels Among Us
The Devil and His Fallen Angels

25

~

Angels Among Us

Do humans become angels at the moment of death?

No! Scripture tells us that Christ created the angels—and He created them *as* angels (Colossians 1:16).

We see the distinction between humans and angels reflected in a number of biblical passages. For example, Psalm 8:5 indicates that man was made lower than the angels. In Hebrews 12:22,23 the "myriads of angels" are clearly distinguished from the "spirits of righteous men made perfect" (NASB). First Corinthians 6:3 tells us that there is a time coming when believers (in the afterlife) will judge the angels. As well, 1 Corinthians 13:1 draws a distinction between the languages of human beings and those of angels. Clearly, human beings and angels are portrayed as different classes of beings in the Bible.

Why are angels called "sons of God" in the Old Testament?

Angels are indeed sometimes referred to as "sons of God" (Job 1:6; 2:1; 38:7 NASB). The words "son of" can carry different meanings in different contexts. A look at any Greek lexicon makes this abundantly clear. Hence, the term can be used in one way in regard to angels and quite another way when used of the person of Jesus Christ.

Angels are sons of God in the sense of being created directly by the hand of God. The phrase *sons of God*, when used of angels, simply denotes spirit beings who were brought into existence by a direct creative act of God.

One must keep in mind that angels do not give birth to other baby angels (Matthew 22:30). Hence, we never read of "sons of angels." Since every single angel was directly created by the hand of God, it is appropriate that they be called "sons of God."

How does this relate to Christ being called the "Son of God"? This is an important question, for Christ is not in the same league as the angels. One will go far astray unless one sees a clear distinction between Christ as the *Son of God* and angels as *sons of God*. The Bible indicates that Christ is *eternally* the Son of God in the sense that He eternally has the nature of God. He is just as divine as the Father is. (I discuss all this in Part 4—the section on Christ.)

When were the angels created?

Theologians have suggested that the angels were created some time prior to the creation of the earth—and I think there is good evidence to support this view. Job 38:7, for example, makes reference to the "sons of God" singing at the time the earth was created. As noted above, many scholars believe these "sons of God" in Job 38 are angels. After all, the term "sons of God" is used elsewhere in Job in reference to angels (see Job 1:6; 2:1).

If Job 38:7 is to be taken as referring to angels, as there is every reason for it to be, then even before the creation of the material universe there was a vast world of spirit beings. These angelic spirit beings sang as a massive choir when God created the earth. What a moment that must have been!

Do all angels have wings?

Scripture indicates that many (if not all) angels have wings. The seraphim described in Isaiah 6:1-5 have wings. The cherubim Ezekiel saw in his vision have wings (Ezekiel 1:6). The angels the apostle John saw in his vision have wings (Revelation 4:8). But many other Bible verses about angels make no mention of wings (for example, Hebrews 13:2). What can we conclude from this?

Though it is possible that all of God's angels have wings, this is not a necessary conclusion. Though many angels are described as winged, we have no assurance that what is true of them is true of all angels. Since there is no explicit reference indicating that angels *as a whole* are winged, we must regard this as, at best, an inference.

How many angels are there?

There has been much speculation regarding just how many angels there are. The great logician Thomas Aquinas believed there are many times more angels than there are human beings.[1] Saint Albert the Great calculated that there were exactly 399,920,004 angels.[2] The Kabbalists of medieval Judaism determined there were precisely 301,655,722 angels.[3]

Clement of Alexandria in the second century A.D. suggested that there are as many angels as there are stars in the stellar heavens.[4] This line of thinking is based on the idea that angels are associated with the stars in Scripture (Job 38:7; Psalm 148:1-3). If Clement is correct, the number of angels would exceed the stars visible to the human eye—approximately six thousand during a year. Scientists say the total number of stars in the universe may run into the billions.[5]

Actually Scripture does not tell us precisely how many angels there are, nevertheless it indicates that their number is vast indeed. Scripture makes reference to "a great company of the heavenly host" (Luke 2:13), and the angels are spoken of as "tens of thousands and thousands of thousands" (Psalm 68:17). Their number is elsewhere described as "myriads of myriads" (Revelation 5:11 NASB). (The word *myriad* means "vast number," "innumerable.")

Daniel 7:10, speaking of God, says that "thousands upon thousands [of angels] attended him; ten thousand times ten thousand stood before him." The number "ten thousand times ten thousand" is 100,000,000 (one hundred million). This is a number almost too vast to fathom. Job 25:3 understandably asks, "Can his forces be numbered?"

Are there ranks among the angels?

Yes. Scripture indicates that the angels are organized by rank. In Colossians 1:16 we read, "For by [Christ] all things were created: things in heaven and on earth, visible and invisible, whether *thrones* or *powers* or *rulers* or *authorities*; all things were created by him and for him." Ephesians 1:20,21 speaks of Christ's authority as being "far above all *rule* and *authority*, *power* and *dominion*, and every title that can be given, not only in the present age but also in the one to come."

What do the terms *principalities*, *powers*, *thrones*, and *dominions* mean in these and other such verses? In the rabbinic (Jewish) thought of the first century, these terms were used to point to the hierarchical organization in the angelic realm. These appellations do not point to different kinds of angels, but simply to differences of rank among them.

Scripture also speaks of other angels who have varying levels of authority and dignity—including the archangel Michael, the cherubim, the seraphim, and Gabriel. The archangel is the highest ranking angel of all (*arche* means first). The cherubim and seraphim rank very high, though we are not told how they relate to the other angels mentioned above. Because Gabriel is the angel God always used in biblical times to deliver important revelations to man, we must assume that he is very high ranking as well.

Are the angels free to do as they please throughout the universe?

No. God's angels act only to carry out God's commands. There is not a single Bible verse that portrays a holy angel of God acting independently from God.

In Scripture angels are most often described in relation to God as *His* angels (for example, Psalm 91:11). It is of great significance that two angelic names mentioned in the Bible—Michael and Gabriel—emphasize this relationship with God with the *el* ending—which in the Hebrew means "God." (*Michael* means "Who is like God?" while *Gabriel* means "Mighty one of God.") Angels are *God's* angels and they exist to carry out *His* purposes. Psalm 103:20 makes reference to God's angels "who do his bidding, who obey his word."

Does God need angels in order to accomplish His work in the universe?

No! God does not *need* angels. In saying this, my intention is not to minimize the importance of what the Bible teaches about angels. I am personally very thankful that God created angels. My point is simply that God does not *need* them as if He could not accomplish His ends without their assistance. Reformer John Calvin says God does not use angels "out of necessity as if he could not do without them, for as often as he pleases, he disregards them and carries out his work through his will alone."[6] Though God does not need angels, He nevertheless created them—for His own pleasure and for His own glory—to carry out various functions in His universe and before His throne.

Does God always answer our prayers by Himself, or does He sometimes use angels?

God often does answer prayers apart from any involvement of the angels (cf. 1 Chronicles 5:20; 1 Peter 3:12). Nevertheless, it is sometimes God's sovereign choice to use angels in answering people's prayers.

One example of this is in Acts 12 where we find Peter wrongfully imprisoned. We read that while Peter was in prison, "the church was earnestly praying to God for him" (verse 5). What happened next? All of a sudden an angel appeared in Peter's prison cell and helped him escape (verses 7-10).

Related to this, it is important that we be aware that just as angels are sometimes used of God to answer prayers, so demons (fallen angels) sometimes seek to thwart the angels God uses in the process of answering a particular prayer. This happened when the prophet Daniel prayed.

According to Daniel 10:13 an angel that had been sent by God to answer Daniel's prayer was detained by a more powerful fallen angel (a demon). It was only when the archangel Michael showed up to render aid that the lesser angel was freed to carry out his task. One thing we learn from this is that we must be fervent in our prayers and not think that God is not listening simply because there seems to be a delay in God's answer.

Do Christians have a single guardian angel that stays with them throughout life?

There are two primary passages in the New Testament that relate to the idea of guardian angels. Matthew 18:10 says, "See that you do not look down on one of these little ones. For I tell you that their angels in heaven always see the face of my Father in heaven." Then, in Acts 12:15, we find a woman named Rhoda recognizing Peter's voice outside the door of the house, and the others inside—thinking Peter was still in jail—said: "You're out of your mind. . . . It must be his angel." A number of theologians have concluded from these two verses that every believer must have his or her own guardian angel.

Based upon Matthew 18:10 and Acts 12:15, it is certainly *possible* that each believer has a specific guardian angel assigned to him or her. However, many theologians argue that this is flimsy support for such an idea. (For example, the angels of the little ones in Matthew 18:10 are said to be *in heaven*, not specifically *with* the little ones.) These theologians argue that Scripture seems to indicate that *many multitudes of angels* are always ready and willing to render help and protection to each individual Christian whenever there is a need.

For example, we read in 2 Kings 6:17 that Elisha and his servant were surrounded by *many* glorious angels. Luke 16:22 indicates that several angels were involved in carrying Lazarus's soul to Abraham's bosom. Jesus could have called on 12 legions of angels to rescue Him if He had wanted (Matthew 26:53). Psalm 91:9-11 tells us, "If you make the Most High your dwelling—even the LORD, who is my refuge—then no harm will befall you, no disaster will come near your tent. For he will command *his angels* concerning you to guard you in all your ways."

How do we reconcile the doctrine of guardian angels with the fact that sometimes bad things happen to us?

If something bad should happen to you (such as a car wreck), you may be tempted to ask, "Where was my angel?" The fact is, God sometimes has a purpose in allowing us to go through tough times. It is well for us to keep in mind that God sometimes uses adversities in our lives to help develop our faith muscles and to make us strong, mature believers (James 1:2-4). And even though

God may not always remove us from the midst of adversity, He will always walk with us *through* the adversity (Psalm 23:4). So, no, your guardian angel is not asleep. He is there. But God may choose to allow a difficult circumstance to come into your life in order to accomplish a greater good.

~

26

The Devil and His Fallen Angels

How did Lucifer fall and become Satan?

Lucifer's fall is described in two key Old Testament chapters—Ezekiel 28 and Isaiah 14. Let's briefly look at both of these.

It would seem from the context of Ezekiel 28 that the first ten verses of this chapter are dealing with a human leader. Then, starting in verse 11 and on through verse 19, Lucifer is the focus of discussion.

What is the rationale for the conclusion that these latter verses refer to the fall of Lucifer? Whereas the first ten verses in this chapter speak about the *ruler* of Tyre (who was condemned for claiming to be a god though he was just a man), the discussion moves to the *king* of Tyre starting in verse 11. Many scholars believe that though there was a human "ruler" of Tyre, the *real* "king" of Tyre was Satan, for it was he who was ultimately at work in this anti-God city and it was he who worked through the human ruler of the city.

Some have suggested that these verses may actually be dealing with a human king of Tyre who was *empowered* by Satan. Perhaps the historic king of Tyre was a tool of Satan, possibly even indwelt by him. In describing this king, Ezekiel also gives us glimpses of the superhuman creature, Satan, who was using, if not indwelling, him.

Now, there are things that are true of this "king" that—at least ultimately—cannot be said to be true of human beings. For example, the king is portrayed as having a *different nature* from man (he is a cherub, verse 14); he had a *different position* from man (he was blameless and sinless, verse 15); he was in a *different realm* from man (the holy mount of God, verses 13, 14); he received a *different judgment* from man (he was cast out of the mountain of God and thrown to the earth, verse 16); and the superlatives used to describe him don't seem to fit that of a normal human being ("full of wisdom," "perfect in beauty," and having "the seal of perfection," verse 12 NASB).

Our text tells us that this king was a created being and left the creative hand of God in a perfect state (Ezekiel 28:12, 15). And he remained perfect in his ways until iniquity was found in him (verse 15b). What was this iniquity? We read in verse 17, "Your heart became proud on account of your beauty, and you corrupted your wisdom because of your splendor." Lucifer apparently became so impressed with his own beauty, intelligence, power, and position that he began to desire for himself the honor and glory that belonged to God alone. The sin that corrupted Lucifer was self-generated pride.

Apparently, this represents the actual beginning of sin in the universe—preceding the fall of the human Adam by an indeterminate time. Sin originated in the free will of Lucifer in which—with full understanding of the issues involved—he chose to rebel against the Creator.

This mighty angelic being was rightfully judged by God: "I threw you to the earth" (Ezekiel 28:18). This doesn't mean that Satan had no further access to heaven, for other Scripture verses clearly indicate that Satan maintained this access even after his fall (Job 1:6-12; Zechariah 3:1, 2). However, Ezekiel 28:18 indicates that Satan was absolutely and completely cast out of God's heavenly government and his place of authority (Luke 10:18).

Isaiah 14:12-17 is another Old Testament passage that may refer to the fall of Lucifer. We must be frank in admitting that some Bible scholars see no reference whatsoever to Lucifer in this passage. It is argued that the being mentioned in this verse is referred to as a man (Isaiah 14:16); is compared with other kings on the earth (verse 18); and the words, "How you have fallen from heaven" (verse 12), is alleged to refer to a fall from great political heights.

There are other scholars who interpret this passage as referring *only* to the fall of Lucifer, with no reference whatsoever to a human king. The argument here is that the description of this being is beyond humanness and hence could not refer to a mere mortal man.

There is a third view that I think is preferable to the two views above. This view sees Isaiah 14:12-17 as having a dual reference. It may be that verses 4 through 11 deal with an actual king of Babylon. Then, in verses 12 through 17, we find a *dual* reference that includes not just the king of Babylon but a typological description of Lucifer as well.

If this passage contains a reference to the fall of Lucifer, then the pattern of this passage would seem to fit that of the Ezekiel 28 reference—that is, first a human leader is described, and then dual reference is made to a human leader *and* Satan.

It is significant that the language used to describe this being fits other passages in the Bible that speak about Satan. For example, the five "I wills" in Isaiah 14 indicate an element of pride, which was also evidenced in Ezekiel 28:17 (cf. 1 Timothy 3:6 which makes reference to Satan's *conceit*).

As a result of this heinous sin against God, Lucifer was banished from living in heaven (Isaiah 14:12). He became corrupt, and his name changed from *Lucifer* ("morning star") to *Satan* ("adversary"). His power became completely perverted (Isaiah 14:12,16,17). And his destiny, following the second coming of Christ, is to be bound in a pit during the 1000-year millennial kingdom over which Christ will rule (Revelation 20:3), and eventually will be thrown into the lake of fire (Matthew 25:41).

Where did the demons come from?

If Lucifer's fall is described in Ezekiel 28 and Isaiah 14, are there any references in the Bible to the fall of numerous angels who became demons? I believe there are some hints in Scripture that help us answer this question.

Many scholars believe the first five verses of Revelation 12 contain a mini-history of Satan. In keeping with this, it would seem that Revelation 12:4 refers to the fall of the angels who followed Satan: "His [Satan's] tail swept a third of the stars out of the sky and flung them to the earth." It has long been recognized that the word "stars" is sometimes used of angels in the Bible (cf. Job 38:7). If "stars" refers to angels in Revelation 12:4, it would appear that after Lucifer rebelled against God, he was able to draw a third of the angelic realm after him in this rebellion. When he sinned, he apparently led a massive angelic revolt against God.

If you're wondering whether God's angels can still "fall" today, the answer is no. Following this angelic revolt, God "elected" or *permanently confirmed* the holiness of the angels who chose to remain loyal to Him (1 Timothy 5:21). God has apparently given them a special grace of perseverance to enable them to permanently retain their position as holy angels.

Does Satan still have access to God's presence in heaven?

Apparently so. It is clear from the events that took place in the Book of Job that Satan has the freedom to appear before God and engage in discourse with Him (see Job 1:6; 2:1). We are told in Revelation 12:10 that Satan is the "accuser of our brethren," which probably involves Satan going before God's throne and making slanderous statements about the saints. In the future Tribulation period, we are told that the devil will be decisively cast out of heaven (Revelation 12:9). Some time later he will be cast into the lake of fire (Revelation 20:10). So his time is definitely limited.

Can Christians become demon-possessed?

I don't think so. Let's begin by defining demon possession. This phenomenon involves

> a demon residing in a person, exerting direct control and influence over that person, with certain derangement of mind and/or body. Demon possession is to be distinguished from demon influence or demon activity in relation to a person. The work of the demon in the latter is from the outside; in demon possession it is from within.[1]

Now, according to the definition given above, a Christian cannot be possessed by a demon since he is perpetually indwelt by the Holy Spirit (1 Corinthians 6:19). I like the way Walter Martin once put it. He said that when the devil knocks on the door of the Christian's heart, the Holy Spirit opens it and says, "Get lost!"

It is highly revealing that there is not a single instance in Scripture of a Christian being said to be demon-possessed. For sure, there are examples of Christians being *afflicted* by the devil—but not *possessed* by the devil.

Christians have been delivered from Satan's domain. As Colossians 1:13 puts it, Christ "has rescued us from the dominion of darkness and brought us into the kingdom of the Son he loves." Furthermore, we must remember that "the one who is in you is greater than the one who is in the world" (1 John 4:4). This statement would not make much sense if Christians could be possessed by the devil.

Having said this, however, we must acknowledge that even though a Christian cannot be possessed, he can nevertheless be oppressed or influenced by demonic powers (see Job 1–2). But the oppression or influence is *external* to the Christian, not internal. The demons seek to work *from outside* the Christian to hinder him; they do not work *from within* him.

What can Satan and demons do to Christians?

Satan and his host of demons are very active in seeking to harm believers in various ways. Satan tempts believers to sin (Ephesians 2:1,2; 1 Thessalonians 3:5), to lie (Acts 5:3), and to commit sexually immoral acts (1 Corinthians 7:5). He accuses and slanders believers (Revelation 12:10), hinders their work in any way he can (1 Thessalonians 2:18), sows weeds among them (Matthew 13:38,39), and incites persecutions against them (Revelation 2:10).

Satan seeks to wage war against believers (Ephesians 6:11,12), opposes them with the ferociousness of a hungry lion (1 Peter 5:8), seeks to plant doubt in their minds (Genesis 3:1-5), seeks to foster spiritual pride in their hearts (1 Timothy 3:6), and seeks to lead them away from "the simplicity and purity of devotion to Christ" (2 Corinthians 11:3 NASB).

No wonder our Lord found it so necessary to provide us with spiritual armor to protect us from these insidious fallen angels (Ephesians 6:11-18).

Are all sicknesses caused by demonic spirits?

No. On the one hand, Scripture portrays Satan and demons as inflicting physical diseases on people (such as *muteness*, Matthew 9:33; *blindness*, 12:22; and *epilepsy*, 17:15-18). They can also afflict people with mental disorders (Mark 9:22; Luke 8:27-29) and can cause people to be self-destructive (Mark 5:5; Luke 9:42).

However, though demons can cause physical illnesses, Scripture distinguishes natural illnesses from demon-caused illnesses (Matthew 4:24; Mark 1:32; Luke 7:21; 9:1; Acts 5:16). In the case of numerous healings, no mention is made of demons. For example, no mention is made of demon affliction in the cases were Jesus healed the centurion's servant (Matthew 8:5-13), the woman with the hemorrhage of 12 years' duration (9:19-22), the two blind men (9:27-30), the man with the withered hand (12:9-13), and those who touched the fringe of Jesus' garment (14:35, 36). Hence, every time you get sick, don't presume you are being afflicted by a demon. You may have just caught a bad bug!

Does Satan have the ability to read our thoughts?

I don't think so. Scripture indicates that only God has the ability to "know the hearts of all men" (1 Kings 8:39). God is portrayed in Scripture as being omniscient (Psalm 139:1-3), and He certainly knows our thoughts: "Before a word is on my tongue you know it completely, O LORD" (Psalm 139:4). Satan, by contrast, is a creature with creaturely limitations.

Nevertheless, Satan is a highly intelligent being (Ezekiel 28:12) who has had virtually thousands of years of experience in dealing with human beings, and thus may give the appearance of knowing your thoughts. Satan is also the head of a vast network of demonic spirits who answer to him (Revelation 12:4, 7), and this too may give the appearance of Satan being omniscient. But again, he is just a creature with creaturely limitations. There is certainly no indication anywhere in Scripture that he has the capability of reading our minds.

What defenses does the Christian have against Satan and the powers of darkness?

We as Christians should be thankful that God has made

provision for our defense against Satan and his fallen angels. What does this defense consist of?

To begin, we must ever keep in mind that twice in the New Testament we are told that the Lord Jesus lives in heaven to make intercession for us (Romans 8:34; Hebrews 7:25). Certainly Christ's intercession for us includes the kind of intercession He made for His disciples in John 17:15, where He specifically asked the Father to keep them safe from the evil one.

Beyond this, God has provided spiritual armor for our defense (Ephesians 6:11-18). "Wearing" this armor means that our lives will be characterized by such things as righteousness, obedience to the will of God, faith in God, and an effective use of the Word of God. *These* are the things that spell defeat for the devil in your life.

Effective use of the Word of God is especially important for spiritual victory. Jesus used the Word of God to defeat the devil during His wilderness temptations (Matthew 4). We must learn to do the same. Obviously, the greater exposure we have to Scripture, the more God's Spirit can use this mighty sword in our lives.

Of course, Scripture specifically instructs us that each believer must be informed and thereby alert to the attacks of Satan (1 Peter 5:8). A prerequisite to defeating an enemy is to know as much as possible about the enemy—including his tactics (2 Corinthians 2:11).

We are also instructed to take a decisive stand against Satan. James 4:7 says, "Resist the devil, and he will flee from you." This is not a one-time resistance. Rather, on a day-to-day basis we must steadfastly resist the devil. And when we do, he will flee from us. Ephesians 6:13,14 tells us to "stand firm" against the devil.

We must not give place to the devil by letting sunset pass with us having unrighteous anger in our hearts toward someone (Ephesians 4:26,27). An excess of wrath in our heart gives opportunity to the devil to work in our lives.

We are instructed to rely on the indwelling Spirit of God, remembering that "the one who is in you is greater than the one who is in the world" (1 John 4:4).

We should pray for ourselves and for each other. Jesus set an example for us in the Lord's Prayer by teaching us to pray, "Deliver us from the evil one" (Matthew 6:13). Jesus also set an example of how to pray for others in His prayer for Peter: "Simon, Simon, Satan has asked to sift you as wheat. But I have prayed for you, Simon, *that your faith may not fail*" (Luke 22:31, 32, italics added). We should pray for each other that we will maintain a strong faith in the face of adversity.

Of course, the believer should never dabble in the occult, for this gives the devil opportunity to work in his life (Deuteronomy 18:10, 11; cf. Romans 16:19).

Finally, we must remember that Satan is "on a leash." He cannot go beyond what God will allow him (the Book of Job makes this abundantly clear). Hence, we should rest secure in the fact that God is in control of the universe and realize that Satan cannot simply do as he pleases in our lives.

Does the reference to "binding" and "loosing" in the New Testament indicate that we have authority over the powers of darkness (Matthew 18:18)?

This is a common misconception. While it is true that God has given us all we need to have victory over the devil (see Ephesians 6:11-18), it's also true that the New Testament verses which speak of binding and loosing have nothing to do with spiritual warfare.

In Matthew 18:18, for example, Jesus said, "Whatever you bind on earth will be bound in heaven, and whatever you loose on earth will be loosed in heaven." The terms "bind" and "loose" were Jewish idioms indicating that what is announced on earth has already been determined in heaven. To *bind* meant to forbid, refuse, or prohibit; to *loose* meant to permit or allow. We can announce the prohibition or allowance of certain things on earth because heaven (or God) has already made an announcement on these matters.

In the context of Matthew 18, Jesus was speaking only about church discipline. The basic idea He was communicating is that those members of the church who sin and repent are to be "loosed" (that is, they are to be restored to fellowship) while those who are unrepentant are to be "bound" (that is, they are to be removed from fellowship). These ideas can be declared on earth because heaven (God) has already declared it.

Part 8

~

The Future Life

The Prophetic Future
The Wonder of Heaven
The Judgment of Humankind
Erroneous Views of the Afterlife
Near-Death Experiences

27

~

The Prophetic Future

What are the different views of the rapture?

There are four primary views. *Partial Rapturism* is the view that only spiritual Christians will be raptured when Christ returns. *Pretribulationism* is the view that Christ will rapture the entire church before any part of the Tribulation begins. *Posttribulationism* is the view that Christ will rapture the church after the Tribulation. *Midtribulationism* is the view that Christ will rapture the church in the middle of the Tribulation period.

I would say that most Christians today are either "pretribs" or "posttribs." Personally, I think the pretrib position is most consistent with the biblical testimony. But it's not an issue worth fighting over. The different views of the rapture may disagree over the *timing* of end-time events, but they all agree on the *big picture*: there will be a rapture and we will live forever with Jesus in heaven. In the long haul (after we've been with Christ for billions of years in heaven), the question of whether the rapture happened before or after the Tribulation period will seem utterly ridiculous. Perhaps we should all keep that in mind the next time we're tempted to get into a heated argument about the timing of the rapture.

What are some of the problems with the posttrib view of the rapture?

Even though I don't think Christians ought to argue about when the rapture occurs, I do think every Christian needs to examine the biblical evidence and come to a conviction on the issue. With that in mind, allow me to share a few of the reasons why I've decided in favor of the pretrib view and against the posttrib (and other) views.

One major problem with the posttrib view is, who will populate the millennial kingdom in mortal bodies? Scripture is very clear that when Christ comes again at the end of the Tribulation period, there will be human beings (Christians) who will enter into the millennial kingdom in their mortal bodies. These people will not be glorified with resurrection bodies at that point. We know this to be true because they will continue to have marriage relationships with their spouses (assuming their spouses are Christians and enter the kingdom), they will continue to bear children during the millennial kingdom (Isaiah 65:20-23; Jeremiah 23:3-6; 30:19,20), and even though longevity will be extended, aging and death will occur among them (Isaiah 65:20-23).

The problem is, then, how can mortal Christians enter the millennial kingdom if the rapture occurs at the end of the Tribulation, thus glorifying *all* believers? There would be no mortal believers left. This obviously is not a problem for the pretrib view, for this view allows for new people to become Christians during the Tribulation period, following the rapture of the church.

Another problem for posttribulationism is, who are the participants in the judgment of the nations (Matthew 25:31-46)? We are told in Scripture that after Christ returns, He will separate the sheep from the goats (who are portrayed as *still being* on the earth) based on how they treated Christ's "brothers." The problem is, if all believers are raptured at the end of the Tribulation, then who are the sheep and the brothers? No separation of the sheep from the goats could occur *on earth*, because all of the sheep (and the brothers) would have *just been raptured and are up in the air with Christ.* They would thus already be separated from unbelievers.

Matthew 25:31-46 just can't be made to fit in a posttrib scenario.

A third problem for posttribulationism is John 14:1-3. This passage cannot be worked into a posttrib scenario. The problem is, at a posttrib rapture, all believers are raptured and meet Christ in the air, only to return *back to the earth* with Christ. But this passage says that Christ will take believers *from the earth to the place Christ is preparing for them*. This passage is not a problem for the pretrib view, which says that Christ will rapture the church before the Tribulation begins and take them to this place He has been preparing.

Having said all the above, what are some good arguments in favor of pretribulationism? For one thing, Revelation 3:10 indicates that believers will be kept from the actual hour of testing that is coming on the whole world. Christians will be kept from the actual *time period* of suffering.

Further, no Old Testament passage on the Tribulation mentions the church, though in some cases the nation of Israel *is* mentioned (Deuteronomy 4:29, 30; Jeremiah 30:4-11; Daniel 12:1, 2). No New Testament passage on the Tribulation mentions the church (Matthew 13:30, 39-42, 48-50; 24:15-31; 1 Thessalonians 1:9-10; 5:4-9; 2 Thessalonians 2:1-11; Revelation 4-18).

Now, Scripture *does* say there will be Christians who live during the Tribulation period. But pretribs believe these people become Christians sometime after the rapture. Perhaps they become Christians as a result of the ministry of the 144,000 Jewish Christians introduced in Revelation 7 (who themselves apparently come to faith in Christ after the rapture).

We are also told that the church is not appointed to wrath (Romans 5:9; 1 Thessalonians 1:9, 10; 5:9). Hence, the church cannot go through the "great day of wrath" in the Tribulation period (Revelation 6:17).

Finally, it is highly revealing that throughout Scripture God is seen always protecting His people before judgment falls (see 2 Peter 2:5-9). Enoch was translated before the judgment of the flood. Noah was in the ark before the judgment of the flood. Lot was taken out of Sodom before the judgment of Sodom and Gomorrah. The firstborn among the Hebrews in Egypt were sheltered by the blood of the lamb before judgment fell. The spies were safely out of Jericho and Rahab was secured before the judgment of Jericho. So, too, will the church be secured safely before judgment falls in the Tribulation period.

What will the future Tribulation period be like?

The Tribulation will be a definite period of time at the end of the age that will be characterized by great travail (Matthew 24:29-35). It is called "the great tribulation" in Revelation 7:14. It will be of such severity that no period in history past or future will equal it (Matthew 24:21). It is called the time of Jacob's trouble, for it is a judgment on Messiah-rejecting Israel (Jeremiah 30:7; Daniel 12:1-4). The nations will also be judged for their sin and rejection of Christ (Isaiah 26:21; Revelation 6:15-17). The period will last seven years (Daniel 9:24, 27).

Scripture indicates that this period will be characterized by judgment (Revelation 14:7), wrath (Isaiah 26:20, 21), trial (Revelation 3:10), trouble (Jeremiah 30:7), destruction (Joel 1:15), darkness (Amos 5:18), desolation (Daniel 9:27), overturning (Isaiah 24:1-4), and punishment (Isaiah 24:20, 21). Simply put, no passage can be found to alleviate to any degree whatsoever the severity of this time that will come upon the earth.

Can you explain the timing of Daniel's 70 weeks (Daniel 9:25-27)?

In Daniel 9 God provided a prophetic timetable for the nation of Israel. The prophetic clock began ticking when the command went out to restore and rebuild Jerusalem following its destruction by Babylon (Daniel 9:25). According to this verse, Israel's timetable was divided into 70 groups of seven years, totaling 490 years.

Now, the first 69 groups of seven years—or 483 years—counted the years "from the issuing of the decree to restore and rebuild Jerusalem until the Anointed One, the ruler, comes" (Daniel 9:25). The "Anointed One," of course, is Jesus Christ. *Anointed One* means "Messiah." The day that Jesus rode into Jerusalem to proclaim Himself Israel's Messiah was exactly 483 years to the day after the command to restore and rebuild Jerusalem had been given.

At that point God's prophetic clock stopped. Daniel describes a gap between these 483 years and the *final* seven years of Israel's prophetic timetable. Several events were to take place during this "gap," according to Daniel 9:26:

1. The Messiah will be killed.

2. The city of Jerusalem and its temple would be destroyed (which occurred in A.D. 70).

3. The Jews would encounter difficulty and hardship from that time on.

The final "week" of seven years will begin for Israel when the Antichrist will confirm a "covenant" for seven years (Daniel 9:27). When this peace pact is signed, this will signal the beginning of the Tribulation period. That signature marks the beginning of the seven-year countdown to the second coming of Christ (which follows the Tribulation period).

What are the main views of Christ's millennial kingdom?

There are three theological views regarding the millennial kingdom:

Premillennialism (the view I think is correct) says that following the Second Coming, Christ will institute a kingdom of perfect peace and righteousness on earth that will last for 1,000 years. After this reign of true peace, eternity begins.

Amillennialism is the view that when Christ comes, eternity will begin with no prior 1,000-year (millennial) reign on earth. Amillennialists generally interpret the 1,000-year reign of Christ metaphorically and say it refers to Christ's present rule from heaven.

The *postmillennial* view says that through the church's influence, the world will be "Christianized" before Christ returns. Immediately following this return, eternity will begin.

I believe the premillennial view is most consistent with a literal interpretation of Scripture.

Should Christians be involved in setting dates for the rapture or the second coming of Christ?

No. Christians can be excited about the coming of the Lord, but they should never set dates. I call date setting "millennial madness."

I can think of at least eight reasons Christians should maintain millennial sanity in the coming years. First, over the past 2,000 years, the track record of those who have predicted and/or expected "the end" has been 100 percent wrong. The history of doomsday predictions is little more than a history of dashed expectations. Though it is possible we are living in the last days, it is also possible that Christ's second coming is a long way off.

Second, those who succumb to millennial madness may end up making harmful decisions for their lives. Selling one's possessions and heading for the mountains, purchasing bomb shelters, stopping education, leaving family and friends—these are destructive actions that can ruin one's life.

Third, Christians who succumb to millennial madness (for example, by expecting the rapture to occur by a specific date) may end up damaging their faith in the Bible (especially prophetic sections) when their expectations fail.

Fourth, if one loses confidence in the prophetic portions of Scripture, biblical prophecy ceases to be a motivation to purity and holiness in daily life (see Titus 2:12-14).

Fifth, Christians who succumb to millennial madness may damage the faith of new and/or immature believers when predicted events fail to materialize.

Sixth, millennial soothsayers tend to be sensationalistic, and sensationalism is unbefitting to a Christian. Christ calls His followers to live soberly and alertly as they await His coming (Mark 13:32-37).

Seventh, Christians who get caught up in millennial madness can do damage to the cause of Christ. Humanists enjoy scorning Christians who have put stock in end-time predictions (especially when specific dates have been attached to specific events). Why give "ammo" to the enemies of Christianity?

Eighth, the timing of end-time events is in God's hands, and we haven't been given the details (Acts 1:7). As far as the Second Coming is concerned, it is better to live as if Jesus were coming today and yet prepare for the future as if He were not coming for a long time. Then you are ready for time and eternity.

Will the second coming of Christ be a physical, visible event, or will it be a spiritual, invisible event, as some cultists argue?

The Second Coming will be a physical, visible event. One Greek word used to describe the Second Coming is *apokalupsis*, which carries the basic meaning of "revelation," "visible disclosure," "unveiling," and "removing the cover" from something that is hidden. The word is used of pulling a cover off a sculpture for everyone to see. The word is used of Christ's second coming in 1 Peter 4:13.

Another word used of Christ's second coming is *epiphaneia*, which carries the basic meaning of "to appear." This word literally means "a shining forth." It is used several times by the apostle Paul in reference to Christ's visible second coming. For example, in Titus 2:13 Paul speaks of "looking for the blessed hope and the *appearing* of the glory of our great God and Savior, Christ Jesus" (NASB). In 1 Timothy 6:14 Paul urges Timothy to "keep the commandment without stain or reproach until the *appearing* of our Lord Jesus Christ" (NASB). Significantly, Christ's *first* coming—which was both *bodily* and *visible*—was called an *epiphaneia* (2 Timothy 1:10). In the same way, Christ's second coming will be both *bodily* and *visible*.

In support of a visible coming of the Lord we must not forget the clear teaching of Matthew 24:29,30:

> Immediately after the distress of those days "the sun will be darkened, and the moon will not give its light; the stars will fall from the sky, and the heavenly bodies will be shaken." At that time the sign of the Son of Man will appear in the sky, and all the nations of the earth will mourn. They will see the Son of Man coming on the clouds of the sky, with power and great glory.

Do cultists legitimately justify their false prophecies by saying that even the biblical prophets made mistakes?

By no means! Cultists typically argue that Jonah made mistaken prophecies. Jonah proclaimed that in 40 days Nineveh would be overthrown by God who would bring calamity on them. What Jonah predicted about Nineveh's destruction did not come to pass. Yet, Jonah was not condemned for this. Hence, false prophecies of cults should not be condemned either.

Note, however, that Jonah did not make a mistake. After all, Jonah told the Ninevites *exactly* what God told him to say (see Jonah 3:1).

It is important to recognize that there was apparently a "repentance clause" built into Jonah's prophecy to the Ninevites. The Ninevites understood Jonah's prophecy to mean that Nineveh would be toppled in 40 days *unless they repented* (Jonah 3:5-9). Based on how the Ninevites responded to Jonah's prophecy, God withdrew the threatened punishment—thus making it clear that even He Himself viewed the prophecy as hinging on how the Ninevites responded.

This is related to something God said in the Book of Jeremiah: "If at any time I announce that a nation or kingdom is to be uprooted, torn down and destroyed, and if that nation I warned repents of its evil, then I will relent and not inflict on it the disaster I had planned" (Jeremiah 18:7,8). This principle is clearly illustrated for us in the case of Nineveh. It is noteworthy that God is often seen showing mercy where repentance is evident (Exodus 32:14; 2 Samuel 24:16; Amos 7:3,6).

The biblical prophets were always 100-percent accurate. In fact, if a prophet was shown to be less than 100-percent accurate, he was to be put to death as a false prophet (Deuteronomy 13; 18:20-22). Cultic prophets are *false* prophets because what they say does not come to pass.

Sometimes Jehovah's Witnesses try to justify their false prophecies of the past by saying that the light is getting brighter today, and hence they now understand prophetic things better. How can we respond to this line of argument?

Jehovah's Witnesses have been prophetically wrong over and over again throughout their history, thereby proving beyond any doubt that the Watchtower Society is a false prophet. For example, the Watchtower Society predicted that the year 1914 would mark the overthrow of human governments and the full establishment of the kingdom of God on earth.[1] (*It didn't happen.*)

Jehovah's Witnesses typically justify such false prophecies by saying the light is getting brighter with each passing day, and hence they understand prophecy better today than in past decades. I generally respond to Jehovah's Witnesses who say this in the following way: "So, conceivably, if the light is getting brighter every day, it is possible that ten years from now you might discover that everything you presently believe is in error, since the light ten years from now will be so much brighter, right?"

(Their response is always interesting.)

I then say, "Now, what if you should die tomorrow? Does this mean you will die having believed the wrong thing, and thus be lost forever and ever?"

(Again, their response is always interesting.)

After making this point, I seek to draw a distinction between the biblical prophets, who are always right, and the Watchtower Society, an organization that has been consistently wrong about prophetic issues. By undermining the Jehovah's Witnesses' confidence in the Watchtower Society, you can help motivate them to discover what the Scriptures really teach, not just about prophetic things, but about Jesus, God, and salvation.

28

~

The Wonder of Heaven

What actually happens at the moment of death?

From a biblical perspective, human beings are made up of both a material aspect (the physical body) and an immaterial aspect (the soul or spirit). When a human being physically dies, his or her spirit departs from the body (2 Corinthians 5:8).

The New Testament word for "death" carries the idea of *separation*. At the moment of physical death, man's spirit separates or departs from his body. This is why, when Stephen was being put to death by stoning, he prayed, "Lord Jesus, receive my spirit" (Acts 7:59). At the moment of death "the spirit returns to God who gave it" (Ecclesiastes 12:7). Verses such as these indicate that death for the believer involves his or her spirit departing from the physical body and immediately going into the presence of the Lord in heaven. Death for the believer is thus an event that leads to a supremely blissful existence (see Philippians 1:21).

For the unbeliever, however, death holds grim prospects. At death the unbeliever's spirit departs from the body and goes not to heaven but to a place of great suffering (Luke 16:19-31).

Both believers and unbelievers remain as spirits (in a disembodied state) until the future day of resurrection. And what a glorious day that will be! God will reunite believers' spirits with their resurrected physical bodies. These bodies will be specially suited to dwelling in heaven in the direct presence of God—the perishable will be made imperishable and the mortal will be made immortal (1 Corinthians 15:53). Unbelievers, too, will be resurrected, but they will spend eternity apart from God.

The Bible speaks of three different heavens. What are we to make of this?

The Scriptures make reference to the "third heaven" (2 Corinthians 12:2)—which is the ineffable and glorious dwelling place of God in all His glory. It is elsewhere called the "heaven of heavens". (Nehemiah 9:6 NASB) and the "highest heaven" (1 Kings 8:27; 2 Chronicles 2:6).

If God's abode is the "third" heaven, then what are the first and the second heavens? Scripture gives us the answer. The first heaven is that of the earth's atmosphere (Job 35:5). The second heaven is that of the stellar universe (Genesis 1:17; Deuteronomy 17:3).

Scripture makes reference to the "old heavens and earth" as well as the "new heavens and earth." What does all this mean?

As we think back to the scene in the Garden of Eden in which Adam and Eve sinned against God, we remember that a curse was placed upon the earth by God (Genesis 3:17,18). Hence, before the eternal kingdom can be made manifest, God must deal with this cursed earth. Indeed, the earth—along with the first and second heavens (the earth's atmosphere and the stellar universe)—must be renewed. The old must make room for the new.

The Scriptures often speak of the passing of the old heaven and earth. Psalm 102:25, 26, for example, says of the earth and the stellar universe: "They will perish, but you [O

God] remain; they will all wear out like a garment. Like clothing you will change them and they will be discarded."

In the Book of Revelation we read, "Then I saw a new heaven and a new earth, for the first heaven and the first earth had passed away, and there was no longer any sea.... He who was seated on the throne said, 'I am making everything new!'" (Revelation 21:1,5).

The Greek word used to designate the newness of the cosmos is *kainos*. This word means "new in nature" or "new in quality." Hence, the phrase "new heavens and a new earth" refers not to a cosmos that is totally other than the present cosmos. Rather, the new cosmos will stand in continuity with the present cosmos, but it will be utterly renewed and renovated. In keeping with this, Matthew 19:28 speaks of "the regeneration" (NASB). Acts 3:21 speaks of the "restoration of all things" (NASB).

The new earth, being a renewed and an eternal earth, will be adapted to the vast moral and physical changes which the eternal state necessitates. Everything is new in the eternal state. Everything will be according to God's own glorious nature. The new heavens and the new earth will be brought into blessed conformity with all that God is—in a state of fixed bliss and absolute perfection.

An incredible thing to ponder is that in the next life heaven and earth will no longer be separate realms, as they are now, but will be merged. Believers will thus continue to be in heaven even while they are on the new earth. The new earth will be utterly sinless, and hence bathed and suffused in the light and splendor of God, unobscured by evil of any kind or tarnished by evildoers of any description.

"Heaven" will thus encompass the new heaven and the new earth. And the New Jerusalem—the eternal city that measures 1,500 by 1,500 by 1,500 miles—will apparently "come down" and rest upon the newly renovated earth (see Revelation 21:2). This city will be the eternal dwelling place of the saints of all ages.

Does the fact that "flesh and blood" cannot enter into God's kingdom mean that our resurrection bodies will not be physical?

No. It is true that 1 Corinthians 15:50 says, "I declare to you, brothers, that flesh and blood cannot inherit the kingdom of God." However, the term "flesh and blood" is simply an idiom used in Scripture to refer to mortal, perishable humanity. This verse is saying that mortal human beings in their present perishable bodies cannot inherit heaven. Mortal humanity must be made *im*mortal humanity in order to survive in heaven. The resurrection body will be endowed with special qualities that will enable it to adapt perfectly to life in God's presence. As 1 Corinthians 15:53 puts it, "The perishable must clothe itself with the imperishable, and the mortal with immortality."

What will Christians do for all eternity in heaven?

There will be no purposeless inactivity in the eternal state. Scripture portrays believers as being involved in meaningful (yet restful) service throughout eternity.

For example, the Book of Revelation portrays believers in the eternal state as offering worship and praise before the throne of God and Christ (Revelation 19:1-6). The worship that takes place in heaven will be ultimately fulfilling. It will not be confining or manipulated, but spontaneous and genuine. We will not find ourselves nodding off to sleep, as we're often tempted to do in church services. Rather, we will virtually lose ourselves in the sheer joy of expressing with our lips the adoration and love we feel for God in our hearts.

Another activity that will occupy us in the eternal state will be the perpetual serving of God and Christ (Revelation 1:5, 6; cf. 22:3). This will not be a tedious kind of service but a joyous one—fully meeting our heart's every desire. There will be no boredom in eternity. Because we will be servants of the Most High, and because there will be an endless variety of tasks to perform, the prospect of heaven is entrancingly attractive.

It would seem that one aspect of our service will involve reigning with Christ. In Revelation 22:5 we are told that believers "will reign for ever and ever." We will be involved in some capacity in the heavenly government.

As well, part of our service will involve judging the angels in some capacity. "Do you not know that we will judge angels?" Paul asks in 1 Corinthians 6:2,3. This is noteworthy because man at present is lower than the angels (see Psalm 8). The situation will be reversed in the eternal state. Angels will be lower than redeemed humanity in heaven.

Another activity we'll be involved in is perpetually learning more about our glorious God. Throughout future ages believers will be shown "the incomparable riches of his grace" (Ephesians 2:7). God is so infinite—with matchless perfections that are beyond us in every way—that we will never come to the end of exploring Him and His marvelous riches.

Do babies and little children go to heaven at the moment of death?

Yes. I believe the Scriptures teach that every infant who dies is immediately ushered into God's glorious presence in heaven. I believe that at the moment of death, Jesus applies the benefits of His death on the cross to that child, thereby saving him or her.

The universal need of salvation. At the outset, we must recognize that the whole of Scripture points to the universal need of salvation—even among little children. All of us—including infants who can't believe—are lost (Luke 19:10), perishing (John 3:16), condemned (John 3:18), and are under God's wrath (John 3:36). In view of this, we cannot say that little children are in a sinless state. That's why it's necessary for Christ to apply the benefits of His death on the cross to each child that dies.

God's purpose in salvation. God's primary purpose in saving human beings is to display His wondrous grace. One must ask, would the "riches of God's grace" be displayed in "wisdom and understanding" (Ephesians 1:7,8) in sending little children to hell? I think not. It would be a cruel mockery for God to call upon infants to do—and to hold them *responsible* for doing—what they *could not* do. At that young age children simply do not have the capacity to exercise saving faith in Christ.

I believe it is the uniform testimony of Scripture that those who are not capable of making a decision to receive Jesus Christ, and who have died, are now with Christ in heaven, resting in His tender arms, enjoying the sweetness of His love. There are numerous factors supporting this viewpoint.

It is highly revealing that in all the descriptions of hell in the Bible, we *never* read of infants or little children there. Only adults capable of making decisions are seen there. Nor do we read of infants and little children standing before the Great White Throne judgment, which is the judgment of the wicked dead and the precursor to the lake of fire (Revelation 20:11-15). The complete silence of Scripture regarding the presence of infants in eternal torment militates against their being there.

Jesus and the children. As we examine instances in which Christ encountered children during His earthly ministry, it would seem that children have a special place in His kingdom. Jesus even said, "Unless you change and become like little children, you will never enter the kingdom of heaven" (Matthew 18:3). He also said, "Whoever welcomes a little child like this in my name welcomes me" (verse 5). I don't think there is any way someone could read through

Matthew 18 and conclude that it is within the realm of possibility that Jesus could damn such little ones to hell!

King David and his son. King David in the Old Testament certainly believed he would again be with his young son who died (2 Samuel 12:22, 23). David firmly believed in life after death. He had no doubt that he would spend eternity with his beloved little one.

The basis of the judgment of the lost. Another consideration that points to the assurance of infant salvation relates to the basis of the judgment of the lost. We read in Revelation 20:11-13 that the lost are judged "according to what they had done." The basis of the judgment of the wicked is clearly *deeds done while on earth.* Hence, infants cannot possibly be the objects of this judgment because they are not responsible for their deeds. Such a judgment against infants would be a travesty.

These and other scriptural factors make it clear that babies and young children go straight to heaven at the moment of death.

Will we recognize our Christian loved ones in the afterlife?

Yes. The Thessalonian Christians were apparently very concerned about their Christian loved ones who had died. They expressed their concern to the apostle Paul. So, in 1 Thessalonians 4:13-17, Paul deals with the "dead in Christ" and assures the Thessalonian Christians that there will indeed be a reunion. And yes, believers will recognize their loved ones in the eternal state.

We are told in 2 Samuel 12:23 that David knew he would be reunited with his deceased son in heaven. He had no doubt about recognizing him. As well, when Moses and Elijah (who had long passed from earthly life) appeared to Jesus on the Mount of Transfiguration (Matthew 17:1-8), they were recognized by all who were present. Furthermore, in Jesus' story of the rich man and Lazarus in Luke 16:19-31, the rich man, Lazarus, *and* Abraham were all recognized by each other in the intermediate state.

Will our children still be our children in the afterlife?

Of course they will! It will always be true that your daughter is your daughter and your son is your son. Receiving a glorified body does not obliterate the fact that in earth-time history a husband and wife conceived and gave birth to a son or daughter.

But in the eternal state, there is a broader relationship in which we are all equally "sons" and "daughters" in God's eternal family. We have each become adopted into His forever family (Ephesians 1:5). We are all children of God!

Will husbands and wives still be married in the afterlife?

It would seem from the scriptural evidence that believers will no longer be in a married state in the afterlife. Jesus said, "At the resurrection people will neither marry nor be given in marriage; they will be like the angels in heaven" (Matthew 22:30).

Of course, it will always be true that my wife, Kerri, and I were married on this earth. *Nothing will ever change that.* And in the eternal state, in the new heavens and the new earth, we will retain our memory that we were married on the old earth. It will be an eternal memory. And what a precious memory it will be.

We should not think of this as a deprivation. It may be very difficult for us to conceive how we could be happy and fulfilled if we were not still married to our present spouse. But God Himself has promised that not only will there *not* be any sense of deprivation, there will be only bliss, and there will be no more sorrow or pain.

My wife and I are part of the glorious church, which, the Scriptures reveal, will one day be married to Christ. This event is referred to as the marriage of the Lamb (Revelation 19:7-9). It is an event to look forward to with great anticipation.

Is it possible that animals have an afterlife like humans do?

That's a tough question. I've had pets who have died and know how emotionally loaded this issue is. I used to be of the opinion that only human beings have an afterlife in the presence of God. But R. C. Sproul has caused me to at least reconsider my position.

It's true that only human beings are created in the image of God (Genesis 1:26). Even though animals *are not* created in God's image, Sproul thinks it's possible that they may have souls. Let me just pass on a few of his thoughts:

> Nowhere does Scripture explicitly state that animals do not have souls.... There's nothing in Scripture I know of that would preclude the possibility of animals' continued existence.... The Bible does give us some reason to hope that departed animals will be restored. We read in the Bible that redemption is a cosmic matter. The whole creation is destined to be redeemed through the work of Christ (Romans 8:21), and we see the images of what heaven will be like; beautiful passages of Scripture tell us about the lion and the lamb and other animals being at peace with one another. Whenever heaven is described, though it may be in highly imaginative language, it is a place where animals seem to be present. Whether these are animals newly created for the new heavens and the new earth, or they are the redeemed souls of our pets that have perished, we can't know for sure.

All of this is sheer speculation, but I would like to think that we will see our beloved pets again someday as they participate in the benefits of the redemption that Christ has achieved for the human race.[1]

How can we be happy in heaven knowing that there are people suffering in hell?

This is a difficult question to answer. In fact, on this side of eternity, we do not have all the wisdom and insight we need to fully answer it. But there are some scriptural considerations that help us keep this question in perspective.

First, God Himself has promised that He will take away all pain and remove all our tears (Revelation 21:4). It is in His hands. We can rest assured that God has the power and ability to do as He has promised. It is a fact that we will be happy in heaven. God has promised it.

Second, we will be aware of the full justice of God's decisions. We will clearly see that those who are in hell are there precisely because they rejected God's only provision for escaping hell. They are those to whom God ultimately says, "Thy will be done."

Third, we will recognize that there are degrees of punishment in hell, just as there are degrees of reward in heaven. This gives us an assurance that the Hitlers of human history will be in a much greater state of suffering than, for example, a non-Christian moralist (Luke 12:47,48).

God is perfectly wise and just. He knows what He is doing! You and I can rest with quiet assurance in God's wisdom and justice.

29

~

The Judgment of Humankind

Is it true that Christians will one day stand before the judgment seat of Christ?

Yes. All believers will one day stand before the judgment seat of Christ (Romans 14:10,11). At that time each believer's life will be examined in regard to the things done while in the body. Personal motives and intents of the heart will also be weighed.

The idea of a "judgment seat" relates to the athletic games of Paul's day. After the races and games concluded, the emperor himself often took his seat on an elevated throne, and one by one, the winning athletes came up to the throne to receive a reward. This reward was usually a wreath of leaves, a "victor's crown." In the case of Christians, each of us will stand before Christ the Judge and receive (or lose) rewards.

This judgment has nothing to do with whether or not the Christian will remain saved. Those who have placed faith in Christ *are* saved, and nothing threatens that. Believers are eternally secure in their salvation (Ephesians 4:30). This judgment rather has to do with the reception or loss of rewards.

What will the Christian be judged on?

The Christian's judgment will focus on his personal stewardship of the gifts, talents, opportunities, and responsibilities given to him in this life. The very character of each Christian's life and service will be utterly laid bare under the unerring and omniscient vision of Christ, whose eyes are "like a flame of fire" (Revelation 1:14 NASB).

Each of our actions will be judged before the Lord. The psalmist said to the Lord, "Surely you will reward each person according to what he has done" (Psalm 62:12; cf. Matthew 16:27). In Ephesians 6:7, 8 we read that the Lord "will reward everyone for whatever good he does, whether he is slave or free."

Also scrutinized will be our *thoughts*. In Jeremiah 17:10 God said, "I the LORD search the heart and examine the mind, to reward a man according to his conduct, according to what his deeds deserve." The Lord "will bring to light what is hidden in darkness and will expose the motives of men's hearts" (1 Corinthians 4:5). The Lord is the one "who searches hearts and minds" (Revelation 2:23).

Finally, the scope of the believer's judgment will include all the words he has spoken. Christ once said that "men will have to give account on the day of judgment for every careless word they have spoken" (Matthew 12:35-37). If even our careless words are carefully recorded, *how much more* will our calculated boastful claims, our cutting criticisms of others, our off-color jokes, and our unkind comments be taken into account.

What kinds of rewards will believers receive at the judgment seat of Christ?

Scripture often speaks of these rewards in terms of crowns that we wear. In fact, there are a number of different crowns that symbolize the various spheres of achievement and award in the Christian life.

The crown of life is given to those who persevere under trial, and especially to those who suffer to the point of death (James 1:12; Revelation 2:10). The crown of glory is given to those who faithfully and sacrificially minister God's Word to the flock (1 Peter 5:4). The crown incorruptible is given to those who win the race of temperance and self-control (1 Corinthians 9:25). The crown of righteousness is given to those who long for the second coming of Christ (2 Timothy 4:8).

It is highly revealing that in Revelation 4:10 we find believers casting their crowns before the throne of God in an act of worship and adoration. This teaches us something very important. Clearly the crowns (as rewards) are bestowed on us not for our own glory but ultimately for the glory of God. We are told elsewhere in Scripture that believers are redeemed in order to bring glory to God (1 Corinthians 6:20). It would seem that the act of placing our crowns before the throne of God is an illustration of this.

Here's something else to think about. The greater reward or crown one has received, the greater capacity one has to bring glory to the Creator. The lesser reward or crown one has received, the lesser his capacity to bring glory to the Creator. Because of the different rewards handed out at the judgment seat of Christ, believers will have differing capacities to bring glory to God.

Still, we shouldn't take this to mean that certain believers will have a sense of lack throughout eternity. After all, each believer will be glorifying God to the fullness of his capacity in the next life. Each one of us, then, will be able to "declare the praises of him who called [us] out of darkness into his wonderful light" (1 Peter 2:9).

How can we be happy throughout eternity if we don't fare well at the judgment seat of Christ?

It seems to be the testimony of Scripture that some believers at the judgment seat of Christ may have a sense of deprivation and suffer some degree of forfeiture and shame. Second John 8 warns us, "Watch out that you *do not lose* what you have worked for, but that you may be rewarded fully" (emphasis added). In 1 John 2:28 John wrote about the possibility of a believer actually being *ashamed* at Christ's coming.

We must keep all this in perspective, however. Christ's coming for us at the rapture and the prospect of living eternally with Him is something that should give each of us joy. And our joy will last for all eternity. How, then, can we reconcile this eternal joy with the possible loss of reward and perhaps even some level of shame at the Judgment Seat of Christ?

I think Herman Hoyt's explanation is the best I've seen:

> The Judgment Seat of Christ might be compared to a commencement ceremony. At graduation there is some measure of disappointment and remorse that one did not do better and work harder. However, at such an event the overwhelming emotion is joy, not remorse. The graduates do not leave the auditorium weeping because they did not earn better grades. Rather, they are thankful that they have been graduated, and they are grateful for what they did achieve. To overdo the sorrow aspect of the Judgment Seat of Christ is to make heaven hell. To underdo the sorrow aspect is to make faithfulness inconsequential.[1]

What is the Great White Throne judgment?

The Great White Throne judgment is the judgment that *un*believers must face (Revelation 20:11-15). (Believers will not participate in this horrific judgment.) Christ is the divine Judge, and those that are judged are the unsaved dead of all time. The judgment takes place at the end of the millennial kingdom, Christ's 1,000-year reign on planet earth.

Those who face Christ at this judgment will be judged on the basis of their works (Revelation 20:12,13). It is critical to understand that they actually get to this judgment because they are *already unsaved*. This judgment will not separate believers from unbelievers, for all who will experience it will have already made the choice during their lifetimes to reject God. Once they are before the divine Judge, they are judged according to their works not only to justify their condemnation but to determine the degree to which each person should be punished throughout eternity in hell.

Is there really such a thing as hell?

The Scriptures assure us that hell is a real place. But hell was not part of God's original creation, which He called "good" (Genesis 1). Hell was created later to accommodate the banishment of Satan and his fallen angels who rebelled against God (Matthew 25:41). Human beings who reject Christ will join Satan and his fallen angels in this infernal place of suffering.

One of the more important New Testament words for hell (in Greek) is "Gehenna" (Matthew 10:28). This word has an interesting history. For several generations in ancient Israel, atrocities were committed in the Valley of Ben Hinnom—atrocities that included human sacrifices, even the sacrifice of children (2 Kings 23:10; 2 Chronicles 28:3; 33:6; Jeremiah 32:35). These unfortunate victims were sacrificed to the false Moabite god Molech. Jeremiah appropriately called this valley "the Valley of Slaughter" (Jeremiah 7:31-34).

Eventually the valley came to be used as a public rubbish dump into which all the filth in Jerusalem was poured. Not only garbage but also the bodies of dead animals and the corpses of criminals were thrown on the heap where they—like everything else in the dump—would perpetually burn. The valley was a place where the fires never stopped burning. And there was always a good meal for a hungry worm.

This place was originally called (in the Hebrew) *Ge[gen]hinnom* (the valley of the sons of Hinnom). It was eventually shortened to the name *Ge-Hinnom*. The Greek translation of this Hebrew phrase is *Gehenna*. It became an appropriate and graphic term for the reality of hell. Jesus Himself used the word 11 times as a metaphorical way of describing the eternal place of suffering of unredeemed humanity.

The Scriptures use a variety of words to describe the horrors of hell—including fire, fiery furnace, unquenchable fire, the lake of burning sulfur, the lake of fire, everlasting contempt, perdition, the place of weeping and gnashing of teeth, eternal punishment, darkness, the wrath to come, exclusion, torments, damnation, condemnation, retribution, woe, and the second death. Hell is a horrible destiny.

Does God really send anyone to hell?

God doesn't want to send anyone to hell. That's why He sent Jesus—to pay the penalty for our sins by dying on the cross (John 3:16,17). Unfortunately, not all people are willing to admit that they sin and ask for forgiveness. They don't accept the payment of Jesus' death for them. So God lets them experience the results of their choice (see Luke 16:19-31).

C. S. Lewis once said that in the end there are two groups of people. One group of people says to God, "Thy will be done." These are those who have placed their faith in Jesus Christ and will live forever with God in heaven. The second group of people are those to whom God says, sadly, "*Thy* will be done!" These are those who have rejected Jesus Christ and will spend eternity apart from Him.

Is the fire of hell literal fire, or is this a metaphorical way of describing punishment?

Scholars are divided on this issue. Some believe the "fire" of hell is quite literal—and that may very well be the case. Others believe "fire" is a metaphorical way of expressing the great wrath of God. Scripture tells us: "The LORD your God is a consuming fire, a jealous God" (Deuteronomy 4:24). "God is a consuming fire" (Hebrews 12:29). "His wrath is poured out like fire" (Nahum 1:6). "Who can stand when he appears? For he will be like a refiner's fire." (Malachi 3:2). God said, "My wrath will break out and burn like fire because of the evil you have done—burn with no one to quench it" (Jeremiah 4:4). Whether the fire of hell is literal or metaphorical, it will entail horrible, horrible suffering for those who are there.

Are there degrees of punishment in hell?

Yes. The degree of punishment will be commensurate with one's sin against the light which one has received.

One good passage that indicates degrees of punishment is Luke 12:47,48: "That servant who knows his master's will and does not get ready or does not do what his master wants will be *beaten with many blows*. But the one who does not know and does things deserving punishment will be *beaten with few blows*. From everyone who has been given much, much will be demanded; and from the one who has been entrusted with much, much more will be asked" (emphasis added). Other verses on this issue include Matthew 10:15; 16:27; Revelation 20:12,13; 22:12.

Will the punishment of the wicked in hell be an eternal punishment, or is it just temporary?

Jesus affirmed that the wicked "will go away to *eternal* punishment, but the righteous to *eternal* life" (Matthew 25:46, emphasis added). Notice that the eternality of the punishment of the wicked equals the eternality of the eternal life of the righteous. One is just as long as the other.

This points to the "forever" nature of the punishment of the wicked. It never ceases.

The eternal nature of this punishment is emphasized all throughout Scripture. The fire of hell, for example, is called an "unquenchable fire" (Mark 9:43 NASB); the "smoke of their [sinners'] torment rises for ever and ever" (Revelation 14:11).

What is the "intermediate state" like for the unsaved? If they're not in hell yet, are they in a place of suffering?

At the moment of death unbelievers go as disembodied spirits to a temporary place of suffering (Luke 16:19-31). There they await their future resurrection and judgment (at the Great White Throne judgment), with an eventual destiny in the lake of fire.

The state of the ungodly dead in the intermediate state is described in 2 Peter 2:9: "The Lord knows how ... to hold the unrighteous for the day of judgment, while continuing their punishment." The word "hold" in this verse is a present tense, indicating that the wicked (nonbelievers) are held captive *continuously*. Peter is portraying them as condemned prisoners being closely guarded in a jail while awaiting future sentencing and final judgment.

While God holds them there, He is said to be "continuing their punishment." The word "continuing" in this verse is also a present tense, indicating the perpetual, ongoing nature of the punishment. But this punishment in the intermediate state is only temporary. As noted earlier, the wicked dead will eventually be resurrected and then judged at the Great White Throne judgment, after which time their *eternal* punishment will begin in the lake of fire (Revelation 20:11-15).

Will unbelievers be resurrected as believers will be?

Yes. Those who participate in the Great White Throne judgment (the unsaved) are resurrected *unto judgment*. Jesus Himself affirmed that "a time is coming when all who are in their graves will hear his voice and come out—those who have done good will rise to live, and those who have done evil will rise to be condemned" (John 5:28, 29).

The Scriptures indicate that there are two types of resurrection—respectively referred to as the "first resurrection" and the "second resurrection" (Revelation 20:5, 6, 11-15). The first resurrection is the resurrection of Christians, while the second resurrection is the resurrection of the wicked.

The "second" resurrection will be an awful spectacle. All the unsaved of all time will be resurrected at the end of Christ's millennial kingdom, judged at the Great White Throne judgment, and then cast alive into the lake of fire (Revelation 20:11-15). They will be given bodies that will last forever, but bodies that are sinful and subject to pain and suffering. Like the devil and his angels, they will exist forever in the lake of fire.

~

30

Erroneous Views of the Afterlife

What is annihilationism, and what do the Scriptures say about it?

The doctrine of annihilationism teaches that man was created immortal. But those who continue in sin and reject Christ are, by a positive act of God, deprived of the gift of immortality and are ultimately destroyed. Consciousness is snuffed out.

There are many passages that refute annihilationism. For illustration purposes, we will select only one primary passage—Matthew 25:46: "Then they will go away to eternal punishment, but the righteous to eternal life."

By no stretch of the imagination can the punishment spoken of in Matthew 25:46 be defined as a nonsuffering extinction of consciousness. Indeed, if actual suffering is lacking, then so is punishment. Punishment entails suffering. And suffering necessarily entails consciousness.

Certainly one can exist and not be punished; but no one can be punished and not exist. Annihilation means the obliteration of existence and anything that pertains to existence, such as punishment. Annihilation avoids punishment, rather than encountering it.

How do we know that the punishment referred to in Matthew 25:46 does not entail an extinction of consciousness and annihilation? There are many evidences. For example, consider the fact that there are no degrees of annihilation.

One is either annihilated or one is not. The Scriptures, by contrast, teach that there will be degrees of punishment in hell (Matthew 10:15; 11:21-24; 16:27; Luke 12:47,48; Hebrews 10:29; Revelation 20:11-15; 22:12).

Moreover, one cannot deny that for one who is suffering excruciating pain, the extinction of his or her consciousness would actually be a blessing—not a punishment (cf. Luke 23:30; Revelation 9:6). Any honest seeker after truth must admit that one cannot define "eternal punishment" as an extinction of consciousness. "It is an odd use of language to speak of an insensate (that is, unfeeling), inanimate object receiving punishment. To say, 'I punished my car for not starting by slowly plucking out its sparkplug wires, one by one,' would evoke laughter, not serious consideration."[1] We repeat, then, that punishment entails consciousness!

A critical point to make in regard to Matthew 25:46 is that this punishment is said to be eternal. There is no way that annihilationism or an extinction of consciousness can be forced into this passage. Indeed, the adjective *aionion* in this verse literally means "everlasting, without end." This same adjective is predicated of God (the "eternal" God) in Romans 16:26, Hebrews 9:14, 13:8, and Revelation 4:9. The punishment of the wicked is just as eternal as our eternal God.

Does consciousness vanish at the moment of death?

No. The Scriptures are clear that the souls of both believers and unbelievers are fully conscious between death and the future day of resurrection. Unbelievers are in conscious woe (see Luke 16:22,23; Mark 9:47,48; Revelation 19:20) and believers are in conscious bliss (Philippians 1:23).

Among the key theological factors that argue against "soul sleep" are: Lazarus, the rich man, and Abraham—both of whom had died—were all fully conscious and fully aware of all that was transpiring around them (Luke

16:19-31). Moses and Elijah (who had died long ago) were conscious on the Mount of Transfiguration (Matthew 17:3). Jesus promised that the repentant thief would be with Him (consciously) in paradise the very day he died (Luke 23:43). The "souls" of those martyred during the Tribulation period are portrayed as being conscious in heaven, talking to God (Revelation 6:9,10). Jesus, in speaking about the Old Testament saints Abraham, Isaac, and Jacob, said that God "is not the God of the dead, but *of the living*" (Luke 20:38). In effect, Jesus was saying, "Abraham, Isaac, and Jacob, though they died many years ago, are actually living today. For God, who calls Himself the God of Abraham, Isaac, and Jacob, is not the God of the dead but of the living."

Does the Bible teach the Roman Catholic doctrine of purgatory?

No. As a backdrop, the Roman Catholic church teaches that those who are perfect at death are admitted to heaven. Those who are not perfectly cleansed and are still tainted with the guilt of venial sins, however, do not go to heaven but rather go to purgatory where they allegedly go through a process of cleansing (or "purging"). Such souls are oppressed with a sense of deprivation and suffer certain pain. How long they stay in purgatory—and how much suffering they undergo while there—depends upon their particular state of sin.

Roman Catholics also teach that a person's time in purgatory may be shortened, and his pains alleviated, by the faithful prayers and good works of those still alive. The sacrifice of the Mass is viewed as especially important in this regard. Catholics find support for this doctrine in the apocryphal book 2 Maccabees 12:42-45.

That purgatory is a false doctrine is easy to prove from Scripture. When Jesus died on the cross, He said "It is finished" (John 19:30). Jesus completed the work of redemption at the cross. In His high priestly prayer to the Father, Jesus said, "I have brought you glory on earth by completing the work you gave me to do" (John 17:4). Hebrews 10:14 emphatically declares, "By one sacrifice he has made perfect forever those who are being made holy." Hence, those who believe in Christ are "made perfect" forever; no further "purging" is necessary. First John 1:7 says, "The blood of Jesus, his Son, purifies us from all sin." Romans 8:1 says, "Therefore, there is *now* no condemnation for those who are in Christ Jesus" (emphasis added).

What's wrong with believing in reincarnation?

There are many problems with the salvation-by-works doctrine of reincarnation. First, there are many practical problems. For example:

1. We must ask, why does one get punished for something he or she cannot remember having done in a previous life?

2. If the purpose of karma is to rid humanity of its selfish desires, then why hasn't there been a noticeable improvement in human nature after all the millennia of reincarnations?

3. If reincarnation and the law of karma are so beneficial on a practical level, then how do advocates of this doctrine explain the immense and ever-worsening social and economic problems—including widespread poverty, starvation, disease, and horrible suffering—in India, where reincarnation has been systematically taught throughout its history?

There are also many biblical problems with believing in reincarnation. For example, in 2 Corinthians 5:8 the apostle Paul states, "We are confident, I say, and would prefer to be away from the body and at home with the Lord." At death, then, the Christian immediately goes into the presence of the Lord, not into another body. In keeping with this, Luke

16:19-31 tells us that unbelievers at death go to a place of suffering, not into another body.

Further, Hebrews 9:27 assures us that "man is destined to die once, and after that to face judgment." Each human being *lives once* as a mortal on earth, *dies once*, and then *faces judgment*. He does not have a second chance by reincarnating into another body.

New Agers argue that Jesus taught reincarnation. How can we respond to this?

New Agers typically point to Matthew 11:14 and John 3:3 in arguing that Jesus taught reincarnation.[2] Let's take a brief look at both of these.

Matthew 11:14 says, "And if you are willing to accept it, he [John the Baptist] is the Elijah who was to come." It is claimed that John the Baptist is a reincarnation of Elijah. However, Luke 1:17 clarifies any possible confusion on the proper interpretation of this verse by pointing out that the ministry of John the Baptist was carried out "in the spirit and power of Elijah." Nowhere does it say that John the Baptist was a reincarnation of Elijah. New Agers conveniently forget that John the Baptist, when asked if he was Elijah, flatly answered, "No!" (John 1:21).

In John 3:3 Jesus said to Nicodemus, "I tell you the truth, no one can see the kingdom of God unless he is born again." New Agers argue that Jesus was referring to "cyclical rebirth" in this verse. However, the context clearly shows that Jesus was referring to a *spiritual rebirth* or regeneration. In fact, the phrase "born again" carries the idea of "born from above" and can even be translated that way. Nicodemus could not have understood Jesus' statement in any other way, for Jesus clarified His meaning by affirming that "flesh gives birth to flesh, but the Spirit gives birth to spirit" (verse 6).

Are the Jehovah's Witnesses right in saying that some of the saved will live forever on a paradise earth and not in heaven with God?[3]

No. This is based on a misinterpretation of a number of key passages from Scripture. Let's take a brief look at a representative example—Psalm 37:9,11,29: "For evildoers shall be cut off: but those that wait upon the LORD, they shall inherit the earth.... But the meek shall inherit the earth.... The righteous shall inherit the land, and dwell therein for ever" (KJV).

A look at the context of Psalm 37 makes it clear that the Psalm is not referring to a distant future time when God will remove all wicked people and allow good people to live on a paradise earth. Rather, the psalmist was speaking of something that people in his own lifetime (and the following generations) would experience. Evil people *in his time* would be cut off; righteous people *in his time* would experience blessing in the promised land.

It is critical to recognize that the Hebrew word for "earth" in this context has reference to *land*—more specifically, the land of Judea, given by God Himself as an inheritance to their fathers and their posterity forever. When the Israelites arrived at the promised land, Moses reminded them that it would be theirs only because the Lord drove out the other nations to "give you their *land* for an inheritance" (Deuteronomy 4:38 NASB).

What, then, does verse 29 mean when it says that "the righteous will inherit the land and dwell in it *for ever*"? The Hebrew word for "forever" often denotes the *unforeseeable future* in the Old Testament.[4] Hence, the phrase "dwell in it *forever*" simply means "dwell in it from the present through the unforeseeable future." The phrase is a Hebraistic way of saying that the *then-living* Israelites would dwell in the promised land their entire lives *as would their children and their children's children* and so forth. From one generation to the next, the righteous would experience blessing in the promised land into the unforeseeable future. This is in noted contrast to the wicked; for, as the previous verse points out, "the descendants of the wicked will be cut off" (verse 28b NASB).

31

~

Near-Death Experiences

What kinds of things happen in so-called near-death experiences?

Based on thousands of interviews with people who have gone through *alleged* near-death experiences, researchers say there are 15 characteristics that commonly occur in a near-death experience:*

(1) *Ineffability*. Most people say that no words can describe the near-death experience. What they went through is said to be inexpressible. Human language is insufficient to depict what occurred.

(2) *Hearing the news*. Individuals typically say they heard themselves pronounced dead by medical personnel. To the doctors and nurses present, death seemed real because the heart and breathing had stopped, and the person appeared to be physiologically dead. But the individual nevertheless claims to have heard him- or herself pronounced dead.

(3) *Feelings of peace and quiet*. Most people who have had a near-death experience say they had sensations of extreme pleasure, peace, and quiet. It is these feelings that often

---

* My listing of these characteristics should not be interpreted to imply my agreement with what is described. I'll evaluate the near-death experience from a Christian perspective later in the chapter.

motivate the individual to want to stay "dead" and not return to earthly life.

(4) *The noise.* During a near-death experience people often hear a noise. Sometimes the noise is pleasant, like rapturous music. In other (most) cases, the noise is harsh and disturbing, like a continuous buzzing or ringing sound.

(5) *The dark tunnel.* A very common characteristic of the near-death experience is that people feel they are being pulled through a dark passageway or tunnel, often while hearing the noise described above.

(6) *Out of the body.* People typically say that they depart from their physical bodies and observe themselves lying on the operating table, while doctors and nurses attempt resuscitation or pronounce death.

(7) *Meeting others.* It is often claimed that there are spiritual entities present to help the newly dead person through the experience. Sometimes these spiritual entities are loved ones who have already passed away.

(8) *The being of light.* One of the most common characteristics of the near-death experience is encountering a being of light. Even though the light emanating from this being is brilliant, it does not hurt the eyes. This being also seems to emanate love and warmth. He communicates not with words but through thoughts. Often the communications deal with the meaning of life.

(9) *The review.* Sometimes individuals in a near-death experience come upon an instant moment in which they witness a vivid review of their entire life. This life-review is said to provoke in them a recognition of the importance of loving other people. The review ends up helping them to understand the true meaning of life.

(10) *The border or limit.* Individuals in a near-death experience often come upon an obstruction that prevents them from going any further in their journey or actually reaching the being of light. Sometimes this border is described as a fence, a door, or a body of water.

(11) *Coming back.* Because of the incredible feelings of peace and tranquility, and because of the love and warmth emanating from the being of light, many individuals in a near-death experience want to stay in the presence of the being of light and not come back. They nevertheless return because they are told they haven't finished their tasks on earth. Other people say they felt obliged to return (without being asked) to complete unfinished tasks on earth. The "return trip" is said to be instantaneous, back through the dark tunnel.

(12) *Telling others.* Most people who go through this experience say they are reticent about disclosing the experience to others. They feel their experience is inexpressible. Moreover, they feel others would be skeptical upon hearing of their experience. Hence, most people choose to remain quiet about what happened.

(13) *Effects on lives.* It is claimed by many researchers that people who go through a near-death experience typically end up having a more loving attitude toward other people. They also have a greater zeal for living. They typically feel they have a greater understanding of the meaning of life.

(14) *New views of death.* Most people who go through a near-death experience say they no longer fear death. But neither do they seek it. They typically come to view death as a simple transition to another form of life. They do not fear any judgment or punishment in the next life.

(15) *Corroboration.* A final characteristic of the near-death experience is that the individual is later able to corroborate specific events (for example, in the hospital operating room) that would have been impossible for him to know about unless he had been consciously observing things.[1]

Now, I need to make very clear that not every person who has gone through a near-death experience reports *all* the characteristics listed above. In fact, most people experience just *some* of these characteristics. No two stories are identical. How many elements a person experiences seems to relate to how deep and how long he or she was apparently "dead."[2] It should also be noted that there are often variations in the order in which the above characteristics are experienced.

How can near-death experiences (NDEs) be explained?

Researchers have suggested a variety of explanations for near-death experiences. Space forbids a detailed treatment of this. But the more popular theories follow:

(1) Some say these experiences can be explained as a result of a lack of oxygen to the brain. This is known as *hypoxia*. It is argued that this lack of oxygen to the brain accounts for sensations like going through a tunnel and seeing a bright light. The problem with this view, however, is that people who have gone through near-death experiences have not been found (in medical tests) to have less oxygen in their blood gases than other people.

(2) Some have suggested that going through a dark tunnel and then seeing a bright light are actually deeply embedded memories of the birth experience. The late astronomer and scientist Carl Sagan held to this view.[3] Critics respond by saying that a memory of birth would be traumatic, not pleasant (like a near-death experience). Further, in the birth experience the baby's face is pressed against the birth canal, conflicting with the rapid transit of going through a dark tunnel. As well, it is argued that the baby's brain is not developed enough to retain such memories.

(3) Other suggested explanations include trauma or injury to the brain, severe psychological stress that may cause the release of chemicals in the brain that could induce certain experiences, or perhaps hallucinations caused by various medications.

Such alternative theories, however, do not really explain the various details of the typical near-death experience. For example, these theories cannot explain how people who were brain dead at the time are later able to describe in vivid detail the attempts of medical personnel to resuscitate them. Could it be that many of these experiences are actually caused by the evil one—Satan, the father of lies, who has the ability to perform counterfeit miracles (2 Thessalonians 2:9)?

Many researchers have noted a clear connection between near-death experiences and occultism. "In large measure the NDE [near-death experience] is merely one form of the occult out-of-body experience (OBE)."[4] As well, "both the NDE and OBE have many other similarities including . . spiritistic contacts, world view changes, and development of psychic powers."[5]

What kinds of psychic powers are we talking about? Some people experience astral travel or out-of-body experiences (that is, the soul leaves the body and travels around the so-called astral realm). Some people develop clairvoyance (the ability to perceive things that are outside the natural range of human senses). Some people develop telepathic abilities (that is, abilities to mystically communicate via thoughts alone). And many people come into contact with spirit guides, who allegedly stay with the person for the rest of his or her life.

Now, here's an important point: Occultism and psychic phenomena are utterly condemned by God in Scripture. Anyone doubting this should meditate on Deuteronomy 18:10-13. In view of this, it is clear that much of what is going on in regard to so-called near-death experiences is in fact not of God. *Reader beware!*

Who is the "being of light" often encountered in so-called near-death experiences? Is it Jesus Christ?

It has been claimed by numerous (not all) individuals who have had near-death experiences that the being of light they encountered was none other than Jesus Christ. As appealing as the idea may initially sound, this identification (at least in *most* cases) seems to be flawed in view of the fact that the so-called being of light typically says and does things contrary to the Christ of the Bible. Since Jesus is the same yesterday, today, and forever (Hebrews 13:8), it would be impossible that these are one and the same Jesus. I believe that many of the individuals who go through near-death experiences actually encounter a *counterfeit* Christ.

The "Jesus" (being of light) typically encountered in near-death experiences teaches such things as:

- ✓ Death is good and is not to be feared.

- ✓ Sin is not a problem. In fact, "Jesus" often responds to human sin and shortcomings with humor.

- ✓ There is no hell to worry about.

- ✓ All people are welcome in heaven, regardless of whether one has placed faith in Christ.

- ✓ All religions are equally valid.

In view of the fact that these ideas clearly go against what the biblical Jesus taught, I think we have good reason to conclude that this "Jesus" is in fact a *lying spirit* (see John 8:44). We must remember that Satan has the ability to appear as an "angel of light" and as a "servant of righteousness" (2 Corinthians 11:14,15). His goal, of course, is to lead people astray. He is happy to mimic a being of light if the end result is that he can lead people away from the true Christ of Scripture.

Is there such a thing as a hellish near-death experience (NDE)?

Yes. Dr. Charles Garfield, who has done extensive research on NDEs, said that "not everyone dies a blissful, accepting death.... Almost as many of the dying patients I interviewed reported negative visions (encounters with demonic figures and so forth) as reported blissful experiences, while some reported both."[6]

Dr. Maurice Rawlings wrote a book entitled *Beyond Death's Door* in which he documented hellish NDEs. He said that about half the NDEs he has researched were hellish in nature. But most people who experience such hellish NDEs end up repressing the memory because it is so awful and traumatic.

Dr. Rawlings (who was not a committed Christian) was once testing a patient on a treadmill when he went into cardiac arrest. Rawlings and his nurse immediately sought to revive the man by massaging his heart and doing CPR. The patient passed in and out of consciousness. Each time he revived, he screamed, "I am in hell!" He pleaded with Rawlings not to let him slip back into unconsciousness.[7]

The patient lapsed into unconsciousness again. When he revived, he said, "Don't you understand? I am in hell. Each time you quit [the CPR] I go back to hell! Don't let me go back to hell!" The man asked how to stay out of hell. Rawlings told the man what he remembered from Sunday school, and led the man in a simple prayer. The man's condition stabilized, and he was taken to a hospital.[8]

A few days later, Rawlings questioned the man about his experience and found that he had forgotten it! Rawlings thinks the experience was so unnerving to him that he repressed it. Even so, the man became a committed Christian and a regular churchgoer after his experience of hell.[9]

Whatever we are to make of such experiences, it is clear from the above account (and others like it) that hellish near-death experiences call into question the claim by many that the afterlife experienced by those who die is *always* positive, tranquil, and peaceful. Not everyone has an experience of being "unconditionally accepted" by a loving being of light.

PART 9

~

APOLOGETIC ISSUES

Apologetics and the Christian
Danger Zone Issues
Confronting Cultic Errors
The New Age Movement
The Word-Faith Movement

~

32

Apologetics and the Christian

Should every Christian be involved in the work of apologetics?

Yes. It is truly unfortunate that many Christians today seem to be secret-agent Christians who have never "blown their cover" before an unregenerate world. The fact is, many Christians have little or no impact on their world for Christ or for Christian values.

The task of apologetics begins with a single person— *you*. A great thinker once said, "Let him that would move the world, first move himself."

"Apologetics" comes from the Greek word *apologia*, which means "defense." Apologetics focuses on the defense of Christianity. There are many benefits of apologetics:

✓ Apologetics provides well-reasoned evidences to the nonbeliever as to why he ought to choose Christianity rather than any other religion.

✓ Apologetics can be used to show the unbeliever that all the other options in the "smorgasbord" of world religions are not really options at all, since they are false.

✓ Apologetics can remove the mental roadblocks that prevent nonbelievers from responding to the gospel.

✓ Apologetics provides not only a defense for the faith, it provides security to Christians who need to be sure that their faith is not a blind leap into a dark chasm, but rather faith founded on fact.

✓ Apologetics demonstrates *why* we believe *what* we believe.

✓ Apologetics does not replace our faith, it grounds our faith.

No wonder God calls each of us to "contend earnestly for the faith which was once for all delivered to the saints" (Jude 3 NASB). As Christians, we are called to contend for the faith by "telling it like it is." Look at it this way: Would we have had a Reformation if Martin Luther hadn't told it like it was to the Roman Catholic church? No, we wouldn't. Luther saw a deviation from "the faith" and he accordingly contended for the faith. We must follow Luther's example.

You and I are called by God to be prepared to give answers. First Peter 3:15 says: "Always be prepared to give an answer to everyone who asks you to give the reason for the hope that you have. But do this with gentleness and respect." The only way to be always prepared to give an answer to everyone is to become equipped with apologetic answers.

Why is the relativistic view of truth wrong?

First, Christianity rests on a foundation of *absolute* truth (1 Kings 17:24; Psalm 25:5; 43:3; 119:30; John 1:17; 8:44; 14:17; 17:17; 2 Corinthians 6:7; Ephesians 4:15; 6:14; 2 Timothy 2:15; 1 John 3:19; 3 John 4, 8).

Second, one must realize that if all truth is relative, then one person's "truth" is just as good as another person's "truth." This ultimately means that any religion's "truth" is as good as Christianity's truth. In moral relativism, there is no way to tell which way is north and which way is south when it comes to right and wrong. As people accelerate down the road where moral relativity takes them, there is no absolute truth, no center stripe down the highway of life. There are many casualties along this highway.

Third, the view that all truth is relative is not logically satisfying. One might understand the statement "all truth is relative" to mean that it is an absolute truth that all truth is relative. Of course, such a statement is self-defeating (since there are supposedly no absolute truths) and is therefore false. Also, one could understand this as saying that it is a relative truth that all truth is relative. But such a statement is ultimately meaningless. No matter how you understand this statement—whether you say it is an *absolute* truth that all truth is relative, or whether you say it is a *relative* truth that all truth is relative—it should be rejected.

As Christians, we believe that absolute morals are grounded in the absolutely moral God of the Bible. Scripture tells us: "Be perfect, therefore, as your heavenly Father is perfect" (Matthew 5:48). Moral law flows from the moral Lawgiver of the universe. God stands against the moral relativist whose behavior is based on "whatever is right in his own eyes" (Deuteronomy 12:8; Judges 17:6; 21:25; Proverbs 21:2 NASB).

Do all religions ultimately teach the same truth?

No. There are many differences in doctrine in each religion that make this view impossible. Consider the doctrine of God—the most fundamental doctrine of any religion.

Jesus taught that there is one and only one personal God who is triune in nature (Mark 12:29; John 4:24; 5:18,19). Muhammad taught that there is only one God, but that God cannot have a son. Confucius was polytheistic (he believed in many gods). Krishna believed in a combination of polytheism (belief in many gods) and pantheism (the belief that all is God). Zoroaster believed in religious dualism—that is, he believed there is both a good god and a bad god.[1]

How can it be said that these religions are teaching the same basic truth when their respective leaders set forth such utterly contradictory and diametrically opposing concepts of God?

Jesus was very exclusivistic in His truth claims, indicating that what He said took precedence over all others. Jesus said He is uniquely and exclusively man's only means of coming into a relationship with God: "I am the way, the truth, and the life; no one comes to the Father, but through Me" (John 14:6 NASB). Jesus' exclusivity caused Him to warn: "Watch out that no one deceives you. For many will come in my name, claiming, 'I am the Christ,' and will deceive many" (Matthew 24:4,5,23).

How can we respond to critics who argue that the miracles recorded in the Bible are the fantasies of ignorant people in biblical times who did not understand the laws of nature?

Such a claim is preposterous. People in biblical times *did* know enough of the laws of nature to recognize bona fide miracles. As C. S. Lewis put it,

> When St. Joseph discovered that his bride was pregnant, he was "minded to put her away." He knew enough biology for that. Otherwise, of course, he would not have regarded pregnancy as a proof of infidelity. When he accepted the Christian explanation, he regarded it as a miracle precisely because he knew enough of the laws of nature to know that this was a suspension of them.[2]

Moreover, Lewis observed,

> When the disciples saw Christ walking on the water they were frightened: they would not have

been frightened unless they had known the laws of
nature and known that this was an exception. If a
man had no conception of a regular order in nature,
then of course he could not notice departures from
that order.[3]

Nothing can be viewed as "abnormal" until one has
first grasped the "norm."

Are there arguments for God's existence, apart from the Bible, that are rooted in God's creation?

Yes, though theologians disagree as to how convincing
these arguments are to unbelievers. Here are the main arguments in a nutshell:

1. *Cosmological Argument.* This argument says that every
effect must have an adequate cause. The universe is an
"effect." Reason demands that whatever caused the universe must be greater than the universe. That cause is God
(who Himself is the uncaused First Cause). As Hebrews 3:4
puts it, "Every house is built by someone, but God is the
builder of everything."

2. *Teleological Argument.* This argument says that there is
an obvious purposeful and intricate design of the world. If
we found a watch in the sand, the assumption would have
to be that someone created the watch because, with its intricate design, it is obvious that all the parts of the watch
couldn't have just jumped together to cause itself. Similarly,
the perfect design of the universe argues for a Designer, and
that Designer is God.

3. *Ontological Argument.* This argument says that most
human beings have an innate idea of a most perfect being.
Where did this idea come from? Not from man, for man is
an imperfect being. Some perfect being (God) must have
planted the idea there. God can't be conceived of as not
existing, for then, one could conceive of an even greater
being that did exist. Thus God must in fact exist.

4. *Moral Argument.* This argument says that every human being has an innate sense of oughtness or moral obligation. Where did this sense of oughtness come from? It must come from God. The existence of a moral law in our hearts demands the existence of a moral Lawgiver (see Romans 1:19-32).

5. *Anthropological Argument.* This argument says that man has a personality (mind, emotions, and will). Since the personal can't come from the impersonal, there must be a personal cause—and that personal cause is God (see Genesis 1:26, 27).

Perhaps Reformer John Calvin's view of these arguments was the best. He said that the unregenerate person sees these evidences for God in the universe with blurred vision. It is only when one puts on the "eyeglasses" of faith and belief in the Bible that these evidences for God's existence come into clear focus.

What can we say to the atheist who flatly asserts that there is no God?

Well, besides taking every opportunity to patiently share the good news of the gospel, you can raise the issue as to how he or she *knows* there is no God. As many apologists have pointed out through the years, one would have to be omniscient (all-knowing) to be able to say from his or her own pool of knowledge that there is no God. The point you want to make is that he or she really doesn't *know* that there is no God. He or she is just *saying* there is no God.

It is helpful to keep in mind that some atheists deny the existence of God because there is some kind of a moral problem in their lives (Psalm 53:1). The twisted logic is that if there is no God, then there is no moral Lawgiver to whom one must answer, and hence one can act as immoral as one wants. But if there is a moral Lawgiver, then one is responsible to obey Him. And hence the immoral things one has done will one day have to be answered for. If you've ever wondered why some atheists respond negatively with such intense emotion when you tell them there is a God, this may be one reason for it.

Atheists often argue their position by saying that the massive amount of evil in the world proves there is no God. *See below.*

Does the fact that there is so much evil in the world prove there is no God?

No. This is a claim that atheists often bring up. The fact is, we wouldn't really know that evil exists in the world unless we had a barometer like the Word of God to show us what is evil. Without an infinite reference point that reveals what is evil, we really have no criteria against which we can judge some things evil and other things good. It would be like trying to determine which direction is north while in a boat without a compass on a cloudy night. With no reference point (like a star or a compass), you can't tell north from south. Without the reference point of God and His Word, you can't tell north from south in terms of what is evil and what is not.

Of course, the Scriptures reveal that God has allowed evil for a purpose. God could have created a bunch of robots that had no choice as to whether or not they obeyed God. But instead God created human beings with free wills—that is, with the ability to choose *for* or *against* God, and with the ability to choose evil or good. Adam and Eve chose evil when they ate the forbidden fruit. And ever since then human beings have continued to use their free wills to make sinful choices. That's why evil exists.

God will one day deal with evil. A day of judgment is approaching when God will right every wrong. Christ will return, strip power away from the wicked, and hold all men and women accountable for the things they did during their time on earth. Justice will ultimately prevail. Those who enter eternity without having trusted in Christ for salvation will understand just how effectively God has dealt with the problem of evil.

33

~

Danger Zone Issues

Is it okay for Christians to get hypnotized?

I wouldn't advise it. When a person is hypnotized, he goes into what is called an "altered state of consciousness." During such a mystical state, when the rational mind recedes, it is possible for demonic powers to afflict the Christian in some way. The Christian may end up compromising his faith.

Besides, the founder of hypnotism, Franz Anton Mesmer, bought into many unbiblical ideas. He taught that health and illness are determined by the flow of "universal fluids" or "heavenly tides" in the body. When these properties are out of balance, a person allegedly becomes sick. By readjusting these properties, he said, one returns to health.[1] Such an idea fits right in with current New Age medicine. *Christians beware!*

What's wrong with "positive thinking" or "possibility thinking"?

Those who subscribe to the "positive thinking" teachings have redefined many key biblical concepts. For example, sin is viewed as any act or thought that robs people of their self-esteem. The core of sin is viewed as a lack of self-esteem. Being "born again" is viewed as a transformation from a negative to a positive self-image. The way of the cross is viewed as pursuing possibility thinking. Unbelief is redefined to mean a deep sense of unworthiness. Hell is redefined to mean the loss of pride that leads to a sense of separation from God. The person "in hell" is one who has lost self-esteem. Obviously, this is not just a distortion of biblical Christianity; it bears no resemblance to it!

Is the phenomenon known as "holy laughter" biblical?

I don't believe it is. I say this for a number of reasons.

First, the Bible admonishes us to test all things against Scripture (1 Thessalonians 5:21; Acts 17:11). I don't see anything that even remotely resembles holy laughter in Scripture.

Second, one fruit of the Holy Spirit is self-control (Galatians 5:23). In the holy laughter phenomenon, people laugh uncontrollably, even when there is nothing funny to laugh about.

Third, I've heard of people laughing at meetings even when the preaching was on hell. But Scripture tells us that God takes no joy at the perishing of the wicked (Ezekiel 18:23, 32). Hence, it would be absurd to say that God was inspiring such laughter in this context.

Fourth, in 1 Corinthians 14:33 the apostle Paul speaks of the need for order in the church. In outbreaks of holy laughter all order is lost in the church. Paul flatly states, "Everything should be done in a fitting and orderly way" (1 Corinthians 14:40).

Fifth, I don't know of a single verse in the Bible that says that when the Holy Spirit comes upon a person, he breaks out into uncontrollable laughter. There are good passages on joy in the Bible (like Psalm 126), but holy laughter advocates who cite such "joy" passages in support of this phenomenon are reading something into the text that simply is not there.

Sixth, during the ministry of our Lord Jesus (who had the Holy Spirit without measure), there is not a single recorded instance of people breaking out into uncontrolled laughter. Neither was there any laughter when the apostle Paul or the apostle Peter ministered in the Book of Acts.

Is it okay for a Christian to become a Mason?

Absolutely not! Masons teach that the Bible is one of many holy books. They teach that Jesus is just one of many ways to the Supreme Being or the "Great Architect of the Universe" (compare with John 14:6; Acts 4:12; 1 Timothy 2:5). They teach that God is known by many names—including Jehovah, Krishna, Buddha, and Allah. Masonry teaches a works-oriented system of salvation, which is a direct contradiction of Scripture (Ephesians 2:8,9). They seek to develop a worldwide religious brotherhood that transcends the sectarian religious beliefs of human beings. They require every member to take oaths that no Christian in good conscience should ever take (such as admitting that they are in spiritual darkness and have come to the Masonic Lodge for light). Further, some rituals in the Masonic Lodge are directly rooted in occultism, pagan religion, and the mystery religions.[2] These and many other factors serve to prohibit the Christian from participating in Masonry.

What do you think about the appearances of the Virgin Mary in such places as Fatima, Lourdes, Guadalupe, and Medjugorje?

I do not believe these were genuine appearances of the Virgin Mary. I say this not because I have anything against Mary (I don't—for she is truly blessed among women, Luke 1:28). I say this because of the scriptural teaching that contact with the dead *in any form* is forbidden by God (Deuteronomy 18:11). We should not expect that God would allow

Mary to do something that He has explicitly forbidden. From a scriptural perspective, we will be reunited with the dead *only* at the second coming of Christ (see 1 Thessalonians 4:13-17), and not before.

Some reputable evangelical scholars who have studied the issue have suggested that people who claim they've seen Mary may have actually encountered a demonic impersonation of Mary.[3] Certainly the powers of darkness are capable of such deceptive acts (see 2 Corinthians 11:14,15). The goal, of course, it to distract people away from the Christ of Scripture.

Was Nostradamus a Christian prophet?

By no means! Nostradamus was a sixteenth-century French astrologer and physician. If anything, he was an occultic prophet, not a biblical prophet. He relied quite heavily on horoscopes and other occult methods of divination.[4] His brand of prophecy thus stands condemned by Scripture (Deuteronomy 18:9-14).

Many of Nostradamus's predictions are esoteric, vague, and open-ended. This is why his predictions have been interpreted in so many different ways by Nostradamus enthusiasts. This is unlike the biblical prophecies, which are much more straightforward and precise. (Micah 5:2, for example, predicted the Messiah would be born *in Bethlehem*. Isaiah 7:14 predicted He would be born *of a virgin*.)

How do we account for the *appearance* of Nostradamus having predicted certain events accurately? There are a number of possible explanations. It may be that Satan inspired these predictions, and even though Satan is not omniscient (all-knowing) like God is, he is a good guesser. Or, it may be that Satan inspired Nostradamus to utter a prophecy and then Satan worked in the world in such a way to bring about some semblance of a fulfillment, thereby lending credence to Nostradamus as a "prophet." Perhaps

Satan's goal was to use Nostradamus as a means of drawing other people into occultism. Clearly, though, he was not a biblical prophet.

UNDERSTANDING UFOS

Is it possible that there is life on other planets?

Though I can't be dogmatic about this, it seems to me that there are several good reasons that point to the likelihood of there being no intelligent life on other planets.

First, though atheistic scientists would scoff at this, Scripture points to the centrality of planet earth and gives us no hint that life exists elsewhere. Relatively speaking, the earth is but an astronomical atom among the whirling constellations, only a tiny speck of dust among the ocean of stars and planets in the universe. To the naturalistic astronomer, the earth is but one of many planets in our small solar system, all of which are in orbit around the sun. But earth is nevertheless the center of God's work of salvation in the universe. On it the Highest presents Himself in solemn covenants and divine appearances; on it the Son of God became man; on it stood the cross of the Redeemer of the world; and on it—though indeed on the new earth, yet still on the earth—will be at last the throne of God and the Lamb (Revelation 21:1, 2; 22:3).

The centrality of the earth is also evident in the creation account, for God created the earth before He created the rest of the planets and stars. One possible reason for this is that in this way God has emphasized the supreme importance of the earth among all astronomical bodies in the universe. Despite its comparative smallness of size, even among the nine planets, to say nothing of the stars themselves, it is nonetheless absolutely unique in God's eternal purposes.

One might ask why God would create such a vast universe of stars and galaxies if He did not intend to populate them. Psalm 19:1 gives us the answer: "The heavens declare the glory of God; the skies proclaim the work of his hands." The sheer vastness of the physical universe points us to the greater vastness and infinity of God Himself.

Related to the issue of possible life on other planets is the question of how unfallen beings (assuming the "aliens" are unfallen) could share the same universe with fallen ones (humans). The effects of Adam's sin seem to pervade the entire universe (Romans 8:19-22). (The second law of thermodynamics—which says that all things tend toward disorganization and death—may be considered the scientific description of the curse God pronounced on creation in Genesis 3:14-19.) It does not seem likely that God would allow the effects of sin to impact a world of unfallen creatures (Revelation 21:4).[5]

In view of these and other factors, it seems to me that from a theological perspective it is improbable that there is intelligent life on other planets in the universe.

Does Ezekiel 1 make reference to a UFO landing?

No. This is not a reference to a UFO but is rather a vision of the glory of God. This is evident for several reasons. First, the text states clearly that "this was the appearance of the likeness of the glory of the LORD" (Ezekiel 1:28). Moreover, it is called "visions" in the very first verse. Visions are usually couched in highly symbolic form (cf. Revelation 1:9-20). Hence, the "likeness" (verse 28) given of things should not be taken literally but symbolically.

It is clear from the context that the "living creatures" were angels, since they had "wings" (Ezekiel 1:6) and flew in the midst of heaven (cf. Ezekiel 10). They compare to the angels mentioned in Isaiah 6:2 and especially the "living creatures" (angels) which are described as being around God's throne (Revelation 4:6).

The message from these beings was from the "Sovereign LORD" of Israel to the prophet Ezekiel (cf. 2:1-4), not one from some alleged UFO beings. The context was a message from the God of Israel through the Jewish prophet Ezekiel to His "rebellious nation" (2:3, 4; cf. 3:4).

Is it true that many alleged UFO abductees have been or are presently involved in the occult?

Yes. Christian UFO researchers have noted that individuals who claim to be contacted by (or become abducted by) UFOs often have a strong prior involvement in some form of occultism. Brooks Alexander of the Spiritual Counterfeits Project said that "many of the reported cases show some kind of occult involvement prior to initial UFO contact."[6] John Weldon likewise notes that "UFO contactees often have a history of psychic abilities or an interest in the occult."[7]

Christian UFO investigator David Wimbish has suggested that interest in UFOs can actually draw one into the occult: "Many UFO investigators have followed a path that has taken them directly into the world of the occult. They believe they are rediscovering ancient spiritual truths and uncovering new realities about the universe. It's more likely that they are getting involved with some ancient deceptions."[8] Indeed, the UFO phenomenon "has led many to experiment with astral projection, to believe in reincarnation, and to get involved in other practices that directly oppose the historic teachings of the Christian church."[9]

Is it possible that UFO citings are actually demonically caused?

Yes. But let me qualify what I mean. Many UFO sightings have a *natural* explanation. Some sightings may even involve deliberate hoaxes. Hence, I don't want to imply that every time someone sees an unidentified flying object that

Satan is at work. However, I think a case can be made that those UFOs that remain truly unidentifiable—and especially those that make "contact," or communicate messages to human beings—are rooted in the work of Satan.

First, the messages communicated by the alleged extraterrestrials consistently go against biblical Christianity.

> The visitors are perfectly in tune with what has become known as "New Age" religion—Eastern mysticism, astral projection, the harmonic convergence, and so on. They are not at all in harmony, though, with Jesus Christ, who said, "I am the way, the truth, and the life." At the very least, they are more interested in steering us away from the truth of the Bible than toward it."[10]

Experts who have long investigated UFOs—both Christian and non-Christian—have noted the strong similarity between the UFO experience and typical manifestations of demonism. John Keel, a respected authority on UFOs, said: "The UFO manifestations seem to be, by and large, merely minor variations of the age-old demonological phenomenon," and "the manifestations and occurrences described in [the literature of demonology] are similar, if not entirely identical, to the UFO phenomenon itself. Victims of [demon] possession suffer the very same medical and emotional symptoms as the UFO contactees."[11]

In support of the idea that UFOs may in fact be manifestations of Satan or demons is the belief by some individuals that the UFOs themselves are alive. Brad Steiger, for example, said: "I have even come to suspect that in some instances, what we have been calling 'spaceships' may actually be a form of higher intelligence rather than vehicles transporting occupants."[12] Likewise, John Keel noted that "over and over again, witnesses have told me in hushed tones, 'You know, I don't think that thing I saw was mechanical at all. I got the distinct impression that it was alive.'"[13]

Jesus clearly warned about religious deception in the last days: "At that time many will turn away from the faith and will betray and hate each other, and many false prophets will appear and deceive many people" (Matthew 24:10,11). Earlier, Jesus warned His followers to "watch out for false prophets. They come to you in sheep's clothing, but inwardly they are ferocious wolves" (Matthew 7:15). Could it be that the so-called extraterrestrials seek to appear as benevolent "brothers," but in fact are ferocious demonic wolves who seek to lead us astray?

The apostle Paul sternly warned: "Satan himself masquerades as an angel of light. It is not surprising, then, if his servants masquerade as servants of righteousness" (2 Corinthians 11:14,15). Appearances can be deceiving. This is why we need to anchor ourselves in the absolute Word of God.

~

Confronting Cultic Errors

What is a cult?

The term "cult" is not intended as a pejorative, inflammatory, or injurious word. The term is used simply as a means of categorizing certain religious or semireligious groups in modern America.

A cult may be defined from both a sociological and a theological perspective. Sociologically speaking, a cult is a religious or semireligious sect or group whose members are controlled or dominated almost entirely by a single individual or organization. A sociological definition of a cult generally includes (but is not limited to) the authoritarian, manipulative, and sometimes communal features of cults. Cults that fall into this category include the Hare Krishnas, The Children of God, and the Unification Church.

Theologically speaking, a cult is a religious group that claims to be Christian but in fact is not Christian because it denies one or more of the essential doctrines of historic, orthodox Christianity (as defined in the major historic creeds of Christianity). Groups that fall into this category include the Mormons and the Jehovah's Witnesses.

What are some specific doctrinal characteristics of the cults?

In terms of doctrinal characteristics of cults, one will typically find an emphasis on new revelation from God, a denial of the sole authority of the Bible, a distorted view of God and Jesus, and/or a denial of salvation by grace.

New revelation. Many cult leaders claim to have a direct pipeline to God. The teachings of the cult often change and hence, they need new "revelations" to justify such changes. Mormons, for example, once excluded African-Americans from the priesthood. When social pressure was exerted against the Mormon church for this blatant form of racism, the Mormon president received a new "revelation" reversing the previous decree.[1]

Denial of the sole authority of the Bible. Many cults deny the sole authority of the Bible. Christian Scientists, for example, elevate Mary Baker Eddy's book *Science and Health* to supreme authority. Members of the Unification Church elevate Reverend Moon's *Divine Principle* to supreme authority.[2]

A distorted view of God and Jesus. Many cults set forth a distorted view of God and Jesus. The Jehovah's Witnesses deny both the Trinity and the absolute deity of Christ, saying that Christ is a lesser god than the Father (who is God Almighty). The Mormons say Jesus is the spirit-brother of Lucifer. The Baha'is say Jesus was just one of many prophets of God. The Jesus of the spiritists is just an advanced medium.[3]

Denial of salvation by grace. Cults typically deny salvation by grace, thus distorting the purity of the gospel. The Mormons, for example, emphasize the necessity of becoming more and more perfect in this life. The Jehovah's Witnesses emphasize the importance of distributing Watchtower literature door-to-door as a part of "working out" their salvation.

What are some specific sociological characteristics of the cults?

Sociological characteristics of cults include such things

as authoritarianism, exclusivism, dogmatism, isolationism, and threats of satanic attack.

Authoritarianism. Authoritarianism involves the acceptance of an authority figure who often uses mind-control techniques on group members. As prophet and/or founder, this leader's word is considered ultimate and final. The late David Koresh of the Branch Davidian cult in Waco, Texas, is a tragic example. Members of this cult followed Koresh to the point of death.

Exclusivism. Cults often believe, "We alone have the truth." The Mormons believe they are the exclusive community of the saved on earth. The Jehovah's Witnesses believe *they* are the exclusive community of Jehovah on earth.[4]

Extreme dogmatism. Closely related to the above, many cults are extremely dogmatic—and this dogmatism is often expressed institutionally. For example, the Mormons claim to be the only true church on earth. The Jehovah's Witnesses claim that the Watchtower Society is the sole voice of Jehovah on earth.[5]

Isolationism. The more extreme cults sometimes create fortified boundaries, often precipitating tragic endings, such as the disaster in Waco, Texas, with the Branch Davidian cult.

Threats of satanic attack. The Watchtower Society is typical of many cults in that it warns new followers that friends and relatives may very well be used by Satan to try to dissuade them from remaining with the Jehovah's Witnesses.[6] Hence, when a friend or relative *actually does* try to dissuade a new member in this way, it makes the Watchtower Society appear to be a true prophet. This, in turn, encourages the new convert to be even more loyal to the Watchtower Society. The Watchtower's warning hence serves as an effective way of keeping new converts so they can be thoroughly indoctrinated into the cult.

Are sincere cultists lost?

Yes, they are. A person can sincerely take a pill that is unknowingly laced with cyanide. All the sincerity in the world is not going to stop that cyanide from killing the person. In the same way, a person can participate in a cult that, unknown to him, teaches all kinds of deadly doctrines. And all the sincerity in the world won't prevent him from going into eternity without Christ. Sincere cultists are indeed sincerely lost.

Paul noted in Romans 10 that the Christ-rejecting Jews were sincerely wrong in their attempt to get a right standing with God by good works. Sincerely believing something doesn't guarantee its truth.

Does Scripture say we should never let cultists into our houses?

The verse generally appealed to in support of this idea is 2 John 10: "If anyone comes to you and does not bring this teaching, do not take him into your house or welcome him." However, this verse does not prohibit Christians from allowing cultists into their homes in order to witness to them. Rather it is a prohibition against giving cultists a platform from which to teach false doctrine.

The backdrop to this is that in the early days of Christianity, there was no centralized church building where believers could congregate. Rather, there were many small house-churches scattered throughout the city. The early Christians are seen "breaking bread from house to house" (Acts 2:46; cf. 5:42 NASB) and gathering to pray in the house of Mary, the mother of Mark (Acts 12:12). Churches often met in houses (Colossians 4:15; 1 Corinthians 16:19). The use of specific church buildings did not appear before the end of the second century.

So, apparently, John is here warning against (1) allowing a false teacher into the church, and (2) giving this false teacher a platform from which to teach. Seen in this way, this prohibition guards the purity of the church. To extend hospitality to a false teacher would imply that the church accepted or approved of his or her teaching. If the church were to extend hospitality to a false teacher, he would be encouraged in his position and take this action as an acceptance of his doctrine. This should never be.

CONTROVERSIAL ISSUES RELATED TO CULTS

Is it wrong to wear a cross, as the Jehovah's Witnesses say?

No. As a backdrop, the Jehovah's Witnesses teach that the cross is a pagan religious symbol. Christians adopted this pagan symbol, we are told, when Satan took control of ecclesiastical authority in the early centuries of Christianity. Jehovah's Witnesses say that Christ was not crucified on a cross but on a stake.[7] That's the correct meaning of the Greek word *stauros*, they say. Hence, for people to wear crosses today dishonors God.

Actually, the Greek word *stauros* was used to refer to a variety of wooden structures used for execution in ancient days. The *stauros* as a wooden structure took on a variety of shapes, including that of the letter T, a plus sign (+), two diagonal beams (X), as well as (infrequently) a simple upright stake with no crosspiece. To argue that *stauros* always referred to an upright beam, as the Jehovah's Witnesses do, contradicts the actual historical facts.

In support of the fact that Jesus died on a cross is the fact that "nails" were used (John 20:25). If Jesus was crucified not on a cross but on a stake, then only a single nail would have been used. It is also significant that when Jesus spoke of Peter's *future* crucifixion, He indicated that Peter's arms would be outstretched, not above his head (John 21:18,19). Further, in keeping with a cross crucifixion instead of a stake crucifixion, we read in Matthew 27:37 that a sign saying "King of the Jews" was put above Jesus' head, not above His hands.

Is it wrong to celebrate birthdays, as some cultists hold?

No. Cultists (like the Jehovah's Witnesses) argue that there are only two references in the Bible to birthday celebrations—Genesis 40:20-22 and Matthew 14:6-10. And in both cases they are presented in an extremely negative light. Indeed, both individuals (Pharaoh in the Old Testament, Herod in the New Testament) were pagans and both had someone put to death on their birthdays. In view of this, cultists say, it is clear that no follower of God should ever celebrate a birthday.[8]

Cultists are here using what is known as "guilt by association." Concluding that a particular day is bad and evil simply because something bad or evil *happened* on that day is truly warped logic. Genesis 40:20-22 proves only that the Pharaoh was evil, not that birthdays are evil. Likewise, Matthew 14:6-10 proves only that Herod was evil, not that birthdays are. Certainly there is no scriptural command to celebrate birthdays, but there is no warrant for saying that celebrating birthdays is forbidden from these passages or any other passage.

A number of scholars believe birthdays are mentioned in Job 1:4: "And [Job's] sons used to go and hold a feast in the house of each one *on his day*, and they would send and invite their three sisters to eat and drink with them" (NASB, italics added; cf. 3:1-3). It is likely that a birthday festival is here intended. When the birthday of one arrived, he invited his brothers and sisters to feast with him; and each observed the same custom.

Nothing in the text indicates that Job's children did evil things on this day. Their celebration is not portrayed as a pagan practice. And certainly Job does not condemn the celebration. If such celebrations of birthdays were offensive to Jehovah, then Job—a man who "was blameless, upright, fearing God, and turning away from evil" (Job 1:1 NASB)—would have done something to prevent this practice among his own children.

There is no reason a birthday cannot be celebrated, like everything else, to the glory of God who created us (1 Corinthians 10:31). And there is nothing wrong with giving proper honor to another human being. The Bible says we should give respect to him who is due respect and honor to him who is due honor (Romans 13:7). Since a typical birthday does not worship another human being, there is no reason we cannot honor him or her on this occasion.

Does it go against the commandments of God for a human being to get a blood transfusion?

No, I don't believe so. Some cults, such as the Jehovah's Witnesses, try to argue that references to "eating blood" in the Bible prohibit receiving blood via transfusion. Among the key passages cited are Genesis 9:4, Leviticus 7:26,27, Leviticus 17:11,12, and Acts 15:28,29.[9]

As a backdrop for answering this question, we must first ask why God prohibited the Israelites from eating blood in the first place. It is a fact that some of the pagan nations surrounding Israel had no respect whatsoever for blood. Such pagans ate blood on a regular basis. Sometimes they did this as part of the worship of false gods; at other times they did this because they thought it might bring them supernatural power. In any event, the prohibition against eating blood set Israel apart from such ungodly nations.

Now, evangelical Christians agree that Genesis 9:4 and other such passages prohibit the "eating" of blood. That is not the issue of debate. The debate focuses on whether "eating" blood is the same as a blood transfusion. It is here that the Jehovah's Witnesses have erred.

The fact is, a blood transfusion treats the blood not with *disrespect* but with *reverence*. A transfusion simply replenishes the supply of essential, life-sustaining fluid that has in some way been drained away or has become incapable of performing its vital tasks in the body. In this context, blood does not function as food. A transfusion simply represents a transference of life from one person to another, and as such is an act of mercy.

Apologist Norman Geisler further points out that "even though a doctor might give food to a patient intravenously and call this 'feeding,' it is simply not the case that giving blood intravenously is also 'feeding.' This is clear from the fact that blood is not received into the body as 'food.'"[11] Indeed,

> to refer to the giving of food directly into the blood stream as "eating" is only a figurative expression.... Eating is the *literal* taking in of food in the normal manner through the mouth and into the digestive system. The reason intravenous injections are referred to as "feeding" is because the ultimate result is that, through intravenous injection, the body receives the nutrients that it would normally receive by eating[12] (italic added).

In view of these facts, Genesis 9:4 and other such passages cannot be used to support a prohibition on blood transfusions, since it is not a form of "eating."

Is it against God's will for Christians to celebrate Christmas? And is this holiday based on a pagan ritual?

There's not a single commandment in Scripture that instructs us to celebrate Christ's birth. But this doesn't mean it's wrong to do it. Scripture indicates that anything is permitted so long as it does not violate biblical principles, and so long as it is done in faith, with love, and in a manner that edifies people (see Romans 13:10; 14:4,5,23; 1 Corinthians 6:12; 10:23; Colossians 2:20,22).

Some have objected that Christ wasn't born on December 25. That's probably true. (His birth likely occurred at a different time of year altogether.) Nevertheless, it is perfectly appropriate for Christians to celebrate the Incarnation, the most incredible event of human history. And it's fine to do it on December 25, even though Christ probably wasn't born that day. (After all, Americans commemorate Washington's birthday on the third Monday of February, even though his real birthday was February 22.)

I know there are those who note that Christmas is celebrated on a day which in the ancient Roman Empire was a pagan holiday linked to the mystery religions. But this doesn't make Christmas a pagan holiday. The fact is, the Christians refused to participate in the pagan ritual. Their attitude was that if the pagans were going to celebrate their false religion, Christians should celebrate the one true religion. And what better way to celebrate than to focus attention on the Incarnation, the event in which eternal God became a man?

Personally I think it brings a smile to Christ's face when Christians celebrate His birth. On the other hand, I think it must sadden Him when He sees Christians focusing exclusively on exchanging gifts with one another, focusing little or no attention on Him.

CULTIC GOSPELS

What is The Course in Miracles that is so popular today?

This 1,200-page spiritual/psychological tome has become an occultic best-seller in New Age circles. This book was allegedly "transmitted" to Helen Shucman in the 1960s via automatic handwriting, a process in which a spirit entity allegedly guides the hand. Shucman claims the source of the words was Jesus Himself.[12]

According to this New Age textbook, the "Son of God" was created by God in a state of "wakefulness." Later, however, the Son fell asleep and had a dream of being separate from God. In the dream, the Son denied that He was created by God, asserting instead that He created Himself. This usurping of God's role as Creator marked the beginning of *ego* and led the Son to conceive of Himself as being *separate* from God.[13]

God then created and commissioned the Holy Spirit to awaken the Son. But the Son wrongly interpreted the coming of the Holy Spirit as judgment from God because the Son thought He was guilty of usurping God's role as Creator. The Son's ego then fragmented into myriads of egos with physical bodies (that is, human beings), each believing himself separate from each other and from God. Humanity's basic problem, then, is its belief in being separate from God. The solution to the problem is a rediscovery of one's Christhood. The *Course* sets out to help people attain this.[14]

What is The Urantia Book?

The so-called "revelations" contained in this 2,097-page book come from alleged extraterrestrial spirit-beings such as Melchizedek of Nebadon, Bagriel of Salvington, and the Chief of the Seraphim. The book sets out to offer those who live on earth ("Urantia," as it is known to these extraterrestrials) "the finest world view of religion available to contemporary man."[15]

The Urantia Book claims that humankind's deepest need is not atonement for sin, but rather a consciousness expanded to realize the fatherhood of God and the brotherhood of man. The book teaches that Jesus is not uniquely the Son of God, for there are allegedly some 700,000 Creator-Sons (Jesus was number 611,121). Jesus differs from us not in kind, but in degree. Christ was divine as we all are. He was able to perfect His divinity by His seventh incarnation. The book also denies Christ's blood atonement and His bodily resurrection from the dead. It blatantly sets forth what Scripture calls "another Jesus" (2 Corinthians 11:4 NKJV) and "a gospel contrary to that which we have preached" (Galatians 1:8 NASB).[16]

Is the Jehovah's Witnesses' New World Translation a reliable translation?

No. It is a terrible translation produced by the Jehovah's Witnesses to support their heretical brand of theology. The translation strips Jesus of His full deity and inserts the term Jehovah throughout the Bible.

Dr. Robert Countess, who wrote a doctoral dissertation on the Greek of the *New World Translation*, concluded that the translation "must be viewed as a radically biased piece of work. At some points it is actually dishonest. At others it is neither modern nor scholarly."[17] No wonder British scholar H. H. Rowley asserted, "From beginning to end this volume is a shining example of how the Bible should not be translated."[18] Indeed, Rowley said, this translation is "an insult to the Word of God."[19]

Dr. Julius Mantey, author of *A Manual Grammar of the Greek New Testament*, calls the *New World Translation* "a shocking mistranslation."[20] Dr. Bruce M. Metzger, professor of New Testament at Princeton University, calls it "a frightful mistranslation," "erroneous," "pernicious," and "reprehensible."[21] Dr. William Barclay concluded that "the deliberate distortion of truth by this sect is seen in their New Testament translation....It is abundantly clear that a sect which can translate the New Testament like that is intellectually dishonest."[22]

Now, in view of this universal "thumbs down" by legitimate biblical scholars, it is highly revealing that the Watchtower Society has always resisted efforts to identify members of the *New World Translation* committee. The claim was that they preferred to remain anonymous and humble, giving God the credit and glory for this translation. However, as former Jehovah's Witness David Reed notes, "an unbiased observer will quickly note that such anonymity also shields the translators from any blame for errors or distortions in their renderings. And it prevents scholars from checking their credentials."[23]

It must have been utterly embarrassing for the Watchtower Society when it became public who the translators of the *New World Translation* were. The reason for this is that the translation committee was completely unqualified for the task. Four of the five men in the committee had no Hebrew or Greek training whatsoever (they had only a high school education). The fifth—Fred W. Franz—claimed to know Hebrew and Greek, but upon examination under oath in a court of law in Edinburgh, Scotland, was found to fail a simple Hebrew test.[24]

Note the following cross-examination, which took place November 24, 1954 in this court (italics added):

> "Have you also made yourself familiar with Hebrew?"
>
> *"Yes."*
>
> "So that you have a substantial linguistic apparatus at your command?"
>
> *"Yes, for use in my biblical work."*
>
> "I think you are able to read and follow the Bible in Hebrew, Greek, Latin, Spanish, Portuguese, German, and French?"
>
> *"Yes."*[25]

The following day, Franz was put on the stand again, and the following interview took place:

> "You, yourself, read and speak Hebrew, do you?"
> "*I do not speak Hebrew.*"
> "You do not?"
> "*No.*"
> "Can you translate that into Hebrew?"
> "*Which?*"
> "That fourth verse of the second chapter of Genesis?"
> "*You mean here?*"
> "Yes."
> "*No.*"[26]

The truth of the matter is that Franz—like the others who participated in the *New World* Translation committee—cannot translate Hebrew or Greek. In fact, he dropped out of the University of Cincinnati after his sophomore year—and even while there, he had not been studying anything related to theological issues.[27] If the average Jehovah's Witness only knew the true history of this translation....

Do the two sticks mentioned in Ezekiel 37 refer to the Bible and the Book of Mormon?[28]

No. The context clearly defines what the two "sticks" are. Ezekiel 37:22 says, "I will make them *one nation* in the land, on the mountains of Israel; and one king will be king for all of them; and *they will no longer be two nations, and they will no longer be divided into two kingdoms*" (NASB, emphasis added). The sticks are not two books but are rather two kingdoms.

The backdrop is that following Solomon's death, Israel became split into two smaller kingdoms (931 B.C.). The Southern Kingdom was called Judah; the Northern Kingdom was called Israel (or sometimes Ephraim). Israel was taken into captivity by Assyria (722 B.C.); Judah was taken into exile by Babylon (605, 597, and 586 B.C.). The division between the kingdoms, however, was not to last forever. The uniting of the "sticks" pictures God restoring His people, the children of Israel, into a single nation again (Ezekiel 37:18-28).

Is it true that there have been virtually thousands of changes made in the Book of Mormon since its original edition in 1830?

Yes! There have been more than 3,913 changes between the original edition of the Book of Mormon published in 1830 and the ones printed and issued through the mid-1970s. The 1981 edition introduced between one and two hundred *additional* word changes.[29]

The Mormon account of how Joseph Smith went about translating the Book of Mormon would seem to disallow *any* possibility of *any* errors or the need for changes—even relating to misspellings and grammar mistakes. Smith was allegedly given the translation supernaturally, letter by letter, word by word. And following the translation of the Book of Mormon, Joseph Smith said he heard a voice from out of the bright light above him that said, "These plates have been revealed by the power of God, and they have been translated by the power of God. The translation of them which you have seen is correct."[30]

In view of this precise and exact process—a process that involved *individual characters* and *specific words*—it would seem there is room for no human error. Yet thousands of changes have been made.

Are there plagiarisms in the Book of Mormon?

Yes. Besides thousands of changes being made in the Book of Mormon through the years, the book is also undermined by the many plagiarisms it contains from the King James Version of the Bible. In fact, there are *whole chapters* that have been lifted directly from the Book of Isaiah.[31]

Here is a thorny issue for Mormons: the Book of Mormon has some 27,000 words directly from the King James Version of the Bible—including *whole verses*.[32] The problem is this: If the Book of Mormon was first penned between 600 B.C. and A.D. 421, as claimed, how could it contain such extensive quotations from the A.D. 1611 King James Version, which was not to be written for another 1,200 to 2,000 years? This is not a subject most Mormons like to talk about.

It is highly significant that in the many King James plagiarisms in the Book of Mormon, even the italicized words from the King James Version were plagiarized. This is relevant because, as noted in the preface of the King James Version, these words were not in the original languages but were added by the King James translators to provide clarity. How could it be that the Book of Mormon was written far, far before the King James Version but contains the King James translators' "inserted clarifying words"?[33]

Is it true that the Book of Mormon does not support many modern Mormon doctrines?

Yes. The Book of Mormon, the "keystone" of the Mormon religion, contains very little in terms of the "Mormonism" as taught by the Mormon church today. Among other things, the Book of Mormon says nothing about Mormon church organization, the "plurality of gods" doctrine, the "God is an exalted man" doctrine, the doctrine that men may become Gods, the "plurality of wives" doctrine, and the doctrine of eternal progression. All of these are distinctive doctrines of the modern Mormon church, yet the Book of Mormon—which is said to contain the "fullness of the everlasting gospel"—does not mention any of these things.[34]

What are we to make of the Mormon claim that the Book of Mormon has good archeological support?

Pure fiction! Down through the years, Mormons have claimed that archaeological finds have proven the veracity and reliability of the Book of Mormon. But there is nothing to such claims.

As a backdrop, one must keep in mind that according to the Mormon Scriptures, the Nephite and Lamanite nations had *huge* populations that lived in *large*, fortified cities in America. They allegedly waged *large-scale* wars with each other for hundreds of years, culminating in a conflict in which hundreds of thousands of people were killed in A.D. 385 near Hill Cumorah in present-day New York State (see Mormon 6:9-15).

One would think that if all this really happened there would be archeological evidence to support it. But there is no evidence that any of this ever happened. While there is massive archeological evidence to support the people and places mentioned in the Bible, such evidence is completely missing in regard to the Book of Mormon and other Mormon scriptures.

In an article published in *Dialogue: A Journal of Mormon Thought*, Dee Green, assistant professor of anthropology at Weber State College, said:

> The first myth we need to eliminate is that Book of Mormon archeology exists....If one is to study Book of Mormon archeology, then one must have a corpus of data with which to deal. We do not....No Book of Mormon location is known with reference to modern topography. Biblical archaeology can be studied because we do know where Jerusalem and Jericho were and are, but we do not know where

Zarahemla and Bountiful (nor any other location for that matter) were or are.[35]

Should we pray about the Book of Mormon when Mormons on the doorstep ask us to?

No. Mormons generally appeal to James 1:5 (which speaks of praying for wisdom) in trying to get people to pray about the Book of Mormon. But that is a misapplication of the text.

One need not pray about whether to commit murder, or adultery, or incest. Why? Because Scripture has already given us biblical commands and principles that instruct us regarding God's mind on these issues.

So it is with the Book of Mormon. We don't need to pray about whether to accept it because God has already made clear His feelings on the matter. Galatians 1:6-8 very clearly reveals God's attitude toward "gospels" that go against that contained in Scripture.

Furthermore, 1 Thessalonians 5:21 instructs us to *test* all things (not *"pray* to see if something is true"). Acts 17:10-12 encourages us to follow the example of the Bereans by testing religious claims against the Bible. The Bereans were certainly believers in prayer, but that was not the measuring stick for truth. They knew only the Bible was the measuring stick for truth, and hence it alone is to be used in testing religious claims.

Here's another observation: When asked to pray about the Book of Mormon, one must wonder, *which* Book of Mormon? The 1830 edition? The 1921 edition? Or today's edition, which has nearly 4,000 changes from the original 1830 edition? Not only that, but even if you *did* pray about the Book of Mormon and received confirmation that it was true, then which church should you join? The fact is, over 100 different churches have been founded that use the Book of Mormon and claim Joseph Smith as a prophet of God.[36]

∾

The New Age Movement

What is the New Age movement?

The New Age movement has been called the fastest-growing alternative belief system in the country.[1] It may be defined as a loosely structured network of individuals and organizations who share a common vision of a New Age of enlightenment and harmony (the "Age of Aquarius") and who subscribe to a common set of religious and philosophical beliefs (that is, "worldview"). This common set of beliefs is based on *monism* (all is one), *pantheism* (all is God), and *mysticism* (the experience of oneness with the divine).[2]

Because it is so broad and organizationally diffuse, the New Age movement, strictly speaking, cannot be categorized as a cult by any accepted sociological definition of "cult." *Cults* are exclusivistic groups made up of individuals who subscribe to a uniform set of beliefs and operate according to a rigidly defined organizational structure. *Movements*, while having an element of unity, are multifaceted—involving a variety of individuals and groups (including cults) whose beliefs, practices, and emphases are distinctive and diverse. This is the case with the New Age movement. To be a New Ager, then, there is no organization one must join and no creed one must confess.

In what ways has the New Age movement penetrated the business community?

The human potential movement blossomed in the 1970s. Since that time, numerous companies have utilized the services of various New Age human potential seminars. One reason so many Fortune 500 companies have been eager to use New Age seminars is that they promise increased productivity, better employee relations, more creativity among workers, and—bottom line—*more sales*. These New Age seminars typically teach attendees: (1) you are your own God; (2) you can create your own reality; and (3) you have unlimited potential.[3] Christians at the workplace have every reason to be concerned.

An important goal of many New Age seminars is to trigger an altered state of consciousness. Seminar leaders first attempt to shred or do away with the attendee's present worldview. An attempt is subsequently made (via a mystical exercise) to trigger an altered state of consciousness in hopes of inducing a mystical experience so potent that it will cause the participant to question or doubt his or her previous understanding of reality.[4]

The participant is then exposed to a New Age explanation that makes sense of the mystical experience. The participant is introduced to a *new* worldview that says that you are your own God and you can create your own reality.[5] Many businesspeople have been drawn into the New Age movement through such seminars.

In what ways has the New Age movement penetrated the public schools of our country?

To begin, it is a fact that curriculum textbooks for public schools have been stripped of Christianity but include many New Age ideas. In his book *Censorship: Evidence of Bias in Our Children's Textbooks*, Paul Vitz provides conclusive evidence that Christianity and Christian values have been systematically stripped from the curriculum books of children.[6] While children's textbooks are silent on Christianity, many of them teach about Buddhism, Hinduism, Eastern meditation, magic, Indian spirituality, and yoga.[7]

It is clear that New Agers have a definite agenda for what they see as important in public school curricula. Marilyn Ferguson says that the New Age educational curriculum includes an emphasis on altered states of consciousness, centering, meditation, relaxation, yoga, and biofeedback.[8]

A key emphasis of New Agers in public schools is what they call right-brain learning. Educators say that the right brain governs man's creative and intuitive abilities. The right-brain/left-brain distinction is not New Age *per se*, but New Agers have appropriated the distinction as a means of justifying bringing "right-brain learning techniques" into the classroom. Supposed right-brain learning techniques include practices such as yoga, meditation, chanting, and visualization. By such practices, children are led to have mystical experiences.

Meditation is also being taught to children in some school districts. A book that made its way into a California school district is *Meditating With Children* by Deborah Rozman. One visualization Rozman recommends is this: "Meditate and go into the Source within, and in that One Source feel that you are One with everyone else's Light, Intelligence, Love, and Power.... Chant 'Om' softly to fill the whole circle and the whole room with your experience of the Source within."[9]

Confluent education is a New Age curriculum developed by Beverly Galyean that has been used in some public schools. Solidly rooted in a pantheistic worldview, confluent education seeks to enable children to recognize and act upon their "inner divinity." Confluent education uses guided imagery and meditation to accomplish its goals.

Galyean says that a key aspect of meditation "is the increased capacity to contact and learn from the source of wisdom, love, and intelligence within us—often called the 'higher self,' God, universal wisdom or spirit, conscience."[10]

Values clarification is another New Age curriculum that has penetrated the public schools.[11] Values clarification seeks to help students discover *their own* values. The idea is that values are not to be imposed from *without* (such as from Scripture or from parents) but must be discovered *within*. The underlying assumption is that there are no absolute truths or values.

What is "holistic" health care? Is this a New Age form of medical treatment?

The word "holistic," when applied to health care, refers to an approach that respects the interaction of mind, body, and environment. Indeed, holistic health focuses on the *whole* person and his surroundings.

As a backdrop, New Agers typically criticize Western medicine as being *reductionistic* in its approach. As Fritjof Capra put it, "by concentrating on smaller and smaller fragments of the body, modern medicine often loses sight of the patient as a human being, and by reducing health to mechanical functioning, it is no longer able to deal with the phenomenon of healing."[12] New Agers claim that reductionistic medicine is disease-centered, not person-centered, and treats *only* the parts of the body that are ailing (the heart, for example).

A holistic approach to health is a "multidimensional phenomenon involving interdependent physical, psychological, and social aspects."[13] The holistic approach seeks to treat the *whole* person—body, mind, and spirit—and also considers the social aspects of the patient's life as a factor to health. Holistic health claims to be person-centered, not disease-centered.

Now, some aspects of holistic health sound reasonable enough and can be accepted by the Christian. However, many New Age health therapies betray a non-Christian worldview. Indeed, the New Age model of holistic health is based primarily on their conception of *energy*, not matter. The editors of the *New Age Journal* report: "All of the healing systems that can be called 'holistic' share a common belief in the universe as a unified field of energy that produces all form and substance."[14]

This energy is not a visible, measurable, scientifically explainable energy. Rather, New Agers speak of a "cosmic" or "universal" energy based on their monistic (*all is one*) and pantheistic (*all is God*) worldview. To enhance the flow of "healing energy" in the body, one must allegedly *attune* to it and realize one's unity with all things.[15] Many New Age health therapies are based on this premise. This monistic and pantheistic worldview is entirely at odds with a Christian worldview, which sees an eternal distinction between God the Creator and the creation (Genesis 1; Isaiah 44:24; Colossians 1:16).

Is it okay for Christians to practice meditation?

Among advocates of Eastern religions, the practice of meditation is said to

> lead to a nondualistic state of mind in which, the distinction between subject and object having disappeared and the practitioner having become one with "god" or "the absolute," conventions like time and space are transcended... until finally that stage is reached which religions refer to as salvation, liberation, or complete enlightenment."[16]

The Christian must not participate in such forms of meditation for at least three reasons. First, Eastern meditation's stated goal of transforming one's state of mind into a monistic (*all is one*) if not an outright pantheistic (*all is God*) outlook lies in direct contradiction to the biblical view of the eternal distinction between God the Creator and His creatures (Isaiah 44:6-8; Hebrews 2:6-8).

Second, Eastern meditation's goal is to provide the practitioner a way (if not *the* way) to ultimate truth and freedom through sheer human effort, thus advocating a form of self-salvation by works over and against what the Bible explicitly teaches (Ephesians 2:8,9). In so doing, it ignores the inability of fallen humanity to independently attain such lofty ends (Romans 3:10-12) and denies Christ's exclusive claim that He alone provides the way to salvation (John 14:6; cf. Acts 4:12; Isaiah 43:11).

Third, such altered states of consciousness can open one up to spiritual affliction and deception by the powers of darkness. This alone should serve to dissuade any Christian from participating in Eastern forms of meditation.

Eastern meditation should be distinguished from biblical meditation. Scripture defines meditation in terms of the individual believer objectively contemplating and deeply reflecting upon God and His Word (Psalm 1:2; 19:14; Joshua 1:8) as well as His Person and faithfulness (Psalm 119; cf. 19:14; 48:9; 77:12; 104:34; 143:5). There is no subjective emptying of the mind in biblical meditation.

Christian meditation calls us to look upward to God so that our minds may be filled with godly wisdom and insight, and so that our hearts may be filled with comfort, happiness, and joy. To echo the opening words of the psalmist, "Blessed is the man...[whose] delight is in the law of the LORD, and on his law he meditates day and night" (Psalm 1:1,2).

Is channeling off-limits for Christians?

Yes. Channeling is a form of spiritism. As such, it is condemned by God as a heinous sin. Deuteronomy 18:10,11 is clear: "Let no one be found among you ... who is a medium or spiritist or who consults the dead. Anyone who does these things is detestable to the LORD."

Related to the above, we must keep in mind that departed humans are not available for spirit contact. Departed human beings are not hovering around in the "great beyond" available for contact from human beings on earth. Departed Christians are in the presence of Christ in heaven (Philippians 1:23). Departed unbelievers are in a place of great suffering (Luke 16:19-31), *confined* until that future day of judgment (Revelation 20:11f.).

Is it okay for Christians to read horoscopes?

No. It is forbidden!

As a backdrop, astrologers believe that man's evolution goes through progressive cycles corresponding to the signs of the zodiac. Each of these cycles allegedly lasts between 2,000 and 2,400 years. It is believed that man is now moving from the Piscean Age (the age of intellectual man) into the Aquarian Age (the age of spiritual man).[17]

Astrology can be traced back to the religious practices of ancient Mesopotamia, Assyria, and Egypt. It is a form of divination—an attempt to seek counsel or knowledge by occultic means—that was very popular among the people of these nations.[18] As such, astrology (including reading horoscopes) is strictly off-limits for the Christian.

In Isaiah 47, we find a strong denunciation of astrologers and their craft. Verse 15 explicitly states that "each of them goes on in his error," and "there is not one that can save you." The Book of Daniel confirms that astrologers lack true discernment, and that the only source of accurate revelation is God Almighty (Daniel 2:2,10).

Is it okay for Christians to participate in visualization?

No, I don't think so. On the one hand, the imagination (which God Himself gave humans) can be used in a very positive way to create great music, art, books, and the like. It is right and good to use the imagination for such creative endeavors.

But the imagination can also be used wrongly—with damaging results. New Agers think they can use the imagination in the sense of "mind over matter." David Gershon and Gail Straub, authors of the best-selling New Age book *Empowerment: The Art of Creating Your Life as You Want It*, say: "Your thoughts are always creating your reality—it's up to you to take charge of your thoughts and consciously create a reality that is fulfilling."[19] Devotees to Seth (an entity that allegedly speaks through channelers) said, "We literally create our reality through the beliefs we hold, so by changing those beliefs, we can change reality."[20]

The attempt to control external reality by the mind is sheer occultism and is hence totally off-limits for the Christian. One must also recognize that man's imagination has been marred and infected by sin (Genesis 6:5). Further, guided imagery sessions can induce an altered state of consciousness that can have extremely dangerous consequences. The fact is, any kind of activity that leads to an altered state of consciousness can open one up to demonic affliction.

All things considered, then, Christians are advised to stay away from all forms of visualization.

~

The Word-Faith Movement

Do the Scriptures teach that human beings are (or can become) "little gods"?

No. If it were true that human beings are "little gods," then one would expect them to display qualities similar to those known to be true of God. This seems only logical. However, when one compares the attributes of humankind with those of God, we find more than ample testimony for the truth of Paul's statement in Romans 3:23 that human beings "fall short of the glory of God." Consider the following:

- ✓ God is all-knowing (Isaiah 40:13, 14), but man is limited in knowledge (Job 38:4).

- ✓ God is all-powerful (Revelation 19:6), but man is weak (Hebrews 4:15).

- ✓ God is everywhere-present (Psalm 139:7-12), but man is confined to a single space at a time (John 1:50).

- ✓ God is holy (1 John 1:5), but even man's "righteous" deeds are as filthy garments before God (Isaiah 64:6).

- ✓ God is eternal (Psalm 90:2), but man was created at a point in time (Genesis 1:1, 26, 27).

- ✓ God is truth (John 14:6), but man's heart is deceitful above all else (Jeremiah 17:9).

- ✓ God is characterized by justice (Acts 17:31), but man is lawless (1 John 3:4; see also Romans 3:23).

- ✓ God is love (Ephesians 2:4,5), but man is plagued with numerous vices like jealousy and strife (1 Corinthians 3:3).

If man is a god, one could never tell it by his attributes!

Man's ignorance of his alleged divinity proves that he is not God. If human beings are essentially God, and if God is an infinite and changeless being, then how is it possible for man (if he is a manifestation of divinity) to go through a changing process of enlightenment by which he discovers his divinity? "The fact that a man 'comes to realize' he is God proves that he is not God. If he were God he would never have passed from a state of unenlightenment to a state of enlightenment as to who he is."[1] To put it another way, "God cannot bud. He cannot blossom. God has always been in full bloom. That is, God is and always has been God."[2]

Did Jesus promise to give us literally anything we ask for in faith?

No. This is a Word-Faith misinterpretation of Mark 11:23,24: "I tell you the truth, if anyone says to this mountain, 'Go, throw yourself into the sea,' and does not doubt in his heart but believes that what he says will happen, it will be done for him. Therefore I tell you, whatever you ask for in prayer, believe that you have received it, and it will be yours." There are limitations on what God will give, indicated by the broader context of Scripture.

To begin, God cannot literally give us *anything*. Some things are actually impossible. For example, God cannot grant a request of a creature to be God. Neither can He answer a request to approve of our sin. God will not give us a stone if we ask for bread, nor will He give us a serpent if we ask for fish (Matthew 7:9,10).

When the rest of Scripture is taken into consideration, there are many conditions placed on God's promise to answer prayer in addition to faith. We must "abide in Him" and let His Word "abide in us" (John 15:7 NASB). We cannot "ask amiss" out of our own selfishness (James 4:3). Furthermore, we must ask "according to His will" (1 John 5:14 NASB). Even Jesus prayed, "Father, *if it is possible,* let this cup [His death] pass from Me" (Matthew 26:39 NASB, emphasis added). We must ever keep in mind that on all except God's unconditional promises, this "if it be Your will" must always be stated or implied.

Does Scripture teach that Christians can receive a hundred-fold return on the money they tithe (Mark 10:30)?

No. In fact, Mark 10:30 has nothing to do with money or riches. It is speaking specifically of those who forsake home and loved ones for the sake of Jesus and the gospel. *These* individuals will receive a "hundredfold return" in the sense that they become a part of a community of believers. It is in this new community that they find a multiplication of relationships, many of which are ultimately closer and more spiritually meaningful than blood relationships (Mark 3:31-35; Acts 2:41-47; cf. 1 Timothy 5:1,2).

Further, God wants us to have a balanced perspective on money. The Bible does not condemn possessions or riches per se. It is not a sin to be wealthy. (Some very godly people in the Bible—Abraham and Job, for example—were quite wealthy.) Rather, God condemns a love of possessions or riches (Luke 16:13; 1 Timothy 6:10; Hebrews 13:5). A love of material things is a sign that a person is living according to a temporal perspective, not an eternal perspective.

What is more, Scripture tells us that a love of money and riches can lead to destruction. The apostle Paul flatly stated that "people who want to get rich fall into temptation and a trap and into many foolish and harmful desires that plunge men into ruin and destruction" (1 Timothy 6:9). Paul also warned that "there will be terrible times in the last days. People will be lovers of themselves, lovers of money...lovers of pleasure rather than lovers of God—having a form of godliness but denying its power" (2 Timothy 3:1-5).

Does 2 Corinthians 8:9 teach that financial prosperity is guaranteed in the atonement?

No. Second Corinthians 8:9 says, "For you know the grace of our Lord Jesus Christ, that though He was rich, yet for your sake He became poor, that you through His poverty might become rich" (NASB). It is telling that if Paul was intending to say that *financial* prosperity is provided for in the atonement, he was offering the Corinthians something that he himself did not possess at the time. Indeed, in 1 Corinthians 4:11 Paul informed these same individuals that he was "hungry and thirsty," "poorly clothed," and "homeless" (NASB). He also exhorted the Corinthians to be imitators of his life and teaching (1 Corinthians 4:16).

In 2 Corinthians 8:9 it seems clear that Paul was speaking about spiritual prosperity, not financial prosperity. This fits both the immediate context in 2 Corinthians and the broader context of Paul's other writings. Certainly if financial prosperity was provided for in the atonement, one must wonder why Paul informed the Philippian Christians that he had learned to be content *even when going hungry* (Philippians 4:11,12). One would think he would have instead claimed the prosperity promised in the atonement to meet his every need.

Does Isaiah 53 teach that physical healing is guaranteed in the atonement?

No. While ultimate physical healing *is* in the atonement (a healing we will enjoy in our future resurrection bodies), the healing of our bodies while in the *mortal* state (prior to our death and resurrection) *is not* guaranteed in the atonement.

It is important to note that the Hebrew word for healing (*napha*) can refer not just to physical healing but to spiritual healing. The context of Isaiah 53:4 indicates that spiritual healing is in view. In verse 5 we are clearly told, "He was pierced through for *our transgressions*, He was crushed for *our iniquities*.... By His scourging we are healed" (NASB, emphasis added). Because "transgressions" and "iniquities" set the context, spiritual healing from the misery of man's sin is in view.

Further, there are numerous verses in Scripture that substantiate the view that physical healing in mortal life is not guaranteed in the atonement and that it is not always God's will to heal. The apostle Paul couldn't heal Timothy's stomach problem (1 Timothy 5:23) nor could he heal Trophimus at Miletus (2 Timothy 4:20) or Epaphroditus (Philippians 2:25-27). Paul spoke of "a bodily illness" he had (Galatians 4:13-15 NASB). He also suffered a "thorn in the flesh" which God allowed him to retain (2 Corinthians 12:7-9). God certainly allowed Job to go through a time of physical suffering (Job 1–2). In none of these cases is it stated that the sickness was caused by sin or unbelief. Nor did Paul or any of the others act as if they thought their healing was guaranteed in the atonement. They accepted their situations and trusted in God's grace for sustenance. It is noteworthy that on one occasion Jesus indicated that sickness could be for the glory of God (John 11:4).

Finally, there are numerous verses in Scripture which reveal that our physical bodies are continuously running down and suffering various ailments. Our present bodies are said to be *perishable* and *weak* (1 Corinthians 15:42-44). Paul said "our outer man is decaying" (2 Corinthians 4:16 NASB). Death and disease will be a part of the human condition until that time when we receive resurrection bodies that are immune to such frailties (1 Corinthians 15:51-55).

Are there apostles today?

No, not in the biblical sense. Scripture indicates that the church was built on the *foundation* of the apostles and prophets (Ephesians 2:20). Once a foundation is built, it does not need to be built again. It is built *upon*.

Biblical apostles had to be eyewitnesses of the risen Christ (Acts 1:21-26; 5:32; Luke 1:1-4; 1 Corinthians 9:1). Paul indicated he was the *last person* to behold the risen Christ and receive an apostolic commission (1 Corinthians 15:8). Moreover, the epistles of 2 Peter and Jude (among the last New Testament books written) exhort believers to avoid false doctrines by recalling the teachings of the New Testament apostles (2 Peter 1:12-15; 2:1; 3:2, 14-16; Jude 3, 4, 17-19). Further, the Book of Revelation indicates that the biblical apostles are accorded a special honor by having their names inscribed on the 12 foundations of the eternal city (Revelation 21:14).

Does Hebrews 11:1 teach that faith is an actual substance that God used to create the universe?

No. Hebrews 11:1 says, "Now faith is the substance of things hoped for, the evidence of things not seen" (KJV). Word-Faith teachers think this means that faith is an actual substance. However, the Greek word translated "substance" is *hypostasis* and literally means "assurance," "confidence," or "confident expectation." Hence, Hebrews 11:1 is simply teaching that faith is the certainty or assurance of things hoped for. This assurance is based on the fact that God's promises never fail (2 Peter 1:4).

When Jesus was "made sin" (2 Corinthians 5:21), did He take on the nature of Satan?

No. This is a Word-Faith misinterpretation of 2 Corinthians 5:21: "God made him who had no sin to be sin for us, so that in him we might become the righteousness of God." Christ did not take on the nature of Satan, for Christ as God is immutable, and cannot change in His divine nature (Hebrews 13:8; cf. Malachi 3:6). In Hebrews 1:12 the Father says of Jesus, "You remain the same, and your years will never end."

Regarding Jesus being "made to be sin," Jesus was always without sin *actually*, but He was made to be sin for us *judicially*. That is, by His death on the cross, He paid the penalty for our sins and thereby canceled the debt of sin against us. So, while Jesus never committed a sin *personally*, He was made to be sin for us *substitutionally*.

One must also keep in mind the Old Testament backdrop of the concept of substitution. The sacrificial victim had to be "without defect" (see Leviticus 4:3, 23, 32). A hand would be laid on the unblemished sacrificial animal as a way of symbolizing a transfer of guilt (Leviticus 4:4, 24, 33). Note that the sacrificial animal did not thereby actually *become* sinful by nature; rather, sin was *imputed* to the animal and the animal acted as a sacrificial substitute. In like manner, Christ the Lamb of God was utterly unblemished (1 Peter 1:19), but our sin was *imputed* to Him and He was our sacrificial substitute on the cross of Calvary. Simply because our sin was imputed to Him does not mean He changed in nature. Christ was not sinful *personally*; He was made to be sin *substitutionally*.

Does Ephesians 4:9 teach that Jesus descended into hell?

No. Ephesians 4:9 says, "What does 'he ascended' mean except that he also descended to the lower, earthly regions?" There are two views as to where Jesus went the three days His body was in the grave before His resurrection.

One position claims that Christ's spirit went to the spirit world, while His body was in the grave. Here, they believe, He spoke to the "spirits in prison" (1 Peter 3:19). According to this view, there were two compartments in Hades (or *sheol*)—one for the saved and another for the unsaved. They were separated by a "great gulf" (Luke 16:26 KJV) which no man could pass. The section for the saved was called "Abraham's bosom" (Luke 16:23 KJV). When Christ, as the "firstfruits" of the Resurrection (1 Corinthians 15:20), ascended, He led these Old Testament saints into heaven with Him for the first time.

A second position holds that the souls of Old Testament believers, as well as Christ, went directly to heaven the moment they died. In support of this view, Jesus affirmed that His spirit was going directly to heaven, declaring, "Father, into Your Hands I commend My spirit" (Luke 23:46 NKJV). Moreover, Jesus promised the thief on the cross, "Today you will be with Me in Paradise" (Luke 23:43 NKJV). But "Paradise" is defined as "the third heaven" in 2 Corinthians 12:2-4.

Further, "descending into the lower parts of the earth" is not a reference to hell, but to the grave. The phrase simply means *caves, graves,* or *enclosures on the earth,* as opposed to higher parts, like mountains. Besides, hell itself is not in the lower parts of the earth—it is "under the earth" (Philippians 2:10 NASB).

Hence, there is no evidence that Jesus went in His spirit to hell during the three days His body was in the grave.

Furthermore, even if it could be shown that Jesus visited the spirit world during this time, the Bible is clear that He was not "born again" while there, nor did He gain victory over the devil at that time. Jesus was not a sinner and, therefore, did not need to be born again (cf. John 2:25; 3:3,6,7). His work for our salvation was completed on the cross (John 19:30; Hebrews 10:14) before He entered the grave.

PART 10

ETHICS

Ethics and the Christian Life
Ethical Issues Related to Death

~

37

Ethics and the Christian Life

Is it ever right for the Christian to lie?

Yes—but I need to qualify what I mean. On the one hand, Scripture forbids lying (Exodus 20:16). Lying is viewed as a sin (Psalm 59:12) and is an abomination to God (Proverbs 12:22). God never lies (Numbers 23:19). Righteous men hate lying (Proverbs 13:5).

On the other hand, there are Scriptures which indicate that under certain circumstances, lying is not condemned. For example, though the Hebrew midwives were commanded by the Egyptian Pharaoh to let newborn baby boys die, the midwives disobeyed the Pharaoh and lied to him when questioned about it (Exodus 1:15-19). To the Hebrew midwives, lifesaving was higher on the ethical scale than truthtelling. God not only did not condemn the midwives for lying, He was kind to them for their merciful act (see verse 20).

A more recent example would be the numerous Christians who lied to the Nazis in order to protect Jews from being captured and exterminated. In such cases lying is permissible because lifesaving is a higher ethic than truthtelling.

Is it ever right for the Christian to disobey the government?

We must answer this question very carefully. I think the biblically balanced answer is that we must obey the government unless the government requires us to disobey the laws of God. Let's look at the details.

The apostle Paul commanded believers to be submissive to the government because authority is ordained of God (Romans 13:1-7). In Paul's argumentation, resistance to government is, in the final analysis, resistance against God (verse 2). Government, Paul says, resists evil (verse 4).

It is noteworthy that some eight years later, after having been imprisoned a number of times by the Roman government, Paul had not changed his mind. He still taught that Christians should obey the government. Maltreatment at the hands of the Roman government had not caused him to alter his view.

Peter, too, wrote about the need to obey the government (1 Peter 2:13-17). Like Paul, he says that obeying God-ordained government shows our obedience to God Himself. All this is significant in view of the fact that both Paul and Peter wrote what they did while living under the reign of the cruel emperor Nero (A.D. 54-68).

Having said all this, there are also clear indications in Scripture that when the government commands a believer to go against one or more of God's commands, one must obey God rather than the government. After being commanded by the Sanhedrin not to preach any further, "Peter and the other apostles replied: 'We must obey God rather than men!'" (Acts 5:29). God commanded Peter and the others to preach; the government commanded them not to preach. So they chose to obey God rather than human government.

We see the same thing illustrated in the Book of Daniel. Shadrach, Meshach, and Abednego righteously disobeyed the king when they were commanded to worship the golden image (Daniel 3). Daniel also righteously disobeyed the government when it commanded him to go against God's revealed will (Daniel 6). In both cases, God confirmed that they had made the right choice by delivering them from the punishment that was afflicted upon them.

Of course, Christians must guard against abusing this principle in Scripture. Scripture indicates that we are to disobey government *only* when it commands us to violate God's commands, not just when we feel the government has personally violated our rights.

What do the Scriptures have to say about drinking?

Drunkenness is forbidden by God all throughout Scripture. It is simply not an option for the Christian. In Ephesians 5:18, the apostle Paul explicitly instructs, "Do not get drunk on wine, which leads to debauchery. Instead, be filled with the Spirit." Paul is telling us to be controlled by the Spirit, not by wine.

While drinking wine *in moderation* is permissible in Scripture (see John 2:9; 1 Timothy 3:3,8), many wine-drinking Christians today are wrongly assuming that what the New Testament means by wine is identical to the wine used today. This, however, is not correct.

Today's wine is by biblical definitions "strong drink." What the New Testament meant by wine was basically purified water. Wine in ancient times was 20 parts water and one part wine. Twenty-to-one water is essentially wine-flavored water. Sometimes in the ancient world they would go as strong as one part water and one part wine—and this was considered strong wine. Anyone who drank wine unmixed was looked upon as a Scythian, a barbarian. So anyone who would take wine unmixed, even the Greeks thought was a barbarian. That means the Greeks would look at our culture today and say, "You Americans are barbarians—drinking straight wine."

Every Christian adult must decide for himself whether or not to drink. A question we must all ask ourselves is:

While drinking may be *permissible,* is it *beneficial* for me to do so? The following verses speak to this issue:

- ✓ "'Everything is permissible for me'—but not everything is beneficial. 'Everything is permissible for me'—but I will not be mastered by anything" (1 Corinthians 6:12).

- ✓ "It is better not to eat meat or drink wine or to do anything else that will cause your brother to fall" (Romans 14:21).

- ✓ "So whether you eat or drink or whatever you do, do it all for the glory of God" (1 Corinthians 10:31).

- ✓ "Each of you should look not only to your own interests, but also to the interests of others" (Philippians 2:4).

Are there any commandments in the Bible against smoking cigarettes?

No. But the Scriptures do indicate that the Christian's body is a temple of the Holy Spirit, and as such, we should seek to glorify God in our body (1 Corinthians 6:19, 20). Of course, this also applies to eating the right kind of food and making sure we stay fit.

Though smoking will not keep you out of heaven, it will probably get you there much quicker. Another thing to keep in mind is that your "secondhand smoke" may send others into eternity (both believers and unbelievers) much earlier than otherwise would have occurred.

What does Scripture say about premarital sex?

God created human beings as sexual beings. But God intended sexual activity to be confined to the marriage relationship. Unfortunately, as is true with so many other things, many people have taken that which God intended for good and have perverted its use. The result: *sexual enslavement.*

Scripture has a lot to say about human sexuality. For example:

1. Scripture is consistent in its emphasis that a sexual relationship can only be engaged in within the confines of marriage (1 Corinthians 7:2).

2. The apostles urged all Christians to abstain from fornication (Acts 15:20). Paul said that the body is not for fornication and that a man should flee it (1 Corinthians 6:13,18).

3. Adultery is condemned in Scripture (Exodus 20:14). In the Old Testament adulterers were to be put to death (Leviticus 20:10). Jesus pronounced adultery wrong even in its basic motives (Matthew 5:27,28). Paul called adultery an evil work of the flesh (Galatians 5:19). John envisioned in the lake of fire some of those who practiced adultery (Revelation 21:8).

Sex within marriage, however, *is good* (see Genesis 2:24; Matthew 19:5). Sex was a part of God's "good" creation. Indeed, God created sex and "everything created by God is good" (1 Timothy 4:4 NASB). But it is good *only* within the confines of the marriage relationship, which He Himself ordained (see Hebrews 13:4).

Is homosexuality acceptable to God?

By no means. The Bible emphatically states that "neither fornicators ... nor homosexuals ... will inherit the kingdom of God" (1 Corinthians 6:9 NKJV). The Scriptures repeatedly and consistently condemn homosexual practices (see Leviticus 18:22 and Romans 1:26). God loves all persons, including homosexuals, but *He hates homosexuality.* The Bible condemns *all* types of fornication—which would therefore include homosexuality (Matthew 15:19; Mark 7:21;

Acts 15:20,29; Galatians 5:19-21; 1 Thessalonians 4:3; Hebrews 13:4).

Is it permissible for the Christian to get divorced?

This is a difficult issue. Scripture is very clear that God Himself created the institution of marriage, and He intended it to be permanent (Matthew 19:4-6). Divorce was never a part of God's original plan. In fact, God hates divorce (Malachi 2:16). The marriage relationship was intended to be dissolved only when one of the marriage partners died (Romans 7:1-3; 1 Corinthians 7:8,9; 1 Timothy 5:14).

When sin entered the world, this affected God's ideal in marriage and many other things. Scripture tells us that even though divorce was not God's ideal, He nevertheless allowed it because of man's sinfulness (Matthew 19:7,8; Deuteronomy 24:1-4).

From a biblical perspective, divorce is allowed only under two circumstances: (1) One of the marriage partners is unfaithful (Matthew 19:9); (2) The unbelieving partner deserts the believing partner (1 Corinthians 7:15,16). Divorce for any other reason is a violation of God's ideal.

Even in cases in which a person clearly has biblical permission to divorce, God's desire is that the person if at all possible forgive the offending spouse and be reconciled to him or her. This follows from God's command to forgive others of their wrongs toward us (Ephesians 4:32; Colossians 3:13).

Of course, God forgives us of all our sins—including the sin of divorce (Colossians 2:13). However, simply because God forgives us does not remove the painful consequences of our actions on ourselves or on others. There is a heavy price to pay for violating God's ideal.

Does the Bible support slavery?

No. From the very beginning, God declared that all humans are created in the image of God (Genesis 1:27). The apostle Paul also declared that "we are the offspring of God" (Acts 17:29 NKJV), and God "has made from one blood every nation of men to dwell on all the face of the earth" (verse 26 NKJV).

Moreover, despite the fact that slavery was countenanced in the Semitic cultures of the day, the law in the Bible demanded that slaves eventually be set free (Exodus 21:2; Leviticus 25:40). Likewise, servants had to be treated with respect (Exodus 21:20, 26). Israel, itself in slavery in Egypt for a prolonged time, was constantly reminded by God of this (Deuteronomy 5:15), and their emancipation became the model for the liberation of all slaves (cf. Leviticus 25:40).

Further, in the New Testament, Paul declared that in Christianity "there is neither Jew nor Greek, there is neither slave nor free man, there is neither male nor female; for you are all one in Christ Jesus" (Galatians 3:28 NASB). All social classes are broken down in Christ; we are all equal before God.

Though the apostle Paul urges, "Bondservants, be obedient to those who are your masters" (Ephesians 6:5 NKJV; cf. Colossians 3:22), he is not thereby approving of the institution of slavery, but simply alluding to the de facto situation in his day. He is simply instructing servants to be good workers, just as believers should be today, but he was not thereby commending slavery. Paul also instructed all believers to be obedient to government (even if unjust) for the Lord's sake (Romans 13:1; cf. Titus 3:1; 1 Peter 2:13). But this in no way condones oppression and tyranny which the Bible repeatedly condemns (cf. Isaiah 10:1; Exodus 2:23–25)

38

~

Ethical Issues Related to Death

What does the Bible say about suicide?

From a biblical perspective, issues of life and death lie in the sovereign hands of God alone. Job said to God, "Man's days are determined; you [O God] have decreed the number of his months and have set limits he cannot exceed" (Job 14:5). David said to God, "All the days ordained for me were written in your book before one of them came to be" (Psalm 139:16).

Moreover, suicide goes against the commandments of God. In fact, the sixth commandment tells us, "You shall not murder" (Exodus 20:13). This command is based on the sanctity of human life. We must remember that man was created in the image of God (Genesis 1:26).

It is important to understand that the command, "You shall not murder," has no direct object. That is, it doesn't say, "You shall not murder someone else," or "You shall not murder your fellow man." It simply says, "You shall not murder." The prohibition thus includes not just the murder of one's fellow man but even the murder of oneself. While suicide is certainly not the "unforgivable sin," we must never forget that God prohibits murder of any kind.

The lives of certain biblical saints are instructive on the issue of suicide. There were times when certain servants of God in biblical times were so severely tested and distressed that they wished for their own death (see 1 Kings 19:4). But

these individuals did not take matters into their own hands
and kill themselves. Instead, in these cases, God always rescued them. We can learn a lesson here. When we despair,
we must turn to God and not commit suicide. God will see
us through.

The apostle Paul certainly went through tough times.
Indeed, in 2 Corinthians 1:8 Paul reflected on his past: "We
do not want you to be uninformed, brothers, about the
hardships we suffered in the province of Asia. We were
under great pressure, far beyond our ability to endure, so
that we despaired even of life."

Nevertheless, Paul did not succumb to breaking God's
commandment against murder and commit suicide. He de-
pended on God, and God came through and gave him all
the sustenance he needed to make it through his ordeal
(1 Corinthians 1:9,10).

Following Paul's example, we must depend on God
when life throws us a punch. And just as God sustained
Paul through his difficulties, so He will sustain us.

Is capital punishment supported by the Bible?

Personally I believe that it is. In Genesis 9:6 we find that
capital punishment is instituted in view of the sanctity of
human life. The underlying basis for this severe punishment is the fact that man was made in the image of God
(Genesis 1:26). Man is so valuable as an individual that
anyone who tampers with his sacred right to live must face
the consequences of losing his own life. The worth of the
individual is so great that the highest penalty is attached to
those who tamper with the life of even one man. This was
true in the Old Testament and it is true today. When a
human being is murdered, this ultimately amounts to an
outrage against God.

Certainly the death penalty was incorporated into the
Mosaic code (see Exodus 21:12; Numbers 35:16-31). And in

Romans 13:1-7 the apostle Paul taught that human government has a God-given right to use force in its resistance of
evil. Romans 13:4 indicates that the government has the
right to take the life of a criminal.

Now, it is true that one of the Ten Commandments says
we are not to murder (Exodus 20:13). However, murder by
a citizen and execution by the government are viewed as
two different things in Scripture. One is a premeditated
crime; the other is a deserved punishment. And since government is set up by God (Romans 13:1-7), it would seem
that capital punishment may be viewed as the enacting of
divine judgment through the instrumentality of the government.

Is cremation following death against God's will for Christians?

In the Bible cremation is portrayed only as an excep-
tional method of disposing of bodies. Most often cremation
took place in the midst of unusual circumstances. For
example, in 1 Samuel 31:12 we read about the men of
Jabesh-Gilead who burned the corpses of Saul and his sons
in order to prevent desecration of their bodies at the hands
of the Philistines.

We don't find cremation mentioned in the New Testament. Burial is the normal method. Moreover, the church
fathers preferred "the ancient and better custom of burying
in the earth."[1]

However, there is no actual prohibition against cremation in the pages of Scripture. And if a Christian does get
cremated, this poses no problem for God in resurrecting that
person's body from the dead (1 Corinthians 15:42-44).

We read in 2 Corinthians 5:1, "Now we know that if the
earthly tent we live in is destroyed, we have a building from
God, an eternal house in heaven, not built by human
hands." It does not matter how our "earthly tent" (body) is

destroyed; all that matters is that God will raise it from the dead. Even those who are buried eventually dissolve into dust and bones. So, regardless of whether we're buried *or* cremated, we can all look forward to a permanent resurrection body that will never be subject to death and decay.

Does a good biblical case exist for self-defense (even to the point of war)?

This is an issue over which Christians have vehemently disagreed for many centuries. Following is a summary of the two basic views:

The path of nonresistance. Christian pacifists believe it is always wrong to injure other humans, no matter what the circumstances. And the same principles supporting pacifism carry over to nonresistance—the belief that any form of self-defense is wrong. This view is usually based on the exemplary life and teachings of Jesus Christ.

According to Christian pacifist John Yoder, Jesus rejected the existing political state of affairs and taught a form of radical nonviolence. Central to Christ's teaching, Yoder says, is His biblical mandate to "turn the other cheek" when encountering violence (Matthew 5:38-48). In Yoder's view, the way to victorious living is to refrain from the game of sociopolitical control. Jesus exposed the futility of the violence engrafted in the present world system by resisting its inclinations even to the point of death. Hence, Christians are to refuse the world's violent methods and follow their Savior to the cross (Matthew 26:47-52).[2]

I don't believe pacifism (or nonresistance) is the essential point of Christ's teaching in Matthew 5:38-42. Nor do I think Christ was teaching to "turn the other cheek" in virtually all circumstances. Even Christ did not literally turn the other cheek when smitten by a member of the Sanhedrin (John 18:22, 23).

The backdrop to this teaching is that the Jews considered it an insult to be hit in the face, much in the same way that we would interpret someone spitting in our face. The principle taught in the Sermon on the Mount would seem to be that Christians should not retaliate when insulted or slandered (cf. Romans 12:17-21). Such insults do not threaten a Christian's personal safety. The question of rendering insult for insult, however, is a far cry from defending oneself against a mugger or a rapist.

In terms of following Christ's example, one must remember that His personal nonresistance at the cross was intertwined with His unique calling. He did not evade His arrest because it was God's will for Him to fulfill His prophetic role as the redemptive Lamb of God (Matthew 26:52-56). During His ministry, however, He refused to be arrested because God's timing for His death had not yet come (John 8:59). Thus, Christ's unique nonresistance during the Passion does not mandate against self-protection.

The biblical case for self-defense. The Bible records many accounts of fighting and warfare. The providence of God in war is exemplified by His name YHWH Sabaoth ("The LORD of hosts"—Exodus 12:41). God is portrayed as the omnipotent Warrior-Leader of the Israelites. God, the LORD of hosts, raised up warriors among the Israelites called the *shophetim* (savior-deliverers). Samson, Deborah, Gideon, and others were anointed by the Spirit of God to conduct war. The New Testament commends Old Testament warriors for their military acts of faith (Hebrews 11:30-40). Moreover, it is significant that although given the opportunity to do so, none of the New Testament saints—nor even Jesus—is ever seen informing a military convert that he needed to resign from his line of work (Matthew 8:5-13; Luke 3:14).

Prior to His crucifixion, Jesus revealed to His disciples the future hostility they would face and encouraged them to sell their outer garments in order to purchase a sword (Luke

22:36-38; cf. 2 Corinthians 11:26,27). Here the "sword" (Greek: *maxairan*) is a "dagger or short sword [that] belonged to the Jewish traveler's equipment as protection against robbers and wild animals."[3] It is perfectly clear from this passage that Jesus approved of self-defense.

Self-defense may actually result in one of the greatest examples of human love. Christ said, "Greater love has no one than this, that he lay down his life for his friends" (John 15:13). When protecting one's family or neighbor, a Christian is unselfishly risking his or her life for the sake of others.

J. P. Moreland and Norman Geisler say that

> to permit murder when one could have prevented it is morally wrong. To allow a rape when one could have hindered it is an evil. To watch an act of cruelty to children without trying to intervene is morally inexcusable. In brief, not resisting evil is an evil of omission, and an evil of omission can be just as evil as an evil of commission. Any man who refuses to protect his wife and children against a violent intruder fails them morally.[4]

RESPONDING TO THE ARGUMENTS FOR ABORTION

How can we respond to the claim of abortionists that the baby in the womb is not really human until it is born?

This is a preposterous statement. If the baby is not human, what is it? A vegetable? Broccoli? A sponge? A monkey? Scripture is clear that everything God has created reproduces *after its own kind* (Genesis 1:21,24). This means that at the moment of conception, what is in the womb is truly human. Certainly Scripture portrays the baby in the womb as a human being (see Psalm 139:13-15; Jeremiah 1:5; Exodus 21:22-24).

One must raise the question of how premature births relate to this issue. Some babies are born months before their due date, and even though they may need medical life support to survive, it is very clear that the baby is a human being. (There have even been cases where babies born in their fourth month have survived!)

Would the abortionist say that a simple change in location is what renders the baby a human being? Such an idea is absurd. The only difference between born and *unborn* babies is their size and location, not their essential nature as a human being.[5]

How can we respond to the claim of some abortionists that because the unborn baby is not conscious, abortion is acceptable?

First of all, medical science has proven that the baby has brain-wave activity at one-and-a-half months following conception. Moreover, the baby responds to external stimuli (which indicates brain activity) at three months.[6]

Beyond these facts, the very idea of "consciousness" as an argument is flawed. Even if we granted that the unborn baby is not conscious, in view of the fact that it is not right (or legal) to kill a *sleeping* person or a *comatose* person, it is not right to kill a baby in the womb. The issue of consciousness is irrelevant to the issue of the morality of abortion.

How can we respond to the claim of some abortionists that because abortions are going to occur anyway, whether we like it or not, we might as well legalize them?

Such a view is the height of folly. Incest is going to happen in our society anyway, but does that mean we should legalize it? Child snatching in our society is going to occur anyway, but does that mean we should legalize it? Murder in our society is going to occur anyway, but does that mean we should legalize it? Theft in our society is going to occur anyway, but does that mean we should legalize it? Of course not. To be consistent, if we legalize abortion we should also legalize all these other crimes, because they're all going to happen anyway.

How can we respond to the claim that having an abortion is more merciful than giving birth to a child with birth defects?

The real issue is whether or not the unborn fetus is a human being, for if it is, then no one has the right to snuff out that life, regardless of whether there are birth defects. From a scriptural perspective, the unborn baby is most certainly a human person (see Psalm 51:5; 139:13; Jeremiah 1:5). To abort the baby therefore amounts to murder.

We can illustrate the absurdity of this position by addressing the situation of an already-born child who has birth defects. Should we execute this child simply because of a missing limb? Why not? Wouldn't it be more merciful for him to not have to go through the rest of his life in such a state?

You see my point. If it is true that the unborn baby is a human person, then to kill the unborn baby is really no different than killing a young child.

One must also keep in mind the scriptural teaching that a person born with a physical deformity may end up glorifying God in a great way. The blind man of John 9 was born blind, and some of the disciples thought it may have been because of sin. But Jesus said, "Neither this man nor his parents sinned, but this happened so that the work of God might be displayed in his life" (John 9:3). This situation led to glorifying God.

How can we respond to the claim of abortionists that because women have the right to control their own bodies, they can therefore have an abortion if the baby is unwanted?

The baby in the womb is not part of the woman's body. The baby has his or her *own* body *within* the womb of the mother's body. It is true that the mother's body sustains the baby's body with nutrients and a protective environment, but it is nevertheless a distinct body from her own body. Hence, for her to have an abortion is not just an operation on her own body but amounts to killing another human being whose body is within her body.

Is abortion okay in the case of rape?

No, it is not. While rape is a terrible indignity, two wrongs never make a right. In fact, the sin of a mother murdering an unborn baby is greater than the sin of the rapist violating a woman. Having an abortion in this situation amounts to punishing an innocent party. It is the rapist who deserves punishment, not the unborn child.

The raped woman who has an abortion must now emotionally deal with two terrible events—the horrible and crushing indignity of being raped, *and* the guilt over killing an innocent human being. Babies who are conceived by rape have every bit as much right to live as any other human being. And to have that life snuffed out is a crime against them and against God.

~

Notes

Chapter 1

1. Norman Geisler and William Nix, *A General Introduction to the Bible* (Chicago: Moody Press, 1978), p. 28.

2. Craig Blomberg, "The Seventy-Four 'Scholars': Who Does the Jesus Seminar Really Speak For?" *Christian Research Journal*, Fall 1994, p. 36.

Chapter 2

1. Donald J. Wiseman, "Archaeological Confirmation of the Old Testament," cited in Norman L. Geisler, *Christian Apologetics* (Grand Rapids: Baker Book House, 1976), p. 322.

2. Nelson Glueck, *Rivers in the Desert* (Philadelphia: Jewish Publications Society of America, 1969), p. 31.

3. William F. Albright; cited in Josh McDowell, *Evidence That Demands a Verdict* (San Bernardino, CA: Campus Crusade for Christ, 1972), p. 68.

4. Gleason Archer, *A Survey of Old Testament Introduction* (Chicago: Moody Press, 1964), p. 19.

5. Dan Story, *Defending Your Faith: How to Answer the Tough Questions* (Nashville, TN: Thomas Nelson Publishers, 1992), p. 35.

6. Greg L. Bahnsen, "The Inerrancy of the Autographa," cited in Norman L. Geisler, ed., *Inerrancy* (Grand Rapids: Zondervan Publishing House, 1980), p. 161.

Chapter 3

1. Norman L. Geisler and Ronald M. Brooks, *When Skeptics Ask*, (Wheaton, IL: Victor Books, 1989), pp. 155-56.

Chapter 4

1. Benjamin B. Warfield, *Biblical and Theological Studies* (Phillipsburg, NJ: Presbyterian and Reformed Publishing Co., 1968), p. 30.

Chapter 5

1. Gleason L. Archer, *Encyclopedia of Bible Difficulties* (Grand Rapids: Zondervan Publishing House, 1982), p. 80.

2. See Ken Ham, *The Lie*, (El Cajon, CA: Creation-Life Publishers, 1987), pp. 123-30.

3. Charles Caldwell Ryrie, ed., *Ryrie Study Bible*, (Chicago: Moody Press, 1994), p. 15.

Chapter 6

1. Walter C. Kaiser, *Hard Sayings of the Old Testament* (Downers Grove, IL: InterVarsity Press, 1988), p. 167.

2. *Reasoning from the Scriptures* (Brooklyn: Watchtower Bible and Tract Society, 1989), p. 76.

Chapter 7

1. Robert M. Bowman, *Why You Should Believe in the Trinity* (Grand Rapids: Baker Book House, 1989), p. 43.

2. Paul G. Weathers, "Answering the Arguments of Jehovah's Witnesses Against the Trinity," cited in Eric Pement, ed., *Contend for the Faith* (Chicago: EMNR, 1992), p. 136.

3. Benjamin B. Warfield, *The Person and Work of Christ* (Philadelphia: Presbyterian and Reformed Publishing Co., 1950), p. 66.

4. Ibid.

5. Lewis Sperry Chafer, *Systematic Theology*, vol. 1 (Wheaton, IL: Victor Books, 1988), 1:181.

Chapter 8

1. Norman L. Geisler and Jeff Amano, *The Infiltration of the New Age* (Wheaton, IL: Tyndale House Publishers, 1990), p. 20.

2. Norman Geisler and Thomas Howe, *When Critics Ask* (Wheaton, IL: Victor Books, 1992), p. 31.

3. Ibid.

4. Walter C. Kaiser, *Hard Sayings of the Old Testament* (Downers Grove, IL: InterVarsity Press, 1988), p. 167.

5. F. F. Bruce, *The Gospel of John* (London: Pickering, 1983), p. 234.

6. Robert M. Bowman Jr. "The Biblical Basis of the Doctrine of the Trinity: An Outline Study" (Irvine, CA: Christian Research Institute, n.d.), p. 3; cf. Geisler and Howe, *When Critics Ask*, p. 417.

7. Ibid., p. 84.

8. Ibid.

Chapter 9

1. William F. Arndt and F. Wilbur Gingrich, *A Greek-English Lexicon of the New Testament and Other Early Christian Literature* (Chicago: The University of Chicago Press, 1957), p. 874.

2. Ibid., p. 146.

Chapter 10

1. Robert Lightner, cited in John F. Walvoord and Roy B. Zuck, ed., *The Bible Knowledge Commentary: New Testament* (Wheaton, IL: Victor Books, 1983), p. 654.

Chapter 11

1. Robert M. Bowman, *Why You Should Believe in the Trinity* (Grand Rapids: Baker Book House, 1989), p. 60.

2. *The Watchtower*, 1 July 1986, p. 31.

3. Benjamin B. Warfield, *The Person and Work of Christ* (Philadelphia: Presbyterian and Reformed Publishing Co., 1950), p. 56.

4. Leon Morris, *The Gospel According to John* (Grand Rapids: Wm. B. Eerdmans Publishing Co., 1971), p. 658.

5. Bowman, *Why You Should Believe in the Trinity*, pp. 14-15.

6. Cf. Robert L. Reymond, *Jesus, Divine Messiah: The New Testament Witness* (Phillipsburg, NJ: Presbyterian and Reformed Publishing Co., 1990), p. 247.

7. David Reed, *Jehovah's Witnesses Answered Verse by Verse* (Grand Rapids: Baker Book House, 1992), p. 97.

8. Ibid.

9. J. B. Lightfoot, *Paul's Epistles to the Colossians and to Philemon* (Grand Rapids: Zondervan, 1979), p. 147.

10. Spiros Zodhiates, *The Complete Word Study Dictionary* (Chattanooga, TN: AMG Publishers, 1992), p. 260.

11. William F. Arndt and F. Wilbur Gingrich, *A Greek-English Lexicon of the New Testament and Other Early Christian Literature* (Chicago: The University of Chicago Press, 1957), p. 112.

12. Zodhiates, *The Complete Word Study Dictionary*, p. 261.

13. Bowman, *Why You Should Believe in the Trinity*, p. 65.

14. Ibid., p. 66.

Chapter 12

1. James Oliver Buswell, *A Systematic Theology of the Christian Religion* (Grand Rapids: Zondervan Publishing House, 1979), 1:105.

2. Charles C. Ryrie, *Basic Theology* (Wheaton, IL: Victor Books, 1986), p. 248; cf. Reymond, *Jesus, Divine Messiah: The New Testament Witness*, (Phillipsburg, NJ: Presbyterian and Reformed Publishing Co., 1990), p. 68.

3. See John F. Walvoord, *Jesus Christ Our Lord* (Chicago: Moody Press, 1969), pp. 22-25.

Chapter 13

1. C. F. Keil and F. Delitzsch, *Commentary on the Old Testament*, vol. 6 (Grand Rapids: Eerdmans Publishing Co., 1986), pp. 273-78; A. R. Fausset, *A Commentary—Critical, Experimental, and Practical—on the Old and New Testaments* (Grand Rapids: Wm. B. Eerdmans Publishing Co., 1973), p. 508.

2. Gleason Archer, *Encyclopedia of Bible Difficulties* (Chicago: Moody Press, 1988), p. 92.

3. Ibid.

4. Norman Geisler, *To Understand the Bible Look for Jesus* (Grand Rapids: Baker Book House, 1979), p. 67.

5. Francis Brown, S. R. Driver, and Charles A. Briggs, *A Hebrew and English Lexicon of the Old Testament* (Oxford: Clarendon Press, 1980), p. 521.

Chapter 14

1. Robert Gundry, *Soma in Biblical Theology* (Cambridge: Cambridge University Press, 1976), p. 168.

2. Norman Geisler and Ronald Brooks, *When Skeptics Ask* (Wheaton, IL: Victor Books, 1989), p. 124.

Chapter 15

1. *Gospel Principles* (Salt Lake City: The Church of Jesus Christ of Latter-day Saints, 1986), p. 9.

2. See David Spangler, *Reflections on the Christ*, (Forres, Scotland: Findhorn, 1981).

3. Shirley MacLaine, *Out on a Limb*, (New York: Bantam Books, 1984) pp. 233-34.

4. Justo L. Gonzalez, *A History of Christian Thought* (Nashville: Abingdon, 1970), vol. 1, p. 129.

5. Louis Berkhof, *The History of Christian Doctrines* (Grand Rapids: Baker Book House, 1981), p. 47.

6. Ibid., p. 47ff.

7. Ron Rhodes, *The Counterfeit Christ of the New Age Movement* (Grand Rapids: Baker Book House, 1991), pp. 18-20.

8. Ibid.

9. Ronald H. Nash, *Christianity and the Hellenistic World* (Grand Rapids: Zondervan Publishing House, 1984), p. 222.

10. Gregory A. Boyd, "Sharing Your Faith with a Oneness Pentecostal," *Christian Research Journal* (Spring 1991), p. 7.

11. Albert Barnes, *Notes on the Old Testament—Isaiah* (Grand Rapids: Baker Book House, 1977), p. 193.

12. Ibid.

13. J. F. Stenning, *The Targum of Isaiah* (London: Oxford Press, 1949), p. 32.

Chapter 16

1. See Robert Lightner, *Evangelical Theology: A Survey and Review* (Grand Rapids: Baker Book House, 1986), p. 180.

Chapter 19

1. John Blanchard, *Whatever Happened to Hell?* (Durham, England: Evangelical Press, 1993), p. 113.

2. Norman Geisler and Ralph MacKenzie, *Roman Catholics and Evangelicals* (Grand Rapids: Baker Book House, 1995), pp. 221-48.

3. John F. Walvoord and Roy B. Zuck, eds., *The Bible Knowledge Commentary: New Testament*, (Wheaton, IL: Victor Books, 1983), p. 851.

4. Kenneth Barker, ed., *The NIV Study Bible*, (Grand Rapids: Zondervan Publishing House, 1985), p. 1894.

5. See Leon Morris, *The Biblical Doctrine of Judgment* (Grand Rapids: Wm. B. Eerdmans Publishing Co., 1960), p. 66.

Chapter 20

1. John F. Walvoord and Roy B. Zuck, eds., *The Bible Knowledge Commentary, New Testament*, (Wheaton, IL: Victor Books, 1989), p. 825.

2. Ibid.

3. Charles Caldwell Ryrie, ed., *Ryrie Study Bible*, (Chicago: Moody Press, 1994), p. 1885.

4. Walvoord and Zuck, eds., *Bible Knowledge Commentary, New Testament*, p. 938

Chapter 21

1. John Calvin, *Commentary on John's Gospel* (Grand Rapids: Baker Book House, 1949), vol. 1, p. 64.

2. Millard J. Erickson, *Christian Theology* (Grand Rapids: Baker Book House, 1985), p. 834.

3. John Calvin, *Commentary on Romans* (Grand Rapids: Baker Book House, 1949), p. 211.

4. Cited in Norman F. Douty, *The Death of Christ* (Swengel, PA: Reiner, 1972), p. 15.

5. Calvin, *Commentary on John's Gospel*, vol. 1, p. 126.

6. Walter Elwell, "Atonement, Extent of the," *Evangelical Dictionary of Theology* (Grand Rapids: Baker Book House, 1984), p. 99.

7. Erickson, *Christian Theology*, p. 832.

Chapter 23

1. See Erwin Lutzer, *Christ Among Other Gods*, (Chicago: Moody Press, 1994).

2. Some years ago, I read an article by Stuart Dauermann in which he outlined how to witness to Jews. I've since lost that article, and have no idea what magazine it was published in. But I do want to credit him for the overall strategy outlined in this chapter.

3. See Geoffrey Parrinder, ed., *World Religions*, (New York: Facts on File Publications, 1971), pp. 485-90.

4. *Draper's Book of Quotations for the Christian World* (Wheaton, IL: Tyndale House Publishers, 1992), p. 106.

5. *Spurgeon Quotes*, electronic media, Hypercard database.

6. Eric Stuyck, "Can Children Be Saved?" Child Evangelism Fellowship of Frederick County, Maryland.

Chapter 25

1. David Connolly, *In Search of Angels: A Celestial Sourcebook for Beginning Your Journey* (New York: Perigee Books, 1993), p. 78.

2. Kenneth L. Woodward, "Angels: Hark! America's Latest Search for Spiritual Meaning Has a Halo Effect," *Newsweek*, 27 December 1993, p. 57.

3. Ibid.

4. Connolly, *In Search of Angels: A Celestial Sourcebook for Beginning Your Journey*, p. 77.

5. C. Fred Dickason, *Angels, Elect and Evil* (Chicago: Moody Press, 1978), p. 86.

6. John Calvin, *Institutes of the Christian Religion*, ed. John T. McNeill, trans. Ford Lewis Battles (Philadelphia: The Westminster Press, 1960), 1.14.11.

Chapter 26

1. Charles C. Ryrie, cited in Paul Enns, *The Moody Handbook of Theology* (Chicago: Moody Press, 1989), p. 298.

Chapter 27

1. *The Truth Shall Make You Free* (Brooklyn: Watchtower Bible and Tract Society, 1943), p. 300.

Chapter 28

1. R. C. Sproul, *Now, That's a Good Question* (Wheaton, IL: Tyndale House Publishers, 1996), p. 291.

Chapter 29

1. Cited in Charles C. Ryrie, *Basic Theology* (Wheaton, IL: Victor Books, 1986), p. 513.

Chapter 30

1. Alan Gomes, "Evangelicals and the Annihilation of Hell," Part Two, *Christian Research Journal*, Summer 1991, p. 11.

2. Shirley MacLaine, *Out on a Limb*, (New York: Bantam Books, 1984), p. 233.

3. *Reasoning from the Scriptures*, (Brooklyn: Watchtower Bible and Tract Society, 1989), p. 76.

4. *Theological Wordbook of the Old Testament*, R. Laird Harris, ed., vol. 2 (Chicago: Moody Press, 1981), p. 645.

Chapter 31

1. Jerry Yamamoto, "The Near-Death Experience," *Christian Research Journal*, Spring 1992, p.2.

2. Ibid.

3. Doug Groothuis, *Deceived by the Light* (Eugene, OR: Harvest House Publishers, 1995), pp. 165-79.

4. John Ankerberg and John Weldon, *The Facts on Life After Death* (Eugene, OR: Harvest House Publishers, 1992), p. 10.

5. Ibid., p. 11.

6. Ibid., p. 28.

7. Recounted by Doug Groothuis, *Deceived by the Light* (Eugene, OR: Harvest House Publishers, 1995), pp. 70, 71

8. Ibid.

9. Ibid.

Chapter 32

1. Erwin Lutzer, *Christ Among Other Gods* (Chicago: Moody Press, 1994).

2. C. S. Lewis, *God in the Dock* (Grand Rapids: Eerdmans, 1972), p. 26.

3. Ibid.

Chapter 33

1. George Mather and Larry Nichols, eds., *Dictionary of Cults, Sects, Religions, and the Occult* (Grand Rapids: Zondervan Publishing House, 1993), p. 184.

2. John Ankerberg and John Weldon, *The Facts on the Masonic Lodge* (Eugene, OR: Harvest House Publishers, 1989), pp. 17ff.

3. Elliot Miller and Kenneth R. Samples, *The Cult of the Virgin* (Grand Rapids: Baker Book House, 1992).

4. See Ron Rhodes, *The Culting of America* (Eugene, OR: Harvest House Publishers, 1994), pp. 205-07.

5. Elliot Miller, "Questions and Answers," *Christian Research Newsletter*, July/September 1992, p. 4.

6. Brooks Alexander, "Machines Made of Shadows," *SCP Journal*, 17:1-2, 1992, p. 11.

7. John Weldon with Zola Levitt, *UFOs: What on Earth Is Happening* (Irvine, CA: Harvest House Publishers, 1975), p. 101.

8. David Wimbish, *Something's Going on Out There* (Old Tappan, NJ: Revell, 1990), p. 158.

9. Ibid., p. 164.

10. Ibid., p. 46.

11. John Keel, *UFOs: Operation Trojan Horse* (New York: G. P. Putnam's Sons, 1970), pp. 215, 299.

12. Brad Steiger, *Gods of Aquarius* (New York: Berkley Books, 1976), p. 6.

13. Keel, *UFOs: Operation Trojan Horse*, p. 143.

Chapter 34

1. Bruce R. McConkie, *Mormon Doctrine* (Salt Lake City, UT: Bookcraft, 1966), pp. 526-28.

2. See Ron Rhodes, *The Culting of America*, (Eugene, OR: Harvest House Publishers, 1994), pp. 97-98

3. Walter Martin, *The Kingdom of the Cults* (Minneapolis: Bethany House Publishers, 1985), pp. 377-85.

4. *Your Will Be Done on Earth* (Brooklyn: Watchtower Bible and Tract Society, 1985), p. 362.

5. *The Watchtower*, 15 January 1917, p. 6033.

6. David Reed, *How to Rescue Your Loved One from the Watchtower* (Grand Rapids: Baker Book House, 1989), pp. 23-24.

7. *The Imperial Bible Dictionary*, I:376; cited in *Reasoning from the Scriptures* (Brooklyn: Watchtower Bible and Tract Society, 1989), p. 89.

8. Davi Reed, *Jehovah's Witnesses Answered Verse by Verse* (Grand Rapids: Baker Book House), pp. 11, 25.

9. *Reasoning from the Scriptures* (Brooklyn: Watchtower Bible and Tract Society, 1989), p. 75.

10. Norman Geisler and Thomas Howe, *When Critics Ask* (Wheaton, IL: Victor Books, 1992), p. 434.

11. Ibid.

12. See Rhodes, *Culting of America*, p. 120.

13. Ron Rhodes, *The Counterfeit Christ of the New Age Movement*, (Grand Rapids: Baker Book House, 1991), p. 224.

14. Ibid.

15. George Mather and Larry Nichols, eds., *Dictionary of Cults, Sects, Religions, and the Occult* (Grand Rapids: Zondervan Publishing House, 1993), pp. 295-96.

16. Ibid.

17. Robert Countess, *The Jehovah's Witnesses' New Testament* (Phillipsburg, NJ: Presbyterian and Reformed Publishing Co., 1982), p. 91.

18. Ibid.

19. Ibid.

20. Julius R. Mantey; cited in Erich and Jean Grieshaber, *Redi-Answers on Jehovah's Witnesses Doctrine* (Tyler, TX: n.p., 1979), p. 30.

21. Ibid.

22. Ibid., p. 31.

23. David Reed, *Jehovah's Witnesses Answered Verse by Verse* (Grand Rapids: Baker Book House, 1992), p. 71.

24. Erich and Jean Grieshaber, *Exposé of Jehovah's Witnesses* (Tyler, TX: Jean Books, 1982), p. 100.

25. Ibid.

26. Ibid.

27. Erich and Jean Grieshaber, *Exposé of Jehovah's Witnesses* (Tyler, TX: Jean Books, 1982), p. 100.

28. LeGrand Richards, *A Marvelous Work and a Wonder* (Salt Lake City, UT: Deseret Book Company, 1973), pp. 50, 67-68.

29. See Ron Rhodes and Marian Bodine, *Reasoning from the Scriptures with the Mormons* (Eugene, OR: Harvest House Publishers, 1995), pp. 116-20.

30. Joseph Smith, *History of the Church of Jesus Christ of Latter-day Saints* (Salt Lake City, UT: Deseret Book Company, 1973), 1:54,55.

31. Rhodes and Bodine, *Reasoning*, pp. 121-25.

32. Ibid., p. 121.

33. Ibid., p. 125.

34. Ibid., pp. 130-32.

35. Dee F. Green, *Dialogue: A Journal of Mormon Thought*, Summer 1969, pp. 76,78.

36. Rhodes and Bodine, *Reasoning*, pp. 105-11.

Chapter 35

1. *The Christian Herald*, Feb. 1988, p. 51.

2. This definition is based on Elliot Miller, *A Crash Course on the New Age Movement* (Grand Rapids: Baker Book House, 1989), p. 15.

3. See Ron Rhodes, *The New Age Movement* (Grand Rapids: Zondervan Publishing House, 1995), pp. 23-24.

4. Ibid., p. 24.

5. Ibid.

6. Paul Vitz, *Censorship: Evidence of Bias in Our Children's Textbooks* (Ann Arbor, MI: Servant, 1986), pp. 18,19, 33-36, 84.

7. Berit Kjos, *Your Child and the New Age* (Wheaton, IL: Victor Books, 1990), p. 26.

8. Marilyn Ferguson, *The Aquarian Conspiracy* (Los Angeles: J.P. Tarcher, 1980), p. 315.

9. Deborah Rozman, *Meditating With Children* (Boulder Creek, CA: University of the Trees Press, 1975), p. 42.

10. Beverly Galyean, "Meditating With Children: Some Things We Learned," *AHP Newsletter*, Aug.-Sept. 1980, p. 16.

11. See Rhodes, *New Age Movement*, p. 21-23.

12. Fritjof Capra, *The Turning Point* (New York: Simon and Schuster, 1982), p. 123.

13. Ibid., p. 322.

14. Rick Fields, et al., eds., *Chop Wood, Carry Water* (Los Angeles: J. P. Tarcher, 1984), p. 186.

15. Miller, *A Crash Course on the New Age*, p. 187.

16. Stephan Schuhmacher and Gert Woerner, eds. *The Encyclopedia of Eastern Philosophy and Religion* (Boston: Shambhala Publications, 1989), p. 224.

17. See Rhodes, *New Age Movwement*, p. 27.

18. Ibid.

19. David Gershon and Gail Staub, *Empowerment: The Art of Creating Your Life as You Want It* (New York: Dell, 1989), p. 21.

20. Jennifer Donavan, "Seth Followers Spoon Up Fun in Their Goal to Enjoy Living," *Dallas Morning News*, July 1, 1986.

Chapter 36

1. Norman L. Geisler and Ronald M. Brooks, *Christianity Under Attack* (Dallas: Quest Publications, 1985), p. 43.

2. Norman Geisler and Jeff Amano, *The Infiltration of the New Age* (Wheaton, IL: Tyndale House Publishers, 1990), p. 18.

Chapter 38

1. Carl F. H. Henry, *Baker's Dictionary of Christian Ethics* (Grand Rapids: Baker Book House, 1973), p. 149.

2. John Howard Yoder, *The Politics of Jesus* (Grand Rapids: Eerdmans, 1972), ch. 2, 5, 8.

3. Myrtle Langley, *The New International Dictionary of New Testament Theology*, ed. Colin Brown (Grand Rapids: Zondervan, 1978), 3:978.

4. J. P. Moreland and Norman Geisler, *The Life and Death Debate: Moral Issues of Our Time* (New York: Praeger, 1990), p. 135.

5. I am indebted to the work of apologist Norman Geisler on the issue of abortion. His class notes from an ethics class at Dallas Theological Seminary have proved to be invaluable.

6. See Frank Beckwith, *Politically Correct Death*, (Grand Rapids: Baker Book House, 1995).

~

Bibliography

Ankerberg, John, and John Weldon. *The Facts on Astrology*. Eugene, OR: Harvest House Publishers, 1988.

———. *The Facts on False Teaching in the Church*. Eugene, OR: Harvest House Publishers, 1988.

———. *The Facts on Life After Death*. Eugene, OR: Harvest House Publishers, 1992.

———. *The Facts on the Masonic Lodge*. Eugene, OR: Harvest House Publishers, 1989.

———. *The Facts on Spirit Guides*. Eugene, OR: Harvest House Publishers, 1988.

Arndt, William. *Bible Difficulties and Seeming Contradictions*. St. Louis, MO: Concordia Publishing House, 1987.

Basinger, David and Randall Basinger, eds. *Predestination and Free Will: Four Views of Divine Sovereignty and Human Freedom*. Downers Grove, IL: InterVarsity Press, 1986.

Barker, Kenneth, ed. *The NIV Study Bible*. Grand Rapids, MI: Zondervan Publishing House, 1985.

Barker, Kenneth L. and John Kohlenberger III, eds. *Zondervan NIV Bible Commentary: New Testament*. Vol. 2. Grand Rapids, MI: Zondervan Publishing House, 1994.

———, eds. *Zondervan NIV Bible Commentary: Old Testament*. Vol. 1. Grand Rapids, MI: Zondervan Publishing House, 1994.

Boyd, Gregory. *Oneness Pentecostals and the Trinity*. Grand Rapids, MI: Zondervan Publishing House, 1992.

Bruce, F. F. *The Hard Sayings of Jesus*. Downers Grove, IL: InterVarsity Press, 1983.

Campbell, Donald K., ed. *Walvoord: A Tribute*. Chicago, IL: Moody Press, 1982.

Clouse, Robert G., ed. *War: Four Christian Views*. Downers Grove, IL: InterVarsity Press, 1991.

Dallas, Joe. *A Strong Delusion*. Eugene, OR: Harvest House Publishers, 1996.

Davids, Peter. *More Hard Sayings of the New Testament*. Downers Grove, IL: InterVarsity Press, 1991.

Ehrenborg, Todd. *Mind Sciences: Christian Science, Religious Science, Unity School of Christianity*. Edited by Alan W. Gomes. Grand Rapids, MI: Zondervan Publishing House, 1995.

Elwell, Walter A., ed. *The Concise Evangelical Dictionary of Theology*. Grand Rapids, MI: Baker Book House, 1991.

Geisler, Norman. *Ethics: Alternatives and Issues*. Grand Rapids, MI: Zondervan Publishing House, 1979.

————, ed. *Inerrancy*. Grand Rapids, MI: Zondervan Publishing House, 1980.

Geisler, Norman, and Ron Rhodes. *When Cultists Ask*. Grand Rapids, MI: Baker Book House, 1997.

Geisler, Norman, and Ronald Brooks. *When Skeptics Ask*. Wheaton, IL: Victor Books, 1990.

Geisler, Norman, and Thomas Howe. *When Critics Ask: A Popular Handbook on Bible Difficulties*. Wheaton, IL: Victor Books, 1992.

Geisler, Norman, and William Nix. *A General Introduction to the Bible*. Chicago, IL: Moody Press, 1978.

Gomes, Alan W. *Unmasking the Cults*. Edited by Alan W. Gomes. Grand Rapids, MI: Zondervan Publishing House, 1995.

Ham, Ken. *The Lie*. El Cajon, CA: Creation-Life Publishers, 1987.

Henry, Carl F. H., ed. *Baker's Dictionary of Christian Ethics*. Grand Rapids, MI: Baker Book House, 1978.

Hoyt, Herman A. *The End Times*. Chicago, IL: Moody Press, 1969.

Hunt, Dave. *In Defense of the Faith: Biblical Answers to Challenging Questions*. Eugene, OR: Harvest House Publishers, 1996.

Kaiser, Walter. *Hard Sayings of the Old Testament*. Downers Grove, IL: InterVarsity Press, 1988.

————. *More Hard Sayings of the Old Testament*. Downers Grove, IL: InterVarsity Press, 1992.

Kreeft, Peter, and Ronald Tacelli. *Handbook of Christian Apologetics*. Downers Grove, IL: InterVarsity Press, 1994.

Lightner, Robert. *Evangelical Theology: A Survey and Review*. Grand Rapids, MI: Baker Book House, 1986.

————. *The God of the Bible*. Grand Rapids, MI: Baker Book House, 1978.

————. *The Last Days Handbook*. Nashville, TN: Thomas Nelson Publishers, 1990.

Mather, George, and Larry A. Nichols. *Dictionary of Cults, Sects, Religions and the Occult*. Grand Rapids, MI: Zondervan Publishing House, 1993.

————. *Masonic Lodge*. Edited by Alan W. Gomes. Grand Rapids, MI: Zondervan Publishing House, 1995.

McDowell, Josh. *The Resurrection Factor*. San Bernardino, CA: Here's Life Publishers, 1981.

McDowell, Josh, and Don Stewart. *Answers to Tough Questions Skeptics Ask About the Christian Faith*. Wheaton, IL: Tyndale House Publishers, 1988.

———. *Handbook of Today's Religions*. San Bernardino, CA: Here's Life Publishers, 1989.

———. *Reasons Skeptics Should Consider Christianity*. Wheaton, IL: Tyndale House Publishers, 1988.

O'Brien, David. *Today's Handbook for Solving Bible Difficulties*. Minneapolis, MN: Bethany House Publishers, 1990.

Passantino, Bob and Gretchen. *Satanism*. Edited by Alan W. Gomes. Grand Rapids, MI: Zondervan Publishing House, 1995.

Rhodes, Ron. *Angels Among Us: Separating Truth from Fiction*. Eugene, OR: Harvest House Publishers, 1994.

———. *Christ Before the Manger: The Life and Times of the Preincarnate Christ*. Grand Rapids, MI: Baker Book House, 1992.

———. *The Counterfeit Christ of the New Age Movement*. Grand Rapids, MI: Baker Book House, 1990.

———. *The Culting of America: The Shocking Implications for Every Concerned Christian*. Eugene, OR: Harvest House Publishers, 1994.

———. *The Heart of Christianity: What It Means to Believe in Jesus*. Eugene, OR: Harvest House Publishers, 1996.

———. *Heaven: The Undiscovered Country—Exploring the Wonder of the Afterlife*. Eugene, OR: Harvest House Publishers, 1996.

———. *Quick-Reference Guide to Angels*. Eugene, OR: Harvest House Publishers, 1997.

———. *Quick-Reference Guide to the Jehovah's Witnesses*. Eugene, OR: Harvest House Publishers, 1997.

———. *Reasoning from the Scriptures with the Jehovah's Witnesses*. Eugene, OR: Harvest House Publishers, 1993.

———. *The New Age Movement*. Grand Rapids, MI: Zondervan Publishing House, 1995.

———. *What Your Child Needs to Know About God*. Eugene, OR: Harvest House Publishers, 1997.

———. *When Servants Suffer: Finding Purpose in Pain*. Wheaton, IL: Harold Shaw Publishers, 1990.

Rhodes, Ron, and Marian Bodine. *Reasoning from the Scriptures with the Mormons* Eugene, OR: Harvest House Publishers, 1995.

Ryrie, Charles C. *Balancing the Christian Life*. Chicago, IL: Moody Press, 1969.

387

Ryrie, Charles C. *Basic Theology*. Wheaton, IL: Victor Books, 1986.

Ryrie, Charles C. *Dispensationalism Today*. Chicago, IL: Moody Press, 1977.

Ryrie, Charles C. *The Holy Spirit*. Chicago, IL: Moody Press, 1980.

Ryrie, Charles C. *You Mean the Bible Teaches That...* Chicago, IL: Moody Press, 1974.

Ryrie, Charles C., ed. *Ryrie Study Bible*. Chicago, IL: Moody Press, 1994.

Saucy, Robert. *The Church in God's Program*. Chicago, IL: Moody Press, 1972.

Sire, James. *Scripture Twisting: 20 Ways the Cults Misread the Bible*. Downers Grove, IL: InterVarsity Press, 1980.

Stein, Robert. *Difficult Passages in the New Testament*. Grand Rapids, MI: Baker Book House, 1990.

Story, Dan. *Defending Your Faith: How to Answer the Tough Questions*. Nashville, TN: Thomas Nelson Publishers, 1992.

Walvoord, John F. *Jesus Christ Our Lord*. Chicago, IL: Moody Press, 1969.

———. *The Prophecy Knowledge Handbook*. Wheaton, IL: Victor Books, 1990.

———. *The Rapture Question*. Grand Rapids, MI: Zondervan Publishing House, 1979.

Walvoord, John F. and Roy B. Zuck, eds. *The Bible Knowledge Commentary: New Testament*. Wheaton, IL: Victor Books, 1983.

———, eds. *The Bible Knowledge Commentary: Old Testament*. Wheaton, IL: Victor Books, 1985.

Youngblood, Ronald, ed. *Nelson's New Illustrated Bible Dictionary*. Nashville, TN: Thomas Nelson Publishers, 1995.

Subject Index

392

Primary Verse Index

Reasoning from the Scriptures Ministries is a discipleship ministry that exists to help you grow strong in the Word of God and equip you to become knowledgeable in the application of biblical wisdom.

We publish a free newsletter and offer numerous materials (many free) on a variety of relevant issues.

If you would like to be on our mailing list, or if we can be of service to you in any way, please don't hesitate to write.

Ron Rhodes
Reasoning from the Scriptures Ministries
P.O. Box 80087
Rancho Santa Margarita, CA 92688